Walking in History: An Autobiography

ROBERT KENNETH WRIGHT

DEDICATION

Dedicated to my elementary school teachers: Carla Monk, Vera Dyer, Sheila Howell, Sallie Sutherland, Corine Stripling, Daphne Singleton, Dr. Gary Jones, Warren Thomas, Cynthia Wells, the late Dorth Blade, Donald Robinson, Margaret Adcock, Sheila Guinn, and Lynda Cookston. For all the years you toiled with me, take a bow. Because of you, the adventure told on these pages could not be possible.

WALKING IN HISTORY: AN AUTOBIOGRAPHY

TWO roads diverged in a yellow wood,
And sorry I could not travel both
And be one traveler, long I stood
And looked down one as far as I could
To where it bent in the undergrowth;

Then took the other, as just as fair,
And having perhaps the better claim,
Because it was grassy and wanted wear;
Though as for that the passing there
Had worn them really about the same,

And both that morning equally lay
In leaves no step had trodden black.
Oh, I kept the first for another day!
Yet knowing how way leads on to way,
I doubted if I should ever come back.

I shall be telling this with a sigh
Somewhere ages and ages hence:
Two roads diverged in a wood, and I—
I took the one less traveled by,
And that has made all the difference.

Robert Frost
"The Road Not Taken"

WALKING IN HISTORY: AN AUTOBIOGRAPHY

CONTENTS

ACKNOWLEDGMENTS

One of my favorite television shows is ABC's "Designated Survivor" starring Kiefer Sutherland as President Tom Kirkman. In 2018, the producers added actress Chelsea Harris to the cast as a White House Staffer. Interestingly, Harris was once the photo subject of one of the favored headshot photographers in Los Angeles. She chose Michael Roud for her photos used in casting. It is her photo that he took that is featured on her IMDB page. Mr. Roud took the cover photo for this book. As I am a photographer, it was an experience being photographed by another professional. Roud's photos have a signature look, and as I observe Harris's photo, I feel a connection to the Roud family, for I took photos in the same scene as she. Many actors in Hollywood have chosen Roud for their casting photos. It was a walk in history that I chose to feature in this presentation.

I would like to acknowledge Lavandolyn Smith and her organization, Never Alone Initiative, for sponsoring the cover art and design. The NAI is active in supporting military spouses and their families. It is also an organization that supports US Veterans. As I am a military veteran, it is an honor to receive her organization's support for the publication of this book.

There are several chapters in this book describing my career as a Hollywood actor. That experience would not have been possible without the assistance of Patricia Matthews and her son, the actor Drew Matthews. They opened up their home to me for many months during my stay and for that I am grateful.

I would like to acknowledge Mr. James Simon and Dr. Claude Minor. These two men have been an asset to my life with support and encouragement without question over the years.

I would finally like to thank my mother, father, and many others who reviewed the text of this publication over the years, providing input and calling to my memory some key events of my past which have shaped the story I tell.

ONE

INTRODUCTION

"See that's what praising God is all about, it's doing your passion…and fulfilling your passion. You know. That's how we're thankful. That's how we say we appreciate the opportunity to be alive."

Lauryn Hill

There is no better way to begin a memoir about a great life than to say thanks to God for the gift of life. I could have been a dog, a tree, a bird, or a deer. However, God allowed me to be a man. It is not a gift I take lightly because many people have misused their time and their abilities and have often overlooked the blessing that human life is.

In this brief pageant of human life, I have never walked on the moon, but I have walked the grounds of three of the planet's seven continents and sailed in the waters of three of the planet's four oceans. I've met thousands of people in my time and have formed lasting relationships with hundreds of them. I have been among the poorest of souls in Indonesia and Thailand and have worked on the scene with the brightest of Hollywood stars like Kerry Washington and Michael Nouri. I've had my photographs published in national magazines with millions of subscribers, and I've berthed for months at sea aboard US naval vessels as a United States Marine. I've crowned beauty queens at pageants and have driven the rich and fabulous in Beverly Hills as an Uber Driver. I've reported the news as a journalist and taught in American public classrooms. It is a blessing to be alive in my given time. Anyone who has ever engaged in travel, exploration, and leaping to try a new thing can agree that having these experience changes everything.

In this memoir, I attempt to share with you the many experiences that I have enjoyed. I am a very blessed individual because many of the experiences you will read about will reveal that I was in the right place at the right time. A great amount of attention will focus on the hundreds of lives that I've encountered that have helped to create this wonderful story. My story is in some part a biography of their lives and how interaction with them shaped my life.

I begin my story with the history of my family. As a historian, I believe it is important for one to know his history before attempting to discover the history of other people, events, and places. So it is with the history of my family that I begin. From there, I categorize my experiences in theaters. They are not chronological, so as you read, time might rewind, but you will discover how these theaters of life fit into the big puzzle.

I have been a record keeper of my life's events since I was a teenager. I've stored books, programs, report cards, certificates, newspapers, letters, yearbooks, and articles of technology that have been beneficial in recalling information from my earlier years. As I've moved around over the years and in my numerous travels from city to city, I've hauled dozens of boxes and hundreds of pounds of items to preserve the history of my time.

There is a scene in the movie *Forrest Gump* where Forrest is seated at a bus stop talking to people about his life. As he is telling his story, the look of disbelief comes on their faces. It isn't until he opens his briefcase and shows them the magazine covers that attest to his many adventures when they begin to take him seriously. Somehow, I feel that much of what I write in these pages will not be believable by many who read it. It is understandable because if I had not lived it, I wouldn't believe it myself. Thus, I am forever grateful that I have been able to live this life.

I've arrived at many forks in the road and have had to make a choice. Some of those choices have led me down some dark valleys, and others have led me into brighter pastures. I don't necessarily regret some of those dark hours of my life, for they have contributed to the perspective I have in the present. We live, we learn, we grow. I have met that point many times in my life, and this is the story of what has transpired as I've decided to take the road by which is less traveled. As the poet Robert Frost described in his literary painting, choosing that road has made all the difference. Join with me as I take you through the journey and you will discover the thrill of life and the excitement one can get if he decides to take that road. In this journey, you will encounter the history of my time as I connect with it. It is my walk in history. The people. The places. The moments.

TWO

A YEAR TO BE BORN

"He who is not courageous enough to take risks will accomplish nothing in life."
Muhammad Ali

Nineteen hundred and seventy-eight was a year of change, challenge, excitement, and sensational upsets. African-Americans gained political power in places that they hadn't before. There were upsets in boxing. Two Popes died, the church elected another within 71 days. Eighteen planes crashed, and there were five earthquakes. A resigned US President resurfaced on the scene after three years in solitude. There were peace accords between Israel and Egypt. The country enjoyed the release of memorable movies at the box office. Here are some highlights of the year I was born and the world into which I was born:

- Jimmy Carter was the President of the United States. Walter Mondale was the Vice-President
- Edwin Edwards was the Governor of Louisiana
- The population of the world was 4.21 billion on January 1
- Mohammad Daoud, the president of Afghanistan, was killed in a military coup d'etat
- Woody Allen dominated the Academy Awards when his movie "Annie Hall" won awards for Best Picture, Best Actress, Best Director, and Best Screenplay
- Argentina won the World Cup Soccer Finals
- The New York Yankees won the pennant against the Boston Red Sox
- The Dallas Cowboys defeated the Denver Broncos 27-10 in Super Bowl XII held in New Orleans
- The Washington Bullets defeated the Seattle SuperSonics to win the NBA Championship game
- Leon Spinks upset boxing defeating the champ Muhammad Ali on February 15 in Las Vegas. The two would fight again

in September at the Louisiana Superdome in New Orleans. Ali reclaimed his title in the rematch.

- Completion of Reunion Tower in Dallas
- Two Popes died, and another was elected all with a 71-day period. Pope VI died on August 6. Pope John Paul I succeeded him on August 26 but died on September 28. The Catholic Church elected John Paul II on October 16.
- Memorable movies such as Grease, Animal House, Superman, Jaws II, and The Wiz screened at the Box Office
- The release of dozens of popular songs including:
  o "Three Times a Lady"- Commodores
  o "We are the Champions"- Queen
  o "Last Dance"- Donna Summer
  o "Always and Forever"- Heatwave
  o "The Closer I Get to You"- Roberta Flack and Donny Hathaway
  o Dozens of hit tracks from the motion picture albums of "Grease" and "Saturday Night Fever."
- Ernest Morial was elected Mayor of New Orleans in May. Succeeding Moon Landrieu, he would be the first African-American to serve in the post.
- Former US President Richard Nixon resurfaced on the public scene after his resignation in 1974.
- The IOC met in Athens, Greece to select Los Angeles, California as the site for the 1984 Olympic Games
- Kodak released the 110 Format Compact Camera
- Twelve days of negotiations occurred at Camp David between Egyptian President Anwar El Sadat and Israeli Prime Minister Menachem Begin. Officials signed a peace treaty on September 17.
- The US Supreme Court upheld affirmative action in the 1978 case *Regents of the University of California v. Bakke*. By doing so, it allowed race to be a factor in college admissions.
- Louise Joy Brown was born on July 25, becoming the world's first "test-tube" baby
- The US Senate approved the creation of the Department of Education on September 28

WALKING IN HISTORY: AN AUTOBIOGRAPHY

- Wallace D. Muhammad, son of Elijah Muhammad, resigned as spiritual leader of the Nation of Islam in October.
- District of Columbia City Councilman Marion S. Barry, Jr. was elected on November 7 and would become the mayor of Washington, D.C., a post he would hold until 1991.

Locally and statewide, events shaped the life of not only the community but of my family. My father was a social activist, and his involvement would ultimately involve me:

- January- The Ouachita Parish NAACP officially opened its business office in the Miller-Roy building on DeSiard Street.
- January- Southern University Marching Band gave a pre-game performance at the Superbowl in New Orleans.
- February- The Tabernacle Players performed James Baldwin's drama "Amen Corner" across the city.
- Judiana Furlough was a finalist for the Miss Northeast Pageant
- April- Dr. Joseph B. Johnson was officially installed as the president of Grambling State University
- April- Dr. Jacqueline Simmons sparked local controversy as she delivered her first sermon, being a female preacher.
- June- Gerald Manning, 18, was found guilty of second-degree murder and attempted aggravated rape in the slaying of Vonda Harris. There was public outcry and a movement led by the NAACP for his defense. Attorney Paul Kidd said that in the history of his law practice, Manning was "the only innocent man I have had convicted."
- June 25- Gospel singer and composer Edwin Hawkins performed at the Carroll High School Auditorium
- July- Dr. Jesse Stone was retained by the Southern University Board of Supervisors as President of the university. At the time, Southern University was the nation's largest predominantly black college.
- August- Abe E. Pierce, III became the Assistant Superintendent of Ouachita Parish Schools.
- August- Ford's Grocery opened for business on Renwick Street.

- August- Judiana Furlough was crowned Miss Black Louisiana at the Monroe Civic Center.
- August- Roy Neal Shelling became the acting principal at Lee Junior High. He told reporters that he was the best disciplinarian in the system, and the school board knew it.
- September- NLU completed its 3rd-floor addition at Sandel Library. It would house serials, microfilm collections, and special collections.
- November- Roosevelt Wright, Jr. was re-elected president of the Ouachita Parish NAACP and elected as regional VP of the Louisiana Conference of NAACP branches in North Louisiana.
- November- Muhammad Ali spoke at Northeast Louisiana University.
- November- Anita Whitaker (future Miss Louisiana) was a member of the Northeast Louisiana University homecoming court.
- November- Derwood Cann became the Mayor of the City of Monroe.
- December- Gregory Hobson retained his post as principal of Berg Jones Elementary School, despite being found guilty of dishonesty and neglect on finance charges.

What an exciting world. Not knowing night from day, a brave new world of politics, entertainment, science, religion, sports, and education was forming around me. It would be years before I was aware of the impact of what was transpiring as I slept in my crib. The history of my family is as fascinating as the events surrounding the year of my birth. In the next chapter, I'll highlight the many years of events that shaped the family to which I was born.

THREE

SON OF A PREACHER MAN
"All of us are products of our childhood."
Michael Jackson

I was born, Robert Kenneth Wright, on Sunday, February 19, 1978, the second son to Roosevelt and Joslyn Marie Adams Wright at the St. Francis Medical Center in Monroe, La. My mother was 27, and my father was 28. My name originated from my mother's father (Robert Adams) and a friend of my mother's family (Kenneth Ocdise). According to my birth certificate, I was born at 12:55 PM, delivered by Dr. Robert Guthrie Jarrell. Jarell was a seasoned physician who received his medical degree from Louisiana State University School of Medicine in New Orleans, Louisiana. It would be another 32 years before I met Dr. Jarrell as an adult. Of course, after delivering hundreds of babies in his time, it was impossible for him to know me from the others. These next few paragraphs include the story as told to me by my father.

I am the grandson of Robert Lee and Alice Irene DeGraffenried Adams. From my mother's lineage, the family line began in Bern, Switzerland. The first written knowledge of the family traces to the year 1191. The "Village of Grafenried" was started by Uolricus and Cuno deGravinsried. He is the 10th generation of the DeGraffenreid family in America. The DeGraffenrieds of white English ancestry attempted to distance themselves from their African-American counterparts by changing the spelling of the name. Most white ancestors used "ried" while African-Americans used "reid.") The Caldwell Parish DeGraffenried (of Louisiana) clan started when one white member of the wealthy DeGraffenried family, William, moved to Caldwell Parish from the family's New England estates. In 1838 he moved from Virginia to Alabama and finally to Caldwell Parish. In 1868 his grandson Edwin Lafayette was born.

Edwin developed a closeness to the Negro community. His generosity was unequaled in Caldwell Parish. The family gave a large block of land to the Negro community. The first Cuba Baptist Church sat on the property for many years until a fire destroyed it and it was rebuilt in another area. The church cemetery still sits on the land donated by the DeGraffenrieds.

Edwin had a fascination with Negro women. He was attracted to the smooth ebony skin that glistened in the sunlight. He fathered a child by a Negro girl named "Sette" and a mulatto child named "Osborned" was born. Another Negro woman named "Dove" bore him a daughter named Bertha. He broke all of the rules of traditional white society and fell in love with a 13-year-old Negro lass, Mary Virginia Davis. He was 25 at the time.

The forbidden love of Edwin DeGraffenried and Mary "Mom Mae" Davis produced nine children, three of whom died at birth. Those who lived began the legacy of the Negro side of the aristocratic DeGraffenried family. Those who lived were: Cora, Bert, Annie Mae, Edward, Lee, and Minnie. For his "crime," several white men of Caldwell Parish called Edwin out in the middle of the night and shot and killed him. Bert Davis-DeGraffenreid (7/12/1896-1/5/1976) married Macie Butler and from that marriage was born a daughter Alice Irene DeGraffenried (born 1/7/1930).

Alice Adams had a hard time raising six children alone. Her husband Robert "Lil Coochie" Adams (born 10/8/1925) died in July of 1960 as a result of a military training accident. Though she had financial assistance from the government, raising six children, who were accustomed to the warm, jovial nature of "daddy" was easier said than done. Sandra, Joslyn, Debra Lissa, Peggy, Carl, and Jerry were a handful, even for two parents.

Alone, Alice had to make ends meet. She was a "kitchen" beautician. From morning until night daily, she washed, set and curled hair. At times, singed hair could be smelled in the yard. Always a fine cook, Alice opened a café next to her house in the quarters. She served tasty food to the neighbors and used the money to supplement the family income.

I am also the great-grandson of Henderson Miller (1862-1960) and Lula Phillips (1892-1983). Lula, although married to Caesar

Wright, birthed a child for Henderson Miller and carried Caesar's last name to be known as Roosevelt Wright, Sr. (1909-1993). The family's roots are in Panther Burn, Mississippi, a small plantation outside of Greenville, Mississippi.

Born into a family of communicators and activists

My father, Roosevelt Wright, Jr. was born on June 29, 1949, in Monroe, Louisiana. He graduated from Northeast Louisiana University in 1972 with a Bachelor of Arts in General Studies-Radio/Television and in 1975 with a Bachelor of Arts in Journalism. Joslyn Wright was born on November 21, 1950, in Monroe, Louisiana. She graduated from Southern University in Baton Rouge with a Bachelor of Arts in Social Welfare and a minor in Psychology.

My father spent a few years in prison as a youth in the Alameda County Home for Boys in California while living with his mother. He was soon sent back to Monroe to live with his father. However, his father did not put the time into rearing him properly, so he allowed the family across the street to take him. So, Roosevelt and Viola Hill, who were deacon and deaconess at the New Tabernacle Baptist Church, reared my father, changing his stars.

He later graduated from Carroll High School and matriculated at Northeast Louisiana University. While a student, he was active in the civil rights movement and participated in sit-ins, protests, and marches fighting for civil rights in the Monroe area. He was jailed sixteen times by the Monroe Police Department, and for the first few years of my life, he was monitored by the FBI for his involvement in the civil rights movement. He was the first African-American radio personality on KYEA radio and began our family's newspaper while a student in college and later became the pastor of the church. During the first few years of my life, he was not only the president of the local NAACP chapter but was the regional VP overseeing twenty NAACP chapters in the Northeast Louisiana region.

I have two brothers, Roosevelt Wright, III and Kita Kenyatta Wright, BNW. Roosevelt III was born October 11, 1976. He attended Southern University in Baton Rouge majoring in Mass

Communications. Kita was born October 3, 1979. He graduated from the Dallas Art Institute with an Associates degree in Video Production and Graphic Design.

Roosevelt III was also a radio personality at my father's previous station KYEA and was there when it switched call signs to 100.1 the Beat. He began a newsmagazine AMPS (African-American People Succeeding) when he lived in Shreveport, Louisiana and later became the pastor of a church in New Orleans.

Kita began his own multimedia company ProWorks Productions after he received his training at the Dallas Art Institute and worked for the television ministry at the Potter's House in Dallas (Bishop T.D. Jakes's church). His photography work caught the eye of the national press and he was hired periodically to take photographs for the Associated Press.

In 2017, my brothers and my cousin Gerald Wright became the founding partners of the online streaming network CONGO. Not only would they be streaming the video content of which filmmakers would pay to get published, but they would also be producing their content. I was proud of them at that moment, for we're a hustling family and we are always busy creating avenues to generate revenue.

My Extended Family

I became the godson to John Joseph Sr. and Mildred James as an infant. The christening ceremony occurred at the New Tabernacle Baptist Church. As their family grew over the years, I became the god-brother of Jolinda, Sera, Beverly, Sheila, Debra, Brenda Josh Omega, Melanie, John Joseph James, Jr. and all of their children.

I was also the "unofficial" godson of Alma Moore, a senior usher at New Tabernacle Baptist Church.

I became closely associated with the Parris family in Chicago. I met them through the Holy Trinity Baptist Church. During my tenure in Chicago, the son and daughters (D'Mari, Parris, and Tatiana) of Latrecia and Mario Parris adopted me as their "godfather."

Another young lady at my church, Berdeisha McClinton, adopted me as her godfather. So she was added to my family of children of which I was in line to care for in case their families were not able to or were not around to care for them.

Childhood and Family Life

My family lived North of the Northeast Louisiana University campus in the Mark IV Apartments during my infant years and later moved to our current residence in the Renwick Street neighborhood.

At home, my brothers and I shared a strict work ethic imposed by our parents. Like many households, we had our share of scheduled chores: washing dishes, vacuuming, raking the leaves, dusting, and taking out the trash. There was limited time for television in the home. Our time was either spent at the family business, at church, or in studies. In fact, we were not allowed to watch television during the week. We could only watch television on the weekend, but since we were active at church, scouting, and community service on the weekends, time still did not present itself for tube consumption.

I spent many days in the summer months at the Tri-District Boys & Girls Club. Ervin Peter Turner operated the center, located on Louberta Street. The building was once the Booker T. Washington Elementary School but later became the club. It was in walking distance from my home. I remember carrying a sack lunch for we would be there for hours. Turner stocked the facility with a host of video games, pool tables, and ping-pong tables. Boys that frequented the club had to stand in long lines for their turns to play, but it was worth our wait. We also played baseball in the club's baseball field. It was a memorable experience.

In the mid-1980s, we were introduced to computers by our father. Unlike my father's childhood experience, he took special care to expose us to all available means of technology preparing us for the future that lay ahead of us. He taught us keyboarding, word processing, and stocked our family's library with books and a 1985 World Book Encyclopedia set. We were allowed to play some video games on our *Atari* and *SEGA* game systems including *Pac-Man* and *Donkey Kong* but had to frequent our cousin's home to play the *Nintendo* games like *Mortal Kombat* and *Street Fighter*. My father thought these games were violent and we could not play them. However, the devil in us gave us such a thirst for blood and that "final blow." *Donkey Kong* was cute, but it didn't end with "FINISH HIM!"

In the early 1990s, my father introduced us to the internet. Although, not a new concept, it had been around since the late 1960s as used by the military. It did not make it to the consumer market until my childhood years. We used our father's internet service *Prodigy*. *Prodigy*, a telecommunications company that began in 1984, was an online service that offered its subscribers access to a broad range of networked services, including news, weather, shopping, bulletin boards, games, polls, expert columns, banking, stocks, travel, and a variety of other features. My brothers and I were in the minority of students who had email addresses and online computer access at home when we were in high school.

Although we slept in the same room for many years, it wasn't until our teenage years that my parents expanded our five room home to 11 rooms. My brothers and I shared an active role in the construction of the home addition, which included four new bedrooms, a library/study, and a great family room. Plumbing was not installed, so out of 11 rooms in our total home, there still only existed one bathroom. I still have a photo of me standing in my room marveling at the construction of it. It was such a thrill to have my space, for we each had our tastes in music and hobbies. In my room, there was classical music. In Kita's room, there was Heavy Metal. In Roosevelt III's room, there was R&B and Gospel. Our parents' room contained the sounds of Luther Vandross (mother) and James Brown (father).

I spent many summers in Columbia, Louisiana (my mother's hometown) and frequently traveled to Mesquite, Texas (where my aunt Debra lived). I also spent many afternoons after school at the residence of Roosevelt and Viola Hill on South 20th Street in Monroe. The Hills were not my biological grandparents but raised my father as a young boy. Coincidentally, the Hill residence was across the street from my paternal grandfather's (Roosevelt Wright, Sr.)

residence. There I spent time with Viola, Roosevelt, and their god-daughter, Carmenita Darrington, who all took part along with my parents, in my rearing.

I can remember many days after school at the Hill's residence eating cereal and watching cartoons (because we couldn't watch TV at home). I used to love *He-Man* and *Thundercats.* With "Nana" (as we called her), I'd enjoy a good episode of *The Price is Right* or *Little House on the Prairie.* We would often have to assist with the in-home care of Mrs. Hill as she was bedridden. With both of her legs amputated, she required assistance getting in and out of the bed when necessary. She could always be seen watching VCR tapes of Rev. Johnnie Coleman's sermons. Her daughter and her husband, Dorothy and Glenn Lanier, lived in Chicago. Dorothy was a school teacher, and Glenn was an officer with the Chicago Police Department. They attended Coleman's Christ Universal Temple and would stock dozens of tapes for Mrs. Hill to watch. She could no longer get out to attend New Tabernacle, so church for her was Coleman during the week, and later Tabernacle's television ministry when it began to air on Sunday nights.

My immediate family

My mother has six siblings:Gerald, Jay, Carl, Peggy, Sandra, and Debra. Their children (my first cousins) include Toria Adams, Gerald Wright, Connie Morgan, Edgar Morgan, Senior Chief Petty Officer Michael Neal, Nikisha Neal, and Travis Carroll.

My father has three brothers and one sister: William Smith, Bruce Kevin Wright, Henry Wilson, Louwanda Smith, Laidia Wilson, and Monica Smith. Their children (my first cousins) include William Broadway Smith, Jonathan Smith, Shelby Smith, and Kevin Wright.

Son of a Preacher Man

As my father was a Baptist minister and pastor of our church, my brothers and I were known as "PKs" (preachers kids). We spent plenty of time undergoing home bible study, bible study on Wednesdays and Sunday school on Sunday mornings. Unlike many of our friends, my brothers and I participated in Bible study on Christmas morning. A tradition in the Wright home was a family gathering around the Christmas tree reading the 2nd Chapter of Luke (the Christmas Story) before we tore into our presents. However, over time, Christmas morning began to lose its bang of excitement, for my dad would awake later and later every year, ever prolonging the gift opening activities. So we eventually would get up around 10 or 11:00 on Christmas morning with little anxiety about presents.

Around town, our father's name and reputation defined us. It had its perks, but it also came with its stereotypical treatment. We were expected to be better than the other children in the church and the community because our father was Pastor Wright. It was irritating hearing that usual statement "Oooooh, I'm telling your dad." As I became older, I would often respond to their statements and would add "Fine, just tell him. Okay. Tell my momma too." There was nowhere we could go in town without someone knowing who I was. "You're a lil Wright aren't you," someone would often ask. I didn't despise my father; I just wanted to have my own identity. I think that would be the greatest inspiration for choosing my path. With every road I would take away from familiar surroundings, I would hear less of my connection with my family, making a name for myself. However, I still carried the family's name and unconsciously had to be careful of not getting tangled up in too many dark adventures to tarnish it.

A leather belt created the King of Pop

A few years ago, I viewed the presentation of *The Jacksons: An American Dream* which aired on ABC in November of 1992. It was the story of the creation of pop music with the life of Michael Jackson and his brothers. In the show, it portrayed Joseph Jackson (Michael's father) as a mean cuss, quick to pick up a belt and whip some butt. The years progressed, and Joe was still at it, beating and fine-tuning. Fast forward twenty years after the Jackson 5 first entered the professional scene, I saw that Joe wasn't just beating his boys....he was creating pop music. Michael had it hidden deep within him, and Joe recognized this. The only way he knew to pull it out was to "beat it" out of him. Joe didn't kill Michael. He only made him stronger and the best, hence why he is the King of Pop and is still the most popular entertainer ever to live.

As I watched the show, I saw elements of my father. I had some tough times growing up in the home of Roosevelt Wright, Jr., the preacher, news publisher, civil rights activist and NAACP leader who'd gone to jail sixteen times fighting and protesting an unjust system of American social and political democracy. He was hard on my brothers and me. His discipline was severe, not to maim or abuse, but enough to get the message across. He knew the life he was reared in before Mrs. Hill and wanted to elevate his sons to an even better future. So he didn't spare the rod. The leather belt was his tool of discipline, that and the bare skin on the buttocks of three little black boys destined for greatness. For many years of my childhood, when we were out of order, we'd be stripped down and given our set of lashings from his belt.

At church, if we were out of order, he'd use a baseball command "Strike One." Everyone at church knew what "Strike Three" meant and when he said, "You're going to get it when we get home." The wait was more annoying than the whipping sometimes because we never knew when our father was coming home for the day. There were even nights that went by that we thought he'd forgotten about his warning. My brothers and I would often lie in bed asking "Ya'll think he forgot." However, to our disappointment, it was still on his agenda. Sometimes it would be 11:00 PM even on a school night when we were supposed to be sleep, the bedroom light would flip on, and there he was standing over us with that belt wrapped around his wrist harking "Get up and get undressed." My mother often couldn't bear the activity and would leave the house, especially in our younger years. We would cry even louder because she was leaving. "Don't leave us with him," we'd cry. As we grew older, she'd say "good riddance" because she'd tell us to do something and we'd disobey and when she had enough of trying to save us from dad's wrath she'd wash her hands with us and let my father have his way.

As the years went by, the whippings were less frequent. I don't know if my father grew tired of the whippings or rather realized that our bodies had become immune to the sting. He normally gave the same amount of hits, and we could calculate it in our minds of how much we had to bear before it was over. Whatever his reason was, the discipline transcended from the belt to punishments. There were some punishments in my late teen years I wished he would have used the belt. Even though he used the belt, he never punched us. He never choked us. He never slapped us around. He never cursed us. He set a procedure for effective discipline early on, and we knew how to respond.

Modern society considers corporal punishment brutal and taboo. The only time-out discipline I encountered with my father was time after the whipping. Time to recover and allow my body to go through the aftershocks of pain. I am no stranger to the effects of using a belt. I know it works, as brutal and medieval as it may seem. I have never sat in the back seat of a police cruiser or had handcuffs placed on me by law enforcement. That I have not done so alone is proof that it works. I hope it never happens and if somehow in the future I encounter a dark period, I know that at least three decades went by as a testament of good parenting and they know that they did their job. My father wanted us to be the best that we could be in our various professions. Today, I can say that I always strive for the best in my works. It's in my blood. Maybe it's just under my skin. I don't know for sure, but a belt created the King of Pop. The belt created the author of this story.

Lessons learned from my Parents

Parents teach lessons to their children either directly or indirectly. Their presence or absence teaches volumes of lessons without them saying anything. If I can say one thing for sure about my parents, they were there. They fulfilled their roles. Although passed on hundreds of lessons, here are just a few that I'd like to document here:

- Think twice before you give your word; come hell or high water you must honor your commitments and keep your promises.

- If you lie, you'll steal. Either one indicates that you have a lapse of moral integrity.

- Never disown your family name. Strive to raise it to the highest level of respect and honor.

- No government agency, church or charitable organization should provide a handout for a struggling family member when there are family members who can provide such assistance.

- Always make your siblings welcome in your home unless they have breached the filial bonds so badly that their presence causes problems.

- The husband is the primary breadwinner of the family; it is his responsibility. It is non-debatable. Your family should not assume any long-term obligations that he alone cannot provide.

- If you hope to achieve your divine purpose, you must believe in God.

- No matter how important you are, you should never forget from whence you have come.

- Be community minded, do your part out of the depths of your heart without using volunteerism as a springboard to special favors.

- Register to vote and vote regularly. You have a responsibility to help shape the government of your community and nation. Your vote does count.

- Birds of a feather flock together. If you hang out with those prone to criminal activity and bad behavior, many will assume you are the same.

- Learn the history and struggles of your race or ethnic group. Read materials that will acquaint you with the particulars of your culture, its contributions, mistakes, and successes.

- If you party, party with a purpose. Make sure the social encounter moves you closer to achieving your purpose in life.

- Choose your battles. If you must fight a battle determine whether the result of the fight is worth the price you will pay for your involvement.

- Before you can lead, you must demonstrate your ability to follow.

- If a police officer stops you, don't be a smart alec or sassy. Even if you disagree with his interpretation of events, you are not in a position to challenge him at that moment.

- You can't fly with eagles if you run with turkeys.

- When the money runs low, be inventive. Create ways to earn money. In America, you can sell just about anything and earn money. Do everything you can to avoid asking others to help you; make that your last resort.

- Keep your living costs less than your income to give yourself room to live without a financial worry in case hard times come.

- Tithe on your income to your church or religious institution then save at least a dime out of each dollar.

Many of these lessons I have learned and have maintained. Some of these and many others I've often strayed from and facing the consequences of them is the obvious result. I can say for sure, however, that my parents helped me build the boat and pushed me out to sea. It is up to me and my connection to God how I maintain the ship's course at sea, whether the current is peaceful or rough.

FOUR

BE PREPARED

"It is risky to order a boy not to do something; it immediately opens to him the adventure of doing it."
Robert Baden-Powell

During the mid-twentieth century, Monroe political activist, World War II hero, and professional tailor Ibra B. January, Sr., worked along with B.D. Robinson and A.V. Turner to develop leadership training for African-American youth in North Louisiana through the scouting program. January believed that the future of the African-American community rested heavily on the training of its men to become leaders. Through the efforts of January, Robinson, and Turner, over 100 boy scout troops for African-Americans began in the Northeast Louisiana area. One of those troops was Troop 65, the one that I would join and have some of the greatest adventures a young boy could experience.

I joined the Boy Scouts of America in 1988 at the age of 10. I held offices of duty such as patrol leader, assistant senior patrol leader, troop quartermaster, and senior patrol leader, and annual summer trip planner. Before I became a troop leader, I was a member of the Panther Patrol. Julius Taylor, Jr. was my patrol leader. When he progressed in rank and office, I became the patrol leader. I earned the rank of Scout on June 10, 1988. I earned the rank of Second Class on July 10, 1988. I earned the rank of First Class on April 8, 1989. I earned the rank of Star on August 10, 1989. My Life Board of Review was held on October 13, 1990, almost one year before I would be approved to earn the rank of Eagle.

In the summer of 1990, I traveled with the troop to Washington, D.C. The "learn-fun" trip involved a study on Booker T. Washington, a tour of his home and the George Washington Carver Museum at the Tuskegee University in Alabama. To qualify for the trip, we had to read Washington's autobiography "Up from

Slavery" and write a report on what we learned from the reading. After we departed Alabama, we toured the King Center in Atlanta, Georgia and took photos by King's tomb. We traveled to DC and toured some sites. We visited the Library of Congress, the F.B.I. Headquarters, the Washington Monument, the Lincoln Memorial, the Vietnam Veterans Memorial, the John F. Kennedy tomb and the Tomb of the Unknown Soldier. This experience would also include my first visit to the White House and the Museum of Natural History.

In the summer of 1991, I traveled with the troop on a tour of Louisiana. During this trip, we completed requirements for merit badges in citizenship and American Heritage. We studied for almost three months in advance of the trip in preparation for what we would see. We read books about Louisiana, black Louisianan sports and entertainment stars, the role of Blacks in the war at Port Hudson and Millikin's Bend, and the impact of the Battle of Vicksburg on the slaves in Monroe. The highlight of our trip was our visit with Louisiana Governor Buddy Roemer. It was an unexpected meeting, but he and son kept their appointment to meet with us in the Governor's Mansion. In our meeting with him, he answered our questions covering subjects including education, school rules, and his job as the governor. We were treated to cookies and punch at the mansion.

On the trip, we visited the gravesite of Louisiana's only African-American Lieutenant Governor P.B.S. Pinchback in New Orleans. I took a photo in front of the tomb which was the subject of a dispute between my 8th grade Louisiana History teacher and I. We took swamp rides in the bayous of New Orleans and stopped in Baton Rouge to visit the Mt. Zion First Baptist Church. It is the church that was pastored by Rev. T. J. Jemison, who orchestrated the civil rights push for the 1955 Baton Rouge Bus Boycott.

Before the troop was able to acquire its travel bus, we operated on an old school bus. We raised the money ourselves and bought it. It was in running condition but was not the best ride. It was cold in the winter and hot in the summer. We painted the bus blue and had an American flag striping on the side. We rode that bus all over the country on our various trips. I remember one trip while riding through Kansas, there was rain in front of us and a tornado forming behind us. To top it off, one of the windshield wipers didn't work and the windshield fogged up, so I had the duty of wiping the fog off of the window so the driver, Mr. Donald Fred Mitchell. Mitchell was the main driver for our trips. He was the assistant scoutmaster and was a beast behind the wheel of a commercial bus. A few years went by, and we were able to purchase a modern travel bus and were riding in a little more comfort as we traveled the highways of the United States.

I spent many Thanksgiving breaks at Camp T.L. James, in Farmerville, for Winter Camp. T.L. James is the official Boy Scout camp of the Louisiana Purchase Council. The site covers over 1,000 acres of land and provides the grounds for a variety of scouting activities including a high-ropes course, boating and swimming, rifle shooting and archery, and a lake for fishing. When I was in scouting, we confronted the challenge of a 25-foot high wall made of wood. It was one of the greatest obstacles to our scouting experience. It required lots of teamwork and maximum effort to get all of the members of a patrol to cross over the top. I think my patrol was able to cross with all members once in my scouting days. It was a very difficult feat. What a scout remembers the most about T.L. James is the entrance to the camp areas. As scouts enter the grounds, there are wooden posts along the road that feature the twelve points of the scout law: Trustworthy, Loyal, Helpful, Friendly, Courteous, Kind, Obedient, Cheerful, Thrifty, Brave, Clean, Reverent. We would look forward to calling out the words as our bus made the trek.

A summer job at Miller Funeral Home

Local businessmen sponsored a scout during the summer and provided a part-time opportunity to work in their establishment, earning money to help offset the costs of our summer learn-fun trips. The summer of my 7th-grade year at Carroll Jr. High school, I worked at Reliable Life Insurance.

Joseph Miller, Sr., who was Ouachita Parish's most prosperous African-American businessman founded Reliable Life Insurance. Along with the insurance company, he created Miller

Funeral Home companies in 1945. I never met the senior Miller, but I knew his son Joseph Miller, Jr. and the rest of the family well. I even took a liking to his granddaughter Crystal, who was a classmate of mine at Carroll Jr. High.

I worked one half of the summer at the insurance office on Jackson Street and the other half of the summer at the funeral home on Renwick Street. At the insurance office, I worked in data entry, keying in information about burial policies of which customers made advance payments. At the funeral home, things became a little more interesting. There I cleaned and maintained the facility and was even allowed to wash the Cadillac hearses. I remember the frightening experience of emptying the trash because of the location of the receptacles in the garage. The only entrance to the garage was through the morgue. There were often dead bodies on gurneys in the morgue covered by white sheets. I quickly dashed through there, emptied the trash and came back in. I don't know what I would have done if one of those bodies had an after-life episode of rigor mortis.

Working for the Millers was a fun experience, and it was interesting being around the history of the place and of the company, seeing a larger-than-life-sized photo of Mr. Miller and his wife Alice hanging in the lobby. I was fortunate that the scouting program allowed me to have this eye-opening gig, my first job outside of working for my family at the newspaper.

Lessons learned from merit badges

I earned twenty-seven merit badges during my time in boy scouts. The badges included: Camping, Cooking, Cycling, Hiking, Citizenship in the Community, Citizenship in the Nation, Citizenship in the World, Communications, Emergency Preparedness, Environmental Science, First Aid, Personal Fitness, Pioneering, Journalism, Art, Orienteering, Music, Photography, Personal Management, Theater, Wilderness Survival, Rifle Shooting, Shotgun Shooting, Safety, Reading, Scholarship, and American Heritage.

To earn twenty-seven merit badges required much work. However, the skills developed through the process would be beneficial for the rest of my life.

Earning the Camping Merit Badge required me to camp at least 20 nights and demonstrate that I could create lashings of wood and other camping skills.

As I earned the Cooking Merit Badge, I was required to plan meals and sample menus, explain the food pyramid, make trips to the grocery store and compare prices and nutritional data, and I had to demonstrate my ability to cook over an open campfire. I was very proficient in building and maintain a campfire, and it became one of the things I loved most about camping, especially on cold nights. There is a certain peace sitting watching the flames, engulfed in the warmth of a fire. The trouble was keeping a reserve of firewood to keep up the blaze.

The Cycling Merit Badge required me to participate in the troop's bike trip and explain my knowledge of bike safety, maintenance, and road rules for bikers.

The Hiking Merit Badge had to be one of my most memorable badges to earn. It took the longest to earn as I participated in a five-day hike. The troop hosted a 50-mile hike. We hiked 10 miles a day for five days with packs and gear. The base camp was in Richwood, Louisiana. We had some irritating mosquitoes at the camp and experienced flooding as the rains came in during our hikes. I can still remember seeing tents floating on the waters and our bodies covered with Calamine Lotion as relief from the mosquito bites. It was very challenging time, but we survived it and had the story to tell.

The three citizenship merit badges would be very beneficial in my future as a working journalist and social studies teacher. They were Citizenship in the Community, Citizenship in the Nation, and Citizenship in the World. The Community badge required me to attend a few local public meetings and interview a member of a branch of government and discuss an issue. One of the meetings that I attended was a meeting of the Ouachita Parish Police Jury. After the meeting, I took my agenda and a host of questions and interviewed Juror Abe E. Pierce, III about some of the agenda items. I was also once asked to lead the Pledge of Allegiance at a Monroe City Council Meeting. I appeared at the request of Mayor Bob Powell in uniform and led the meeting's pledge.

The Citizenship in the Nation merit badge required us to visit federal buildings and to write a letter to an elected official on the federal level. I earned this merit badge during my troops trip to Washington, DC. I wrote to US Senator John Breaux, and his office allowed visiting it in the Capitol.

The Citizenship in the World merit badge is one for which I would ultimately become an adult counselor. As a scout, I had to apply for a US Passport, understand and explain the citizenship process. I also had to study various types of governments, the United Nations, and human rights organizations around the world.

The Communications merit badge required me to write a five-minute speech. I do not remember the topic of my speech, but I delivered it before my church congregation during a Sunday morning worship service. I also had to write a letter to the editor of a local newspaper. This requirement came easy since I knew the editor of a local paper and getting my article published was not difficult.

The Emergency Preparedness merit badge required me to know emergency situations and responses to fire, flood, tornado and auto accidents. I had to demonstrate my ability to communicate with rescue planes using signals and my ability to transport an injured person using First Aid maneuvering procedures.

I had to learn about ecosystems, land pollution, erosion, and air pollution during the study for the Environmental Science merit badge. We met the requirements for this badge during our camping events as we were in nature, the place to study the environment.

Earning the First Aid merit badge was a very important step to advancement in the scouting program. I had to learn CPR, various carries to transport injured victims, procedures to give aid to bone fractures, and had to learn how to treat emergency situations like hypothermia, burns, and dehydration. A bulk of my study and training took place with Dr. Henry Bonner, who operated the local Red Cross unit in Monroe, which visiting the Red Cross was one of the requirements for the badge.

The Journalism, Art, Music, and Theater merit badges came easily to acquire for me as my real-time participation in these three fields were almost an automatic completion of the requirements. I was a youth reporter for the local newspaper, I was an art student in the school system's Talented Art Program, and I took regular piano lessons and played with the youth choir at my church. I participated in the annual dramatic productions at the Monroe Civic Center Theater. I wrote the music for the plays, coached the actors who sang songs and conducted the band during the live performances. These all met the requirements for me to earn the Theater merit badge.

The Wilderness Survival merit badge was not an easy one to acquire, for it required me to camp out in the outdoors under the elements. The troop hosted "Wilderness Survival Camps" in my scouting days. We learned survival skills, camped without tents, lit a fire without matches, found our hidden food through the use of land navigation skills, and had to cook our food on an open campfire.

Pinned as an Eagle Scout

I earned the rank of Eagle Scout in Top Gun Troop 65 at the age of 13, after completing a community service project that cost over $5,000. My project entailed the design and construction of a canal ditch walk bridge. I received assistance from the Engineering Department of the City of Monroe, with funds used from a CDBG (Community Development Block Grant) grant. Monroe Mayor Bob Powell and Assistant Scoutmaster Jamie Mayo (later Mayor Jamie Mayo) attended the ribbon-cutting ceremony. I passed the Eagle Board of Review on October 28, 1991. At my Eagle Scout Court of Honor, in December of 1991, I was pinned and given a briefcase with $1,000 in cash and a Bible, the traditional award for Top Gun Eagle Scouts. The funds were placed in a mutual fund of which I would have access to when I graduated from high school.

After I earned the rank of Eagle Scout, I continued to serve as troop guide and later served as Assistant Scoutmaster.

In the summer of 2010, I became a merit badge counselor for the Citizenship in the World Merit Badge. I taught 20 students in the three-week course. Of the 11 students that continued in the course, seven completed the final exam. I awarded them with a free trip to the Tinseltown movie theater in West Monroe, Louisiana to see the movie "The Karate Kid" starring Jaden Smith and Jackie Chan.

In June 2015, I became an authorized merit badge counselor for the Citizenship in the World, Citizenship in the Nation, Citizenship in the Community, American Heritage, and Photography merit badges with the Southeast Louisiana Council of BSA.

During the Winter Camp of 2016, held at the Chemin-A-Haut State Park in Bastrop, Louisiana, I served as the Citizenship in the Community and Citizenship in the Nation merit badges to 25 campers. Only seven completed the Citizenship in the Community requirements, and only four completed the Citizenship in the Nation requirements.

FIVE

TALES OF A CHURCH MUSICIAN

"Most importantly for me growing up, it was a spiritual, it was the gospels, it was James Cleveland, Aretha Franklin, Marion Williams…that music helped me preserve my sanity."

Cornel West

In the summer of 1985, I began playing the piano at the age of 7. One evening after a youth musical, I sat on the piano at my church and began playing the tune of one of the songs that was performed at the musical. The name of the song was "Father We Come." The lyrics to the song read: "Father we come to glorify thy name. Father we come to give your name a praise. For you're worthy of our praises, today, forevermore that's why we praise you and glorify thy name." My parents realized I had an ability; I've been playing piano since then.

I sang in the church youth choir as a tenor until 1987, when I began playing the keyboard for the Tabernacle Baptist Church youth choir under the direction of Mrs. Brenda Kyles. At the age of 10, I started testing out my skills on the Hammond organ.

GMWA

The Gospel Music Workshop of America was founded in 1967 by Rev. James Cleveland and Albertina Walker. It hosts an annual convention in August where some 15,000 gospel music delegates from around the country converge to attend seminars and workshops, learning the newest trends and samples of the latest gospel songs. The first workshop was held in Detroit at the King Solomon Baptist Church with almost 3,000 delegates. From there it grew to the massive convention it is today.

In 1987, Brenda Kyles and organist Leatrice Morrison led the New Tabernacle Baptist Church music department. It was a charter member of the Gospel Music Workshop of America. A group of choir members traveled to the GMWA annual convention in Detroit, Michigan that year. In Detroit, I witnessed thousands of people engaged in workshops and seminars on gospel music. I enjoyed the exhibition hall where vendors sold everything from choir robes to sheet music. I sang in the youth choir at the finale musical. It would be the first of many experiences singing with such large bodies of singers.

Piano training

I took piano lessons at Dew Music School (the former Zeagler Music on North 18th Street). Soon after, my father gave me music instruction for some years. Though he wasn't a piano player, he was a musician and understood the theory. In high school and college, he was a percussionist. His ability to read music afforded him the ability to tutor me and make sure I knew how to count and play in time.

As with many young piano students, I did not like practicing, and the continued scrutiny by my father to aim for perfection worked some nerves in me. I would cry day after day when I was forced to sit and practice. My father bribed me with chocolate candy sometimes to get me to practice. He'd put a candy bar on the edge of the keyboard and promise that I could eat it once I'd finished my practicing for the day. As I recall, I went through a lot of candy bars as a young musician.

As time commenced, my father continued to search for a real piano teacher that would give me quality instruction. He wanted the instruction of a church musician. That piano player would be none other than Ellis Carter, the dynamic piano player at First Missionary Baptist Church, where Rev. Andrew Mansfield was the pastor. I didn't learn under Carter for more than a year. He would often be away at workshops or had other music duties and would not be available for lessons, so my father ceased the training under his tutelage.

During my high school years, I received piano training under Jessie Stewart. Stewart was an elderly white woman who taught me out of her home in Swartz, Louisiana. There, she taught me the rudiments of music theory and harmony. Mrs. Stewart was a religious woman, so she knew the hymns of the Baptist Church. She introduced me to new hymns used at predominantly white congregations (unlike those used in my predominantly black church). Songs like "A Church's one foundation" "No not one" and "There's Just Something About that Name" were just a few of the hymns I learned under her tutelage.

In 1995, I received a Superior Rating in Hymn Playing at the National Federation of Music Club's Junior Music Festival held at Northeast Louisiana University. I also participated in two public recitals held at the university. Under Mrs. Stewart, I learned arranged versions of Beethoven's "Moonlight Sonata" and "Fur Elise." It is also through my training under Mrs. Stewart that I developed an interest in the celebrity pianist Dino Karsonakis

Kartsonakis was trained at Julliard and was the pianist for Kathryn Kuhlman, a Pentecostal television evangelist. Her show "I Believe in Miracles" appeared weekly during the 1960s and the 1970s. Dino was the religious version of Liberace, for his religious performances were filled with complex classical arrangements. His concerts included all of the showmanship of Liberace, fabulous costumes and light shows. I always dreamed of being a performing piano player like Dino.

In 1995, West Monroe's First Baptist Church brought Kartsonakis to perform at its church. Their grand piano sat in the pulpit where Dino played the songs from his cassette tapes. My parents took me to see Dino on both nights of his performances. I met him, bought one of his cassette tapes and he signed it for me. Today it is still in my collections as one of my more prized possessions.

Youth Musician at Louisiana Baptist Youth Encampment

In 1991, I became a youth camper at the Louisiana Baptist Youth Encampment. The encampment was an end-of-the-summer week-long convention for the Black Baptist youth from around the state of Louisiana. Rev. Dr. T. J. Jemison, of the Mt. Zion Baptist Church in Baton Rouge, Louisiana, was the president of the Louisiana Baptist State Convention at the time. The convention was the umbrella organization for the encampment. Churches who were members of the Baptist Convention would register their youth to attend the annual session. Southern University A&M College in Baton Rouge hosted the encampment on its campus every year. There were almost 2,000 teenagers and their church sponsors at the encampment every year.

Of those, 500 of them sang in the camp choir. I sang in the choir my first year. It was the largest choral gathering I had seen since attending the James Cleveland Gospel Music Workshop in Detroit back in 1987. Greg Jones, a Baton Rouge church musician, was the director of the encampment music ministry. He was one cool guy that was beloved by the choir members. Mrs. Kyles, my choir director back home, had her funny way of keeping the youth choir involved and interested, making it fun to participate, but Jones was on another level. This guy was phenomenal. To the youth, he was the James Cleveland of gospel music. The songs he would introduce to us every summer were fun, required lots of memorization of words and required lots of moving that was syncopated with the action of the song. Though we only had four days to learn the words to eight brand new songs, Greg made it exciting enough to make us excited to return to choir rehearsal the next day. We were eager for more. When we returned home from camp, we would sing camp songs taught by Jones for months and sometimes all the way up until the following camp.

Camp leaders requested youth musicians who desired to play musical instruments with the camp music staff. My second year as a camper, I answered to the call and on Sunday night following the Convocation service, Greg and his brother Jason, who was the drummer, met with all the eager musicians who thought they had what it took to play in his band. We would all soon find out that it would be no easy task. I was only 14 at the time, but I had been a church musician for almost half my life. Certainly, this would be a walk in the park. Not so.

Greg was very demanding. He could sing, play keyboards, organs, and also knew how to play the drums. Our eyes were wide open in every moment of his presence. Although we were Christians and understood that there was to be 'no god other than God,' we for moments of time forgot all about that commandment. Greg Jones was a god, in a musical sense, and we were willing to do whatever it took to please him. He became a great mentor, and the music that he taught was on another level as compared to what we sang back home at church.

At 9:00 AM on Monday morning of the 1992 summer camp, we met in the F.G. Clark Activity Center at Southern for musician's rehearsal. It was an hour of musical power. When people come to hear a choir sing at a musical, little do they know of the time it takes to put the elements together to make the sound we call Gospel Music. Although it looks easy, it is very complex and organizing such a group of drummers, keyboard players, and a horn section takes a master musician. Greg was such a person.

There were no guitars in the band. So, that year I was placed on keyboards. My task was to play the bass line. Greg referred to me as RobBass. I wondered if I would ever learn how to play like Greg for he never taught me the chords to the songs….only the bass line. Playing the bass line would be a skill that I would later master and one that would play a significant role in my musical repertoire.

The bass line, as I learned, is one of the most important aspects of gospel music. Without it, the song is empty and is impossible to build the other elements of the sound. The bass line is also the feeder for the beat. A bass guitar player or keyboard player who runs the bass line well and with a little creativity will work wonders for a good percussionist. It is the groove that permeates the music scene that allows the gospel music drummer to create dynamic sequences of beats. It is that groove which musicians refer to as "the pocket." Once a drummer is in that zone, it's on. Sit back and watch the drumsticks travel at rocket speed.

That was my responsibility. It would not be an easy one either, for Jason, the band leader, was quite different than Greg. Greg was the good cop, and Jason was the bad cop. Greg had fun with the choir members and was more involved with the singing and choral movements. Jason, on the other hand, had full control of the beat, the sound, and the musicians. If a youth musician couldn't cut it, there was no sense in crying to Greg. If Jason said you were out, you were out. Greg gave him control of that aspect, and when we realized this, we were more compelled to please Jason than Greg.

Playing the bass line for Jason was crucial. As he scolded me so many times, I had reflections of my father. Jason was more demanding than Greg. They were both perfectionists, but he was also Greg's choice for band leader. As church musicians know, there are a number of guys lining up to play drums. If one can't fulfill the duties, it's easy for the director to say 'get up' and put someone else on the seat to play the beat. Although the two were brothers, I don't think Greg would hesitate to replace Jason if it got to the point that he couldn't hold his end.

There I was, learning new material and playing in the band. Though Greg was over the choir, he didn't normally participate in the music at the other parts of the encampment. Throughout the day, there were worship services and assemblies that required music. This task was left up to those musicians that Greg had selected as camp musicians. Everett Parker, a music professor at LSU, was the General Camp Music Director. He would provide the music and organize choral arrangements for the day services. During the day he would allow the youth musicians to play along with him. On the main platform, there was a row of chairs along the rear railing. The young musicians would sit here and wait for their opportunity to play. We were like musical vultures, awaiting a cue to play in front of a 2,000 member audience.

The first time I was allowed to play the organ during the day service I thought I was in heaven. This was major for me. I couldn't play chords in the band for the musical, but having that opportunity to play the hymns of the church during worship services made up for the lacking. It was a very enjoyable experience.

As the years progressed, I continued to play the bass line for Greg's band until 1995. That year he began allowing me to play chords on his songs. You couldn't tell me anything. I had made it.

In 1996, there was a change of direction at the encampment. My father was named the Director of the Encampment. The

Christian Education deans changed, the music staff changed, and the whole operation of the encampment went through a period of transition to what was known as the "Circle of the Chosen." Greg moved to California the previous year. He was flown in to head up the music for the encampment for one more year. This would be the last year I would play in Greg Jones' Youth Encampment band.

I was charged by my father to score the tune to lyrics he wrote as the theme song for the encampment. The song was entitled "We are the Chosen." Our church choir director Brenda Kyles directed the song at the encampment that year; I played the grand piano during the singing. In retrospect, it was a rough rendering of the song, for it was first performance. We made it through, and the audience received it well. However, it wasn't until 2000, when the true essence of what I wrote in 1996 came to life. I was in the military at the time and was home for leave during the encampment week. Herman Finley was the music director that year. The camp produced a live recording, and I was asked to teach the song to the 2000 choir and direct it during the musical. I conducted my band rehearsal, taught the song to the choir and received a standing ovation from the audience at the closing of the song. That arrangement of the song was more of an accomplishment to me than writing it in the four years that proceeded it.

The year 2004 was my last year as a musician at the Louisiana Baptist Youth Encampment. During my final year, Herman Finley directed the music department. Although Finley led the music department, like Everett Parker in the mid 90's, it was Sheridan Royce Mosely who organized and directed the musical. Mosely, a very talented church musician at the Lone Wa Missionary Baptist Church in Monroe (at the time) would also become my mentor. Like Greg from previous years, he knew how to work the youth singers into excitement and made us all eager to come to rehearsal to see what more he had for us. And like my experience with Greg, I was excited to play for Royce. He was one of those musicians who didn't care for other musicians playing the chords to his song. He knew what he wanted and what sound he required to deliver the song, and if he couldn't have it, he'd be better off playing it himself. He was known and still is known for directing from the piano. He'd sing the solo, play the music, and direct a 300 member choir with power and passion. It was very effective, and I was shocked in 2004 when he got up from his chair during the song, "And He Blessed My Soul" and asked me to take over while he directed the choir. It was another one of those moments I was blessed to work with such talented musicians who thought I was good enough to play their music.

Mosely would later become the General Overseer of Music and Worship Arts at the Mt. Zion Baptist Church in Nashville, Tennessee. Bishop Joseph W. Walker, III is the pastor of the church.

Over time, a 15-year-old boy playing the bass line for Greg Jones' band developed into a 26-year-old assistant director and staff musician for the Louisiana Baptist Youth Encampment. I carried lessons learned at the camp with me throughout the rest of my musical career.

The Chaplain's Musician

In 2000, On my second deployment with the Marines, aboard the USS Duluth, I volunteered to play music for the weekly Protestant worship services, held in the ship's chapel. Along with my musical duties, I also served as one of the Chaplain's assistant, aiding in storage and maintenance of supplies used for the services such as Bibles and communion supplies. It was no coincidence that I'd taken hymn playing study under Mrs. Jessie Stewart in my teenage years that I'd be using these songs learned for the Chaplain's services. He gave me the use of the Chaplain's assistant's room, which was a real luxury for me aboard the vessel. Many of my superior enlisted officers didn't have their personal office space on the ship, and there I was, a junior Corporal, with a private office on a Navy ship.

Mt. Olive Baptist Church- Greenwood, LA

I served as a church musician at the Mt. Olive Baptist Church in Greenwood, LA under Pastor Theron Jackson (2005 – 2006) where I worked with Organist Marcus Franklin. Franklin introduced me to the Yamaha Motif, a new keyboard that was on the market. The keyboard's Grand Piano sound became a favorite and must-have for me. I'd played on Yamaha's Ensoniq and the Fantom keyboards in the past. I get irritated with "computer" sounding piano tones in keyboards. The Motif had a very distinct sound that I liked. Marcus would play the organ, and I'd play on the Motif. Jackson was a social activist and a Shreveport City Councilman. That I had a similar interest in politics and history, we would often sit in the pastor's study and talk politics. He was also a powerful speaker. Although short in stature, he could reach mighty high with his preaching ability.

Holy Trinity Baptist Church- Chicago, IL

I served for one year at the Holy Trinity Baptist Church in Chicago, IL under Pastor Charles Cherry (2006- 2008) where I worked with Organist Walter Miller. At Holy Trinity, I played for both the massed choir and the "Angelic Choir." For over two decades, my style of Hammond organ playing consisted of full chords on the right hand and one note on the left hand followed by bass tones. Miller introduced and instructed me on the skill of playing left-handed chords, a feat that I'd had found difficult to master. It was through Miller's famed rendition of "Pray for Me" that I was able to begin the practice of chording with my left hand and playfully "whining the Hammond" with single notes played on the right hand. This was a style I would continue and perfect for the rest of my time in churches.

The Holy Trinity congregation welcomed me. It sometimes felt like I was their long-lost relative who finally got on a train and traveled up north from the deep south. I enjoyed working with Miller and the many talks with the pastor's son Frederick. We had a lot in common, being preachers' kids, so we had plenty of fun fellowships.

Back at New Tabernacle in 2008

I returned to New Tabernacle Baptist Church in Monroe in January 2008 to resume a post I left four years earlier.

In January 2010, the church created a praise team under the direction of Crystal Winfield. I served as the musician of the team along with my duties as Church Musician.

On November 14, 2010, I gave a recital at New Tabernacle Baptist Church to commemorate my 25th year as a musician. The church rented a black "Young and Chang" baby grand piano on which he performed. Many notable church musicians including Roosevelt Pine, Samuel Douglas, and Eddie Bilberry attended the event.

Playing with great musicians and singers

During my time as a musician, I also worked with many other notable gospel musicians including Herman Finley, S. Royce Moseley, Ahmad Smith, Everett Parker, Michael Jackson, Seane Kelley, Eddie Billberry, Samuel Douglas, and drummers Osaro Kyles, Josh Smith, Jonathan Newman, and Ashton Howell. I received private instruction at the homes of accomplished Monroe musicians Roosevelt Pine and Richard Miles. Pine had a black Baby Grand piano in his salon and Miles had a Hammond Organ in his music room. Miles had a habit of clearing his organ registrations after he would leave the organ, a practice of many seasoned organists. Miles was the former Assistant Superintendent of the Monroe City School District. Somehow, I found myself in the homes of these great educators before I developed a desire to teach. It was time well spent, for I learned a lot from them. I also met and received an autographed cassette tape from renowned gospel songwriter and pianist Glenn Burleigh. I still play and direct songs he composed in choral renderings.

I've also accompanied many talented singers in my time as a musician. I've been a director and a solo musician on many occasions, but there is a certain freedom of expression that I get when I accompany a singer. It's as if I'm a much better musician when I'm serving others and not receiving attention on a musical pedestal. Of all the people I've heard sing "The Lord's Prayer" none have been able to put out the power and expression other than Brittney Jones Williams. She sang in the praise team at Tabernacle, and it was a joy working with her. Renee Broadnax gives a one-of-a-kind delivery of "Precious Lord" by Thomas Dorsey. She even sang it in a 2018 heritage production at the Monroe Civic Center when she played the role of Marian Anderson. Carolyn Taylor, another lady from my church, always liked to sing "My Tribute" and even as her voice aged, she could still hit some high notes.

There are three male singers from my community of which I've accompanied on many occasions that have great voices. Those are Mr. Andrew Hill, David Brownfield, and Pastor Oliver W. Billups, Jr. Hill was a choice for many funerals and social programs. He has a classic voice and a command presence and can hit a pretty good falsetto. Hill always liked to sing "He's there all the time" and "There's a bright side somewhere." Brownfield was known for his falsetto delivery at church services and had a favorite song that he sang "Jesus Purchased My Salvation." The song could not conclude until he softly sang "Jesus Purchased." Pastor Billups was great anytime he stepped in front of a microphone. There were many instances in which I heard him sing of which he didn't need music. He asked me to play for him at a funeral, and I was too excited. He sang "King Jesus will Roll the Tears Away" and brought the church to a shout. He too sang "My Tribute" as Mrs. Taylor and gave a command performance. There were many others of which I've worked with and accompanied, but these few are the standouts over decades of musicianship.

New Beginnings Worship Center- Monroe, LA

In September 2011, the New Beginnings Worship Center, where Prophetess Dr. Janet Floyd was the pastor, hired me as its musician. I remained there until my departure for California in December of 2012. Floyd was one of those inspiring individuals that made you want to stand when she walked in the room. When she spoke, she spoke with conviction and confidence. She would look you in the eye and sometimes would be preaching to you. Floyd had a favorite song "Living He Loved Me" of which she sang and danced to for almost 20 minutes in an extended melody. This was a very high spirited Pentecostal praise song that required a lot of energy from the organist and the drummer. I always wanted to travel with her on her road trips, for she would be all over the country preaching at megachurches, and then be back in Monroe for Sunday services.

One of the rituals at Floyd's church was the washing of the feet. It was a humbling practice for the pastor as she would reduce herself in stature to that of a lowly servant capable of washing the feet of her members. The musician was not exempt from this gesture, as I would find out. After washing the feet of the members, Floyd would come over to the organ as I was playing music and pull off a sock and shoe and would wash my foot. It was the strangest thing to me, for I'd always hoped she would pass me. She wouldn't have it any other way. Members had to always to be ready for foot washing for we never knew when Floyd was going to pull out her pan and I had to learn how to play the organ while someone was washing my foot.

St. Andrew Baptist Church- Braithwaite, LA

In June of 2015, I was hired as the organist at the St. Andrew Baptist Church in Braithwaite, LA, where the Rev. Merlin Flores was the pastor. I worked under the direction of choir director Trina Payne and with pianist Charles Jackson. In May 2016, the church presented me a plaque and flowers in appreciation for my "Spirit of Excellence" rendered to the church. This came one week before my final Sunday at the church, and the pastor decided to commend me for my work over the year I served. My last Sunday at St. Andrew was May 29, 2016.

Flores was a new pastor when I began in 2015. However, he had been a preacher for years as well as a musician. He was a very strong preacher and could get those older preachers to stand in awe. He was that good. When he and I had our initial meeting, he was very interested in hearing me play the organ, for that is what he was most needing. That he was an organist as well meant that he knew what to listen for when I played. I passed his test, and he instantly gave me the job. We had a very cordial working relationship. Sometimes he had to fuss when things didn't go as he needed it for the services. And then we'd be back to laughing and joking as ministerial partners. He was one cool preacher with whom to work.

New Light Baptist Church- Monroe, LA

In October of 2016, I responded to an advertisement for the job of Minister of Music/Organist at the New Light Baptist Church in Monroe. This is the church where my high school choir director, Mr. Pine, played at for over forty years. New Light was known for singing the traditional style of gospel worship, as was the preference of Pine. That they needed someone to fill in the void to provide similar services appealed to me, as I was one of the few musicians from the area that could get close to Pine's delivery. I never would compare myself to Pine, as he was my teacher. However, I could take a lot of what he taught me back to the place that he called home for many decades.

I spoke with Mr. Andrew Hill and told him of my interest in the position, and he invited me to come and play for the church to evaluate my abilities. Within two weeks, I was sitting before the musician search committee in an interview for the position. The committee asked me a series of questions such that it could make a recommendation to the church.

I had never been regretful of my past or my many adventures as I was in that moment, for I always thought my ability to do so much in so many places was rather impressive. However, my resume also spoke of my inability to remain in a place for an extended period. This was a cause to pause for me as I had to face the music that it was time to cease with moving around from church to church and be consistent with at least one area of my life. These people were about to give me a handsome salary to do a job I knew all too well. In return, they wanted something I had not been able to give anyone else.....a promise of stability. But I'd seen the way that Mr. Pine and Mr. Samuel Douglas lived. I'd visited their homes. These gentlemen lived very well in small town Monroe. The thing that made their kingdoms possible was that they were committed, they remained loyal servants in their posts, and their posts rewarded them for that. I took all of this into consideration and decided it was time.

My first service at New Light was on Sunday, October 23, 2016. What I presented to them was acceptable and the Pastor, James

B. Johnson, was delighted to have me accompanying his ministry. Within a month, I was already preparing for a musical; as the church has it's annual Christmas Cantata on the 2nd Sunday in December.

The Cantata took place on Sunday, December 11, 2016. It would be my first musical as Minister of Music for the church, and it expected much of me. We put in a lot of hours of rehearsal time in addition to the regular rehearsals for Sunday worship services. The choir sang with great power and excitement as we progressed from hymns to a testimonial selection at the closing of the event.

On April 22, 2017, the choir traveled to Thomasville, Alabama to worship with the New Greater First Baptist Church. We lodged at Hometown Inn and worshipped in song service the next day. I drove to Thomasville from New Orleans, as my fraternity's regional convention was the previous day in New Orleans. Afterward, I took the six-hour voyage from Thomasville back to Monroe.

I directed my second Christmas musical at New Light on December 10, 2017. We sang a number of selections, and I asked my friend and fellow musician Ahmad Smith to accompany me. He played the organ for the program. He's one of those organists an organist wants behind him. His playing allowed me to direct with ease, for I knew he knew how to deliver a quality sound.

Louisiana Baptist State Convention Choir

During the spring months of 2017, I began rehearsing with the choir organized to sing for the Louisiana Baptist State Convention. The convention convened in Monroe in July 2017. It was a choir that was formerly under the direction of my mentors Roosevelt Pine and Samuel Douglas. This would be the first convention musical in Monroe since the death of the two. So it was sentimental to me to participate in the event. The musical was under the direction of Rev. John L. Russell, Jr. The choir sang 15 songs in three parts. They began with a Tom Fettke arrangement of "The Prayer." They continued with: "Enter his gates" sung with soloist Melissa Riley, "The King of Glory" with soloist Carolyn P. Armand, "Ain't He Good", "Holy, Holy, Holy" with soloist Corine

Henderson, "Even Me" with soloist Charlene Jackson, "When He Calls Me" with soloist Patricia Keys, "He is the Keepuh" with soloist Minister Tina T. Withers, "God will bring you out" with soloist Kema Dawson-Robinson, "All the Praises" with musical songwriters singing solo Dexter Moffit and Crystal Gayle Williams, "Not for Our Glory", "A Change" with soloist Rev. Henry Yearby, and "Sold out for Christ" with soloist Muriel Finley.

A memorial period was held to honor the musical legacy of past convention directors and musicians. Pastor Ike Byrd, III led the memorial service to commemorate the contributions of Dr. Samuel Douglas, Dr. Roosevelt Pine, Gwendolyn Douglas, Nellie Moore, and Dr. C. V. Rodgers. During the period two selections were sung by a quartet including Janice Fleming, Andrew Hill, Patricia Keys, and Rev. John L. Russell, II. They sang a Donald Vails arrangement of "When we all get to heaven" and "Thank you Jesus" a song written by Dr. Roosevelt Pine.

Russell was assisted in directing the choir by Dexter Moffitt, of Calvary and St. James Baptist Churches, Rev. Seane T. Kelley, of First Missionary Baptist Church, David Starr, Sr., of Mt. Olivet Baptist Church, Charles Lacy, of Zion Traveler Baptist Church, and Terrance Smith, musician at True Vine Baptist Church. Moffitt, Starr, myself, Ahmad Smith, Pastor Michael Thompson, and Blake Wright played the music for the event.

More than thirty years have passed, and I've been the musician at six churches, directed a 500-member choir, written religious song material, and have mustered a tutelage of ten beginner piano students. I began by playing the hymns, anthems, spirituals, and contemporary gospels. I play by ear and read music and have entered the technological world of being the iPad Church Musician, where I have iTunes running, my digital hymnal, and YouTube religious videos operating as the pad sits on that old Hammond organ. It has been a wonderful experience that has taught me many lessons about being technically proficient, a well dressed and mannered professional, and how to be an effective accompanist. It has also taught me how to let the spirit flow, how to work with a preacher and how music aids in their delivery of the word. It has taught me how to spice up the worship experience with a little showmanship and excitement that lifts up bowed down heads, brings tears of joy to the surface, and leaves a weary soul returning home uplifted.

The charge and duty of a church musician are two of great importance. Music plays a chief role in the worship service and right below the preacher, the church musician can either kill or elevate the service. It is a serious role that many either are naive to its importance or never learn to master to their full potential.

SIX

EDUCATION STORY: BEING A CARROLL BULLDOG

"Gathered all together, we will not say goodbye. For it is our thoughts of you that will never die."

Dr. Shamalon Johnson

I was supposed to have been a Neville High School Tiger. However, factors out of my hands would not allow me to walk through the halls of Neville and hear Coach Roosevelt Rankins say "Get down Tiger." I'd spent my first six years of grade school in Neville feeder schools (Sallie Humble, J.S. Clark, and Georgia Tucker). Then I received the heart crushing news from my father that I'd be going to Carroll. "My sons will graduate from Carroll," he said. So there would be a period of transition as I would be in a school environment comprised of kids with whom I was not familiar.

I began my journey as a Carroll Bulldog in August of 1990. At Carroll Junior High I trained under Alma White (Homeroom), Leonard Clark (Reading/English), Pat Duke (Louisiana History), Patsy McClanahan (Earth Science), Kathy Monohan (Algebra I), Moses Farris (Physical Education), and Janet Maxwell (Talented Art). The principal was Jimmy Jones. At Carroll Junior High, I was a member of the Student Council and participated annually in the school's Science Fair.

A referral was written to me in my 8th grade Louisiana History class for being disrespectful to my teacher. The incident grew from a discussion on the burial site of former governor P.B.S. Pinchback. My teacher, Duke, argued that Pinchback was buried in New York. However, I argued that he was buried in New Orleans. So a battle ensued between he and me in front of the class. So, Duke wrote the referral and sent me to the office for challenging his authority. I visited the site of P.B.S. Pinchback's burial site in New Orleans on a trip there with the boy scout troop. I even took a picture standing next to the tomb. Even this was not convincing enough for Duke. Pinchback died in 1921 in New York. However, his body was returned to New Orleans and was placed in the family's tomb in Metairie.

I had a memorable physical education teacher. Coach Moses Farris was a no-nonsense teacher. He had simple rules and dire consequences for breaking them. "White t-shirt, gold gym shorts....or I'mma get my board," Farris would say. As long as the students were dressed out in P.E. attire and participating, they were okay in Coach's book. He did not hesitate to use his paddle, as corporal punishment in those years was accessible as a tool of behavioral correction in every classroom. I used to dislike dressing out for I was a very tiny fellow. As my adolescent growth spurt had not set in, I did not look like the boys who had developed, so naturally, I was self-conscious about my small frame and skinny legs.

Dr. Leonard Clark was my English teacher. He had a level of style and sophistication that exceeded many of his colleagues at Carroll Junior High. Clark's room was immaculate, and he spent plenty of time watering his plants and wiping down furniture. He dressed well and always chose his words wisely. Later in life when I went to college, he would become my advisor. In his office at the University of Louisiana at Monroe, there were elements of his classroom. Clean, neat, and sophisticated. I felt like I was back on the Renwick Street campus. This was Clark's style, and he will always be remembered for it.

At the High School

I began my high school education in 1992 at the age of 14. I attended Carroll High School and received training from a number of teachers including: 9th Grade- K. Phillips (Homeroom), L. Richards (Civics), Brenda Dixon (Biology), Walter Rush (Algebra 2), Juanita Rambo (English I), Albert Hartwell (Physical Education), Sylvia White (French I), and Darryl Tripplet (Talented Art); 10th Grade- Walter Rush (Homeroom), Terry Kent (Geometry), Wayne Brown (Chemistry), Marsha Ayers (English II), Sylvia White (French II), Ernest White (World Geography), Janice Fleming (Consumer Home

Economics/Food & Nutrition), Maydell Spears (Physical Education); 11th Grade- Walter Rush (Homeroom/Advanced Math), James Allen (Business Math), Stacy Guillory (English III), David Breighthaupt (American History), L. Richards (Free Enterprise), Brenda Dixon (Biology 2), and Jana Chowns (Keyboarding I); 12th Grade- K. Medley (Fine Arts Survey), Advanced Choir (Roosevelt Pine), English IV (Lynetta Coates). The principal was Julian Gray.

I enjoyed my English course with Ms. Rambo. Ms. Rambo was a no-nonsense kind of educator. She rarely cracked a smile, and when she did, you felt a certain peace. She would write out her problems and assignments on the board. Most of them were essay type questions of which I enjoyed. When she would sneeze, students would respond "Bless you." Ms. Rambo would return "No, sweetie, you don't have the power to." I have used this line time and time again. Such a cold, short statement. I also remember reading Romeo and Juliet in her class. We read the text, and at the conclusion, we viewed the 1968 film by director Franco Zeffirelli….however, not the entire movie. The movie starred Leonard Whiting as Romeo and Olivia Hussey as Juliet. There was a scene in the movie where the two stars were naked in bed. Rambo stood up from her seat and stood in front of the screen so we couldn't see it, then moved out the way when it was complete. That didn't help my situation for now I was destined to go find a copy of the movie and see what it was Ms. Rambo was hiding. Well, I saw it. Not too bad. I also loved the theme song from the movie "Love theme from Romeo and Juliet" ("A Time For Us") by Henry Mancini. It is a single from the album "A Warm Shade of Ivory." The song was a number-one hit song in the United States in 1969 and topped the Billboard Hot 100 singles in June of 1969. Because of my time in Rambo's class, exposure to it made it one of my favorite songs to play on the piano.

One of my more memorable teachers at Carroll was Mr. Walter Rush. He taught me Algebra 2 and Advanced Math. Rush also taught my father when he was a student at Carroll in the 1960s, evidence of Rush's tenure at the school. He would have a unique vernacular of which everyone who has taken his class would recognize. "Uhhhhh sir, where's your notebook," he would ask when students found difficulty in solving problems. He wanted to see if they took notes during his lecture. Rush taught more life skills than he did mathematics. He would often sit on the edge of his desk with white chalk all over his hands and talk about life outside of school. He would discuss citizenship and encouraged us to be productive citizens. He would often get irritated by intercom interruptions or at students making unnecessary noises in class. When students would tap on their desks he'd hark "Uhhhhhh sir, if you want to play the drums, go see Claverie (the band director). This is not the place." Rush gave two-four question tests on legal sized paper. More often they would be two-question tests, one math problem on the front and one on the back. "Uhhhh, sir...if you can't do two problems why should I waste time checking twenty," he would explain.

Mrs. Fleming taught me how to sew. Even though my mother is an expert seamstress, I never learned the skill from her. It was Fleming who would put me behind a sewing machine, show me how to read a pattern and make a garment. Home Economics was divided into two semesters. We operated in the kitchen during the first semester. During my semester of in the sewing lab, Fleming guided me in making a pair of spandex shorts. I was fascinated by the Soloflex workout machine advertised on TV. The actors in the commercials always wore spandex shorts. So, when I finally purchased a used Soloflex, I worked out in my white spandex shorts, made from a pattern bought at Hancock's Fabrics.

Mr. Ernest White taught the AP World Geography class. This class would open a door that would expose me to the future, and I didn't even know it at the time. Every day in his class we watched a syndicated TV show called "Channel One." It featured the highlights of news from around the world as we focused on the politics and geography of Earth. The class was small since it was an honors course. I learned a lot, and I used a photo we took in class in my classroom when I became a geography teacher, some 20 years later.

Mrs. Coates was my English Teacher during the junior and senior year. There were many papers to write in her class, but the time in her class was sweet as we would always have access to Peanut M&Ms. When I took courses at the University of Louisiana at Monroe, I would often have Mrs. Coates to review my papers before I submitted them. She told me to use her as a resource and that she'd gladly take the time to assist me in being successful. When I later became a teacher, I would continue this practice for my former students when they needed assistance.

At Carroll High School, I was a member of the National Honor Society, student council, National Beta Club, FBLA, and the Carroll High School Choir, under the direction of Mr. Roosevelt Pine. I also served as a volunteer with the football team as team videographer and assistant manager, under Coach John McCaa. However, my extra-curricular activities came with some temporary suspensions when my grades began to lag. I brought home a D in Science on a progress report, and as a punishment, my father forced me to read Alex Haley's "Roots," a 688-page novel. I had to write a report following every chapter and could not engage in any extra-curricular activities until the assignment was complete. After I handed my father the reports, he took them and threw them in the garbage. I was shocked and asked why he did such a thing. He responded, "Those were for you, not for me." It took me many years to understand the importance of that experience, but I finally understood what he meant.

I attended the annual Literary Rally held at Louisiana Tech University. In 1993, I participated in the French I division and 1994 in the French II division. In April of 1994, I attended the 6th Annual SAAD "Taking a Stand" Youth Conference in Baton Rouge, LA, held at the Jimmy Swaggart Worship Center. On the trip back from Baton Rouge, I rode with Ms. Sandie Lollie. She gave me advice on being successful in school. She would later become the President of the Monroe Federation of Teachers union. When I became a teacher with the Monroe City Schools, there were a few other unions I could have joined. However, I remembered the seed planted in me by Lollie when I was just a teenager. I paid back the debt of investment and joined her union.

Singing in the school choir was a very rewarding experience. We sang under the direction of Mr. Roosevelt Pine. He was the Minister of Music at New Light Baptist Church, and he was a very strict master teacher. We sang many spirituals (his favorite) by Moses Hogan. We competed at the Louisiana High School Rally at Louisiana Tech University. The Boys Quartet won a Superior Rating.

We also competed at the Louisiana High School Rally at Louisiana State University in Baton Rouge. The rehearsals leading up to the competitions were more rewarding than the trophies and ribbons. During rehearsals, we had an opportunity to see Mr. Pine in his element. He would often say "Stretch," and when I'd get off focus he would bellow "ROBERT!" Mr. Pine would often take off his belt and placed it on the piano. When he became upset, he would plead with us to straighten up "Here's my right hand to God," he would pray to hold his peace from not using his belt.

My most memorable event during football season was a trip to Bastrop High School. The Bulldogs played against the Rams and beat them on their turf. When we were leaving, their fans started throwing rocks and bottles at our bus. Coach Patrick Taylor (who would later become principal) told the players "Y'all better put them helmets on!" We were all down on the floor trying to avoid getting hit with bottles and rocks.

Our band was good. Directed by Elmo Claverie, it could keep rhythm, play, and dance simultaneously. It was our high school version of the famous college band Southern University Human Jukebox. They always played "Friends." I grew tired of hearing them play that song. Another song of which the band wore out was the gospel song "Call Him Up."

I spent a considerable amount of time with the school's dance line, The Carrollettes, during my junior and senior years. They even named their wardrobe and supply bag after me. They called it "Robert" a name given by the sponsor Judianna Cotton. It was unusual, and a few of the girls were alarmed at first that a guy was always in their dressing room. I guess many assumed I was gay. They would often say "Oh that's just Robert…he's harmless." Contrary to their assumption, I wasn't gay. It was cool, however, having the finest girls in the school call your name and even recognize your presence. That I was such a nerd, this level of recognition would never have been possible in any other way.

The Senior Year homecoming game featured a rivalry between the Bulldogs and Green Oaks. It was our best game of the year of which the score was 56-6. Our worst game during senior year was against Neville High School. They defeated us with a score of 30-6.

The homecoming theme was "Bulldog Pack…Back on Track." Monday featured Flashback Day/Radio Day. We dressed in clothes from the past and music was played over the intercom during transitions. Tuesday featured Imitation Day. We dressed as our favorite celebrity. Wednesday was Skip Day. We were given a pass to skip one class, reported to the gym, and had refreshments. Thursday featured Senior Takeover Day. Senior students portrayed the faculty. Friday was Blue and Gold Day.

I went to the senior prom alone. I wanted to go to the prom with my high school crush, Crystal Miller, however, she told me I waited too late to ask her and that she was going with someone else. I would later find out, she was already dating a guy and her prom date was her boyfriend; it wouldn't have mattered if I had asked in advance. So I went stag. The theme was "Wish Upon a Star." My father allowed me to drive the family's Lincoln Town Car to the prom. It was held at the Monroe Civic Center Conference Hall. I wore a black Oscar de la Renta Tuxedo with a gold vest. The royal court included: King Damian Webb, Queen Demetria Moses, Duke Montrell Harris, Maid of Honor Ericka Standifer, Princess Katasha Cherry, and would you guess, they voted me as Prince. I had a chance to dance with a pretty girl after all. So I danced with Katasha Cherry, the Prom Princess on prom night. She would later develop into one fine woman, an officer with the Monroe Fire Department. After the prom, I decided to eat at Shoney's, but when I saw everyone else there with their dates, I felt out of place. So I went home. I arrived back home at 11:45 PM.

The senior class traveled to Cocoa Beach, Florida for our trip. We sold bar-be-que plates to raise money for the trip. We must have bar-be-qued all day. I don't think I'd ever seen so many beans and so much potato salad in my life, and I grew tired of looking at the chicken.

My goal in life at graduation (as written in my memory book) was: "to go to school, get further educated, get certification for a profession, work in that field, marry a very beautiful, attractive, successful black woman (who works and is independent), have children, make a name for myself, be successful in my career, help others in their lives, train up another generation of humans and hopefully retire and vacate." My dream career was to be the Superintendent of a public school district making $85,000 a year. I wanted to drive a Toyota 4-Runner and a Lexus LS400 and live in either Dallas, Atlanta or anywhere in the northern United States.

Graduation

My high school commencement ceremony took place on Wednesday, May 15, 1996, at the Monroe Civic Center Theater. The Carroll High School Concert Band led the processional of graduates to the tune of "War March of the Priest" arranged by E. DeLanister. Crystal Miller led the invocation, and Shamalon Johnson gave the welcome. I sang two songs with the choir, led by Mr. Roosevelt Pine. We sang "Glorious Everlasting" and "Elijah Rock." Addresses were given by the Salutatorian, Alford Cherry, Jr., and Valedictorian, Roy Garrick Sims. I was presented the Morris Henry Carroll Scholarship Fund Award by Abe Pierce, who had recently won his campaign for Mayor of Monroe. The award was given to a high school graduate with aspirations of becoming a teacher. At the end of the ceremony, I joined the choir for two final selections "The Lord Bless You and Keep You" and the "Sevenfold Amen." My classmate Demetria Moses gave the benediction. We recessed to the tune of "The Thunderer."

The Carroll High School Class of 1996 included: Shataqua Abraham, Toria Abraham, Carmen Allen, Damien Allen, Leonard Atkins, Jr., Tyesha Baker, Oliver W. Billups, III, Taticasejuana Bobo, Garzy Brisco, Rashunda Broadnax, Yogunda Brooks, Christine Brown, Hope Brown, Keisha Brown, Nadia Brown, Oliver Brown, Ricky Brown, Jr., Michael Buie, Kymekha Butler, Kenneth Cahn, Jr., Yolanda Caldwell, Antonio Carter, Audrey Carter, Angela Chatman, Alford Cherry, Jr., Katasha Cherry, La'China Clay, Rhonda Coleman, James Collins, Sherifa Cotton, Anita Davis, Corey Davis, Robin Dickson, Shanta Dickson, Yakena Edwards, Latisha Eleam, Antoine Ellis, Lanella Ellis, Telithia Epps, Amy Filhiol, Milini Gaines, Jacoby Gibson, Shannon Gix, Malvin Goldman, Sharalyn Gospel, Dometa

Griffin, Tracee Griffin, Fanta Hardwell, Damian Harris, Montrell Harris, Latron Henderson, Tamika Hogg, Rochanda Horne, Andrea Hunt, Lakesha Ivory, Michael Jackson, Tashayla Jackson, Taieesha Jamerson, Alonzo Johnson, Camille Johnson, Eric Johnson, Jr., Shamalon Johnson, Sheareem Johnson, Shermell Johnson, Trasheki Johnson, Cedric Jones, Lakeisha Keys, Deborah King, Daleicia Land, Tawanna Landers, Lisa Lewis, Shonnica Lewis, Lakeisha Logwood, Rontarrius Logwood, Clarcinda Long, Jennifer Louis, Mia Marshall, Wynois Martin, Keith Matthews, Altrecheia McFee, Amanda McFee, Latora McFee, Sonja Menyweather, Crystal Miller, Brandy Mitchell, Demetria Moses, Omeka Nash, Bolivia Newton, Vincent Newton, Rekita Owens, Linh Pham, Ronald Powell, Gladesha Pratt, Teresa Rachal, Shunta Randle, Keetron Rasco, Trinesha Robertson, Kenya Robinson, Latasha Robinson, Lennon Robinson, Shawana Robinson, Quianna Rogers, Sallie Saulsberry, Harold Sellers, Rosheda Sims, Roy Sims, Erica Standifer, Latedra Tate, Ida Thomas, Chyetra Tucker, Jamal Vaughn, Brian Washington, Damian Webb, Terrence White, Gerald Williams, Linda Williams, Rodney Williams, Tedrick Wilson, Luwjonia Wright, and myself.

Our class motto was "There are no limits on our future if we put no limits on our education." The Senior Class Officers included: President Shamalon Johnson, Vice President Roy Sims, Recording Secretary Ericka Standifer, Corresponding Secretary Demetria Moses, Treasurer (Myself), Chaplain Dometa Griffin, and Sergeant-at-Arms Yakena Edwards.

In time, I learned to love being a Carroll Bulldog. Many of the associations made there and lessons learned, whether academic or social, have shaped the person I am today. My teacher Mrs. Fleming ensured that we learned the words to the Alma Mater. I have carried them with me on my walk as an adult. One of the most powerful lines in the song says "You will always be a mighty force in this great nation all the world can see." Many educators, doctors, lawyers, engineers, architects, professional football players, and actors can attribute their beginnings at Carroll. The world has tasted and has seen its mighty works. I'm glad my father chose for me. I'm forever proud to be a Bulldog!

SEVEN

EDUCATION STORY: BEING A ULM WARHAWK

"The buildings and bayou represent ULM's external beauty-but its heart and soul is found in its people."

ULM President Dr. Nick J. Bruno

I returned to college as a 31-year-old. I made numerous attempts at obtaining my Bachelor's Degree over the years. However, everytime I matriculated, I would soon drop out and take up another adventure. In July of 2009, I decided that it was time to get the job done. It would be a three-year commitment, but I was ready to meet the challenge.

Freshman Year 2009

In the fall of 2009, I once again enrolled at the University of Louisiana at Monroe. I had debts at the university from a few years before when I dropped classes after the drop date. The university did not erase these debts from my record, and I had no other way of coordinating a funding source for tuition. So at the fork in the road, I made a decision. I sold my car, furniture, and many other items to pursue my collegiate education. After the debt had been cleared, the Registrar allowed a one-time GPA wipe of my previous classes. I had originally completed 12 hours of coursework. To re-instate me to a clean GPA, all of those classes would have to be eliminated, and I had to start from the beginning. So I did. Back to one.

During my first semester in school, I lived in Madison Hall. It was a bit of a culture shock, but I wanted the full college experience this time. The dorms, the fraternity parties, the events, gym, games, and everything that encompassed campus life. I was much older than my fellow students, but I wanted to fit in as much as I could.

The classes I took during my Freshman year included: Dr. H. P. Jones (History 111- Western Civilization to 1648), Dr. Brian Bramstedt (Psychology 201- Introduction to Psychology), Robert Williamson (Kinesiology 201- First Aid), Dr. Mike Beutner (Curriculum 285), Suzy Seebers/Amanda Carter (Math 111- College Algebra), and Dr. Kevin Unter (Political Science 201- National Government). Dr. H.P. Jones (History 112- Western Civilization since 1648), Dr. Minton Russell (Biology 101), Dr. Neil White (Sociology 101), Frances Gregory (English 101), Christy Riser (Educational Foundations 201). Dr. James Cofer was the university president during my Freshman Year.

In September 2009, I was hired as a student worker at the university to serve as the photographer for the Office of University Relations. My supervisors were Laura Woodard and Michael Echols. Echols would later become a Monroe City Councilman. I took the official activity and portrait photographs for the University of Louisiana at Monroe. However as my academic requirements increased, I became unable to maintain the duties of both student and worker. In January of 2010, I resigned from the post. Many of my photographs are documented in the 2010 Chacahoula Yearbook, with name credits by them.

During the Spring Semester of 2010, I'd had enough of Madison Hall and desired to live in the Bayou Apartments on Campus. So I made arrangements for the move. I moved into Building 5, the structure next to the Schulze Cafeteria. There were four rooms which shared a kitchen and living room area. The two adjacent rooms shared a bathroom on both sides of the center suite area. It is during my stay in the apartments that I began a friendship with Trevarious Imari Hall. Hall was a very exciting individual. He was a very popular guy on campus, and many flocked to be in his presence. He didn't mind an old guy like me sharing living space with him. However, his friends weren't all so welcoming. It was very obvious that my living there was an interruption into their youthful flow. When I decided to move off campus in the Summer, they naturally followed me…only because I moved into a house. They found me and the first thing they did was arrange a party at the house of a guy they didn't always appreciate living amongst them on campus. I also met and began a lasting friendship with Mateo Jose Lopez. We would eventually become history teachers together at

Excellence Academy Charter School. Lopez graduated a few semesters before me with a History degree. He offered advice and even reviewed some of my papers and offered suggestions for revision.

During my Freshman year, I had the privilege of being taught Western Civilization by Dr. Horace P. Jones. Jones was in his 80s when he taught the survey course. He was a United States Marine Korean War Veteran. On the first day of class, Jones entered the classroom with an old worn black commencement gown, walking to the tune of the Rocky "Eye of the Tiger" Theme, and had a prosthetic leg filled with tootsie rolls, of which he threw out as if he were in a parade. My immediate thoughts were that this guy was looney and that the class was going to be a waste of time. However, after he began to talk and deliver the material, I found a certain appreciation for him. His introductory story entailed his world travels of which he came in with a Marine backpack filled with items one would use in the field. These were items he used during his voyages of which he began in Paris on a bicycle and moved all the way through the bottom of Southeast Asia where he embarked on a boat and sailed back to the United States. His story was filled with adventure and daring tales of a guy who lived on the street, fought with savages and screamed at the heavens at night. It was a story I will never forget.

Jones was a poet, and he would often stop his lectures to read poetry to his pupils. Some would be on paper, and some, he would recite from memory. There would even be times where Jones would tear up and become emotional as many of the poems and writings were reflective of his long life's journey. One poem he recited the most was "The Road Less Traveled" by Robert Frost. It was Jones that inspired me to take the journey and see more of the world than I had already seen. It was also Jones who convinced me to change my major to History. I wanted to go on that adventure and come back to be a History Professor, just like him.

At Homecoming 2009, Seth Hall and Lindsey Eickman were presented as King and Queen. Others on the court included: Jessica Gilbert, Verlencia Jordan, Chasline Fontenot, Kelsea McCrary, Lauren Carnahan, Lauren Rosson, Megan Boullard, and Maggie Warren. ULM defeated FIU 48-35 at the Homecoming game.

In the Fall, Kelsi Crain was crowned Miss ULM. Other contestants included: Chris Jeansonne, Katlyn Wilson, Rachel Hornsby, Evan Lane, Brandi Stout, Karmen Rubin, Lindsey Eickman, Heather Clapp, and Heather Wardlaw.

The President's Lyceum Series was held in December. The special guest was best-selling author Thomas Friedman. I attended a class session Mr. Friedman gave in Stubbs Hall. After hearing him speak, I purchased a copy of his book "The World is Flat," and it became one of my favorite books to read, packed with valuable insights to the reality of the modern world.

Sophomore Year 2010

I continued into my Sophomore year in the Summer of 2010, since I did not take the summer off from coursework. I lived in my brother's house in Town & Country and commuted to and from campus to complete the six hours of coursework. Those classes included: Dr. Terry White (History 201- American History), Dr. Barbara Cottingham (Psychology 301- Educational Psychology). In the fall, I continued full time with five classes including: Dr. Sean Chenoweth (Geography 1001- Regional Geography), Dr. Robert Eisenstadt (Economics 2001- Macroeconomics), Dr. Brian Bramstedt (Psychology 2005- Adolescent Psychology), Nicole Smith (English 1002), Dr. Richard Chardkoff (History 2002- American History). In the fall of 2011, I changed my major concentration to a study in History, with a minor in Criminal Justice.

Dr. Cofer resigned that year, and Dr. Stephen Richters served as Interim President until Dr. Nick Bruno was selected and installed as the 8th President of the University. One of my classmates, Jaden Leach, was crowned Miss ULM 2010. I took two classes with her, Louisiana History and a Middle East Politics course. Leach was a Freshman when she won the title, competing against eleven other contestants. The other winners were Brittany Jordan- 1st Runner-up, Nicole Tucker- 2nd Runner-Up, Kylie Stracener- 3rdd Runner-Up, and Kristen Meier- 4th Runner Up.

During Spring Fever that year, Country Music artists Sara Evans and Josh Turner performed at the Fant-Ewing Coliseum. Homecoming was held in November, with Brooke Dugas as the Homecoming Queen and Ahmaad Solmone as the Homecoming

King. Others on the court included: Jensen DeGroot, Kelsey Williams, Jessica Gilbert, Monica Zeno, Brittany Jordan, Ciera Paul, and Marnecia Hall. The Warhawks played Troy for Homecoming and won 28-14.

One of my more memorable professors during this year was Dr. Robert Eisenstadt. He taught me Macroeconomics. I remember him beginning the course with a lecture on time management. Eisenstadt said, "We have twenty-four hours in a day, eight devoted to sleep, eight devoted to work, two for bathing, eating, and getting prepared for work or school…what are you doing with the remaining hours." He challenged us to use our time wisely and not waste it. It was his icebreaker into the discussion on scarcity and limited resources, as time was one he considered limited. I didn't make a high grade in his course. I hated supply and demand curve charts and could never figure them out on exams. However, I learned a great deal about economics through his lectures and discussions.

Dr. Richard Chardkoff was another impressionable professor. He taught American History 2002. It was a coincidence that I was taking his course because he also taught my father when he was a student at the university. He recognized the name and made the connection. Chardkoff taught history as it related to presidential administrations. This would have an impression on my appreciation for the Presidents and the Oval Office. His exams were usually multiple choice, but the choices one had to choose from were not so simple. You had to know all factors dealing with the question to get a decent grade on the exam.

Junior Year 2011

I began my Junior Year in the Spring of 2011. I studied under a number of professors including: Mr. Jerry Dahl (Math 1016- Statistics), Dr. Karl Kogut (Economics 2002- Microeconomics), Frances Gregory (English 2005- American Literature), Dr. Sean Chenoweth (Geography 1002- Regional Geography), Dr. Ralph Brown (History 4047- US Military History since 1865). Junior Year (Summer 2011): Dr. Monica Bontty (Anthropology 2001), Dr. Ralph Brown (History 4030- World War II), Lauri Anderson (Geology 1001). Junior Year (Fall 2011): Glenda Swan (Art 1009- Art

Appreciation), Dr. Terry Jones (History 3005- Louisiana History), Dr. Gene Tarver (Political Science 2002- State and Local Government).

In the Spring of 2011, World-renowned journalist Dan Rather was the special guest at the President's Lyceum held at Brown Auditorium. At the event, he shared his career highlights and spoke about his experiences during the Clinton impeachment, his interview with Saddam Hussein, and 9/11.

Homecoming 2011 featured Jessica Gilbert and Benjamin Young as King and Queen. To an upset, ULM lost the football game in overtime to Western Kentucky 31-28.

The Miss ULM Pageant was held in the fall. Gilbert, who was the Homecoming Queen, also took the crown in the Miss Louisiana Preliminary.

The Spring Fever event was held in conjunction with the City of Monroe's Delta Fest. Held in the Civic Center Arena, the pop-rock band The Fray, was the headliner at the concert. I attended this concert while taking photographs as the Civic Center's house photographer. The group gave an awesome show.

It was during the junior year that I encountered Dr. Bontty. I took her online Anthropology course but would soon learn that she was a no-nonsense kind of professor. I once heard a student refer to her as Mrs. Bontty in the hall and she was quick to correct him with "It's Dr. Bontty." True enough, in her professional setting, that is the title she is deserving, and she did not hesitate to remind students. In class, she didn't ask for much discussion and was quick to get to the point and move on without a long deliberation on student questions. She was a hard one to get used to, but she knew her history, so you really couldn't get upset with her.

Senior Year 2012

My final year was my most challenging year. My Military GI Bill funds were depleted, and I needed more cash to pay tuition. I did not like the idea of graduating with student loans or debts. I wanted to walk across the stage at commencement with my tuition paid in full. So, I moved out of the house and lived in my office building that I was leasing to operate my photography business. It was a very challenging process, but it was one that I managed to undertake. I rented out two lockers in the university's activity center and took showers at the center every day, sleeping in the office suite at night.

The office suite was in a building on Royal Ave. off of North 18th street in Monroe. It was on the other side of town, and transit to and from the University took on an adventure of its own. For about three months of my senior year, my driver's license was suspended, due to an insurance lapse. So, as a result, I bought a bicycle from Wal-Mart and rode it to school. I obtained a monthly bus pass from the Monroe Transit Authority, and daily I put my bicycle on the front rails and transited to the university. Often I'd ride the bicycle back when I didn't want to wait for the bus.

Laundry duties required creativity as well. Since I had no washer and dryer in the building, I used the coin laundry a few blocks from the office suite. I'd pack all of my soiled garments in plastic bags and ride them on my bicycle to the laundromat. I had time during this operation to read and complete assignments. The lack of a kitchen was not a major concern, as I ate in the cafeteria on campus. I did stock the suite with a microwave and coffee maker, so I was able to snack and enjoy convenient meals when time did not permit me going to the campus.

The experience was a great lesson in frugality and determination. I was going to graduate on time, and I didn't allow even living accommodations to stand in the way of reaching that goal. I often hear people complain about why they can't find the time or the means to get a college degree. On many times I've shared my senior year story and advised that one must do whatever is necessary, even if that means relocating or trimming the fat off of life's creature comforts.

I took the maximum number of courses such that I could reach the finish line in December of 2012. I took a number of classes including: Senior Year (Spring 2012): Quentin Holmes (Intro to Criminal Justice), Katherine Dawson (CMST 2001- Public Speaking), Dr. William Ryan (English 2006- American Literature), Fredrick Adams (French 1001-Elementary French), Dr. Ralph Brown (History 3099- Historian's Craft), and Dr. Monica Bontty (History 4076- Ancient Rome). Senior Year (Summer 2012): Dr. Jeffrey Anderson (History 3010- African American History), Dr. John Sutherlin (Political Science 1001- Intro to Political Science), Fredrick Adams (French 1002- Elementary French), Dr. Roger Carpenter (History

4049- Native American History). Senior Year (Final Semester Fall 2012): Lauri Anderson (Geology 1002- Historical Geology), Dr. Jeffrey Anderson (History 4040- New South), Dr. Christopher Blackburn (History 4088- Revolutionary France), Robert Noel (Political Science 4013- Constitutional Law: Gov. Powers), Dr. Joshua Stockley (Political Science 4020- Louisiana Government and Politics), Dr. John Sutherlin (Political Science 4044- Middle East Politics).

In February, bestselling author Nicholas Sparks was the featured guest at the President's Lyceum Series. He spoke to ULM students about his career and how he became one of the most celebrated romance writers in the country. He's known for such books as "A Walk to Remember" "Message in a Bottle" and the memorable book that became a sensational heartthrob movie "The Notebook."

In March, Marlon Jackson, of the Jackson 5, made an appearance at the Beidenharn Recital Hall and spoke to fans. I attended this gathering and took photos. Although there was a large gathering, I would have expected more people to be in attendance, as his name and relation to the world's most famous entertainer should have carried more appeal. But to those who came out, it was still exciting to be in the presence of a member of the famous singing group many grew up watching on TV.

During Homecoming, Kylie Stracener and Henry Mitchell, IV, were crowned King and Queen. Others on the court included: Kemper Block, Kelsey Williams, Raegan Trusty, Chelsea Wyatt, Kristen Meier, Lauren Harper, Adrian Lejeune, and Candice Johnson. At the Homecoming Game in October, ULM won over South Alabama 38-24. Amy Matherne was crowned Miss ULM 2012 at the Fall Pageant held at Brown Auditorium.

Dr. Sutherlin's Middle East Politics course was one of my more memorable courses from the fall semester. This subject is one of the most challenging for Americans or anyone with a vested interest in the region. I took the course with a' fellow US Marine, Aaron Word, and one of my longtime colleagues, the former Miss ULM and Miss Louisiana Jaden Leach. I was fortunate to be taking the class during the time of the Benghazi massacre of US Soldiers and the assassination of Ambassador Chris Stephens. In September, members of the Ansar al-Sharia group coordinated an attack on US government facilities in the Libyan city. Earlier, in the summer of 2012, a trailer for a film entitled "Innocence of Muslims" was uploaded to YouTube. It depicted the Islamic prophet Muhammad as a fool and even showed him in sexual situations. Many believed this was one of the factors that prompted the assault on the West. We watched this video and many others in the fall course. In the course, I also took part in a team project of which we had to either be for or against an Iranian nuclear program. I was on the proponent side and argued that the Shah of Iran was once celebrated in the United States and we once had a political love affair with the nation, boasting its nuclear program. To say that a sovereign nation did not have the right to defend itself was not fair and we as a nation had no grounds to make such a demand. Well, this was my argument anyway. I created flyers to pass out, and the group gave a formal presentation to the class defending our position.

I found the Historical Geology course by Professor Lauri Anderson to be very informative. Lessons learned in this course would prove very beneficial in later years as I became a World Geography teacher. She taught a great lesson about global warming and the notion that humans were killing the planet. After viewing some videos and hearing lectures, she concluded that the planet had been reset many times over and that it is impossible to kill the planet, although possible to kill human life on it.

I didn't necessarily like the English Literature course taught by Dr. Ryan. For an entire semester, we focused on the theme of "The Others." To the unenlightened mind, this would seem like a legit analysis. However, a closer look at the idea exposes an element of prejudice on the part of the professor. We studied the literary works of African-Americans, Native Americans, and Hispanics. To Dr. Ryan, these were considered "the others." I guess I was an other, according to his theme. No doubt, this was a classic example of a Eurocentric curriculum. I will always believe that I was a victim of the most prejudiced course of my undergraduate experience.

But Dr. Ryan's "others" course would be balanced by the no-nonsense political science course taught by Dr. Joshua Stockley. He taught Political Science 4020, which was Louisiana Government and Politics. There was a textbook associated with the course, but Stockley only used it as a base. He had two other books for us to read and discuss in class. Those books are still on my bookshelf. He brought the books to life as we discussed everything from poverty to rednecks in trailers tailgating at an Alabama football game. Stockley, a Democrat, was very critical of all things conservative and he didn't hold his tongue when making his claims about society. There were some interesting discussions in class as he would pose political questions to Republicans in the room. They would give him a run for his money, but Stockley had the evidence and the many years of research to back his claims. He left many speechless. He was a white guy who could talk bad about white people, from a political and social perspective. So, naturally, he was to be taken seriously. We had discussions entitled "The Deep-Fried, Double-Wide Lifestyle" "Republicans by Default" and "Road trip into the heart of fan mania." Stockley is the local news media's go-to guy for political insight. I still engage in discussions with him, and he's a good source of information.

The night before my commencement exercise, I hosted my own "Bachelor Party." Of course, I wasn't getting married, but the name was fitting the occasion. It was a very wild unforgettable night of which I have a limited recollection. I woke up late the next morning and had to rush to the Coliseum to a mix of emotions. One part of the mixture was an element of inebriation, and the other was the feeling of accomplishment as I was about to make that walk across the stage. I think I was holding it together until the brass ensemble began its "Pomp and Circumstance" and I walked by my professors. There among them was my 7th grade English teacher and college advisor, Dr. Lenard Clark, with a smirk on his face, a look that brought tears to my eyes. Here he was, at the college level, witnessing one of his junior high pupils get a college degree, and knowing that he played a major role in making it happen. It is a look that is burned in my memory. That's how I want to look at my pupils. That's the impact I want to have on them. Open the door for them, expose them to the idea of learning, and then watch them go forth. That's the value of a good teacher. And at that moment, Dr. Clark captured that image for me, and he made that hour memorable.

On December 8, 2012, I graduated from the University of Louisiana at Monroe with a Bachelor of Arts Degree in History. Dr. Nick Bruno was the president, and it was a pleasure to walk across the stage and shake his hand, completing the challenge I undertook in 2009. My cumulative GPA was 3.4. The commencement speaker at the ceremony was Louisiana State Representative Katrina Jackson. The theme of her commencement address was to "Dance with Time." She spoke about the many graduates who made sacrifices to complete their educational requirements. She even called my name, to my surprise, and spoke of my prior military service. I thought it was cool to have the commencement speaker call my name during her address. Afterward, I walked out and greeted family and friends. My parents had the same big grin on their faces as they did in San Diego after watching me graduate from Marine Boot Camp. I'd made them proud again. I was the first of their sons to earn a Bachelor's Degree, and they were both alive to see it happen.

EIGHT

BECOMING A US MARINE

"Some people spend an entire lifetime wondering if they made a difference in the world.
But, the Marines don't have that problem."
President Ronald Reagan

In May of 1997, I enlisted in the United States Marine Corps. I completed recruit training at the Marine Corps Recruit Depot in San Diego, California. The training lasted 90 days and tested me both mentally and physically.

My decision to join the military was similar to that of many of the men in my family. My mother's father was in the Army and my uncle Gerald also served in the Army. My cousin Michael enlisted in the Navy. Michael was stationed on the USS George H.W. Bush (CVN 77) and later became a Master Chief Petty Officer. My aunt Debra was enlisted in the Air Force and retired after 20 years of service. My grandfather, Roosevelt Wright, Sr., signed up for the military during WWII but was rejected. My father's brother, Bruce, enlisted in the Marines, only to serve six months and a day, long enough to get full benefits, then faked a knee injury. He came home with boot camp tendencies in him, like flipping a quarter on the bed to test whether the spread was pulled tight enough. My father signed up for the draft in 1968, during the Vietnam conflict. Each registrant was assigned a number by lottery from 1-366. His number was 365. However, the draft ended when the numbers pulled were in the 120s, so he did not have to go to fight in Vietnam.

Recruit Training

Recruit training for those enlisted in the United States Marine Corps includes a thirteen-week process during which I became cut off from the civilian world and was forced to adapt to a Marine Corps lifestyle. During training, drill instructors trained us in a wide variety of subjects including weapons training, Marine Corps Martial Arts Program, personal hygiene and cleanliness, close order drill, and Marine Corps history. The training emphasized physical fitness, and we had to attain a minimum standard of fitness to graduate by passing a Physical Fitness Test. We also had to meet minimum combat-oriented swimming qualifications, qualify in rifle marksmanship with the M16A2 service rifle, and pass a 54-hour simulated combat exercise known as "The Crucible."

Unlike training at Parris Island, we had to leave the depot to conduct field training. The final three-week phase occurred at Edson Range on Marine Corps Base Camp Pendleton, where we qualified on the rifle range, conducted field training, and underwent the Crucible. At the conclusion, we returned to MCRD San Diego for graduation.

At the MCRD San Diego, I was assigned to First Recruit Training Battalion., Series 1101, Platoon 1101. My drill instructors were: Ssgt J. W. Bone (Senior DI), Sgt. C.D. Demuro, Sgt S. Monzon, and Sgt. J.A. Morales.

I began my training on May 7, 1997. I remember the drill instructor arriving at the San Diego airport, ordering us to get on the bus. The anxiety built along the ride as we were told to be quiet, close our eyes, and keep our head down until we arrived at the depot. On arrival, we were ordered to stand on a group of yellow footprints that had been painted. It was at this point when I thought to myself, "What did I just get myself into." Then the three months of training began.

Receiving week began with a literal strip down. Every recruit was put online in the holding barracks and told to strip down nude. All of our civilian garments were put in a box, and we were rushed through a receiving line to receive a military issue of briefs, t-shirts, socks, shorts, and athletic shoes. We would not yet receive the BDUs or boots. There was a lot of noise from the initial drill instructors as we attempted to adjust to what would be our way of life for the next three months.

During receiving week, we were sized for uniforms, received our issue of gear, had our initial haircuts, shots, dental checkups, and medical evaluations. We also received our initial strength test, the

Initial PFT. These procedures were completed as we anticipated "Pickup." Pickup was the day we were assigned to our formal platoon and the day we met the four drill instructors that would be in our face 24/7 for the next 12 weeks. We assembled on the quarterdeck of the squad bay (the main foyer area) and sat with our legs crossed, back straight, eyes forward listening to our commanding officer welcome us to our assigned platoon. Once he introduced us to the platoon, he turned directions over to the Senior Drill Instructor. The SDI seemed like a nice guy. He had a daddy complex, but that's how it was arranged for training. After a week of receiving with the initial drill instructors, he was a breath of fresh air. But that would last only a few moments, for after he completed his briefing, he turned the house over to our three drill instructors, then all hell broke loose. I would not be lying if I said I was scared out of my mind of these guys. They would be the deviled dogs that would be on my case for a while.

Recruit Training- Phase One

Phase One of training included four weeks of training from history classes to combat swimming. We received instruction on military history, customs and courtesies, bayonet training, first aid, military uniforms, and core values. We began training on a number of combat skills including bayonet training, pugil sticks, and hand-to-hand combat. I had one of my first real fights during this phase of training. Although it was discontinued a year after my boot camp experience, Combat Hitting Skills was a celebrated feature of training. It was a boxing match between two opponents. The drill instructors placed us in a small ring of which we each took turns in the offense and the defense. The drill instructors taught us the art of offensive punching and that of defensively "bobbing and weaving." One recruit had a minute to punch offensively while the other had to defend himself without punching back. After the minute expired, the two alternated. Then for a minute, we both had to compete with both skills against each other. For someone who had never been in a fight before, I took a few good blows, but I didn't get knocked out.

The Marine Corps eliminated Combat Hitting Skills from practice at recruit training in 1998. Two recruits at the Parris Island Recruit Depot were injured during training. One received severe brain damage, and the other had serious injuries but recovered. I considered the training to be one of the most important exercises we had, for we needed to feel a real punch. I expected my drill instructors to punch me in the face and slap me around, as I witnessed in the movie "Full Metal Jacket." However, legislation was passed that prohibited physical abuse by drill instructors to recruits. So, at least I was afforded a chance to undergo this training before it was eliminated.

One of the most difficult aspects of Phase One for me was Swim Week. The training taught us how to survive in deep waters with equipment strapped to our backs and a rubber M-16 rifle to simulate combat situations. I had learned swimming in the boy scouts and could swim from one end of the pool to the next easily. However, treading water was not my strong suit, and I struggled with it. I was initially afraid of the 15-foot free fall dive, but I eventually shrugged the fear and mastered it. When the drill instructor put that pack on my back and ordered me to tread for a few minutes, that's when I found myself in a tough situation. I eventually lasted long enough to pass the requirement, but it was a tough battle.

Recruit Training- Phase Two

During Phase Two, we competed against other platoons in close order drill. This was another feature I was familiar with before I arrived, as we marched as a troop in parades during my days as a boy scout. There was more to it than what we did in the scouting program, and that is what I encountered with formal precision drill with the Marines. After initial drill, the platoons loaded on buses to go "up north" as we called it. Up North was simply being transported to the training facility at Camp Pendleton, California, the Marine Base. The drive would take an hour, about 48 miles north of San Diego.

When we arrived, we had new squad bays to which we had to get accustomed quickly. Before our rifle shooting training began, we spent a week in mess duty. We endured sixteen hour days of working in the chow hall (cafeteria) of which we could not sit down or break until it was our time to eat. We did the cleaning, loading, and maintenance work required to operate the center while other recruits were going through their rifle training. That soon ended and it became our time to train.

During grass week, we realized why drill instructors made us sit with our legs folded, with our backs straight, eyes forward, for the previous weeks. It would get us prepared for shooting positions. Nearly everything we did back at the San Diego Depot was training us to be a shooter, the most important aspect of being a Marine. For as we learned, every Marine is a Rifleman, regardless of his occupational assignment. If he or she can't shoot, he's no good to the Corps.

So we snapped in at a can for hours at times in different positions. It was long and boring, but had we not gone through the disguised training before, it would have been uncomfortable and irritating. The KD Range is where we would make our marks as either marksmen, sharpshooters, or expert riflemen. 500 yards of shooting space. At the target area, there was a bunker of which the recruits made the targets and replaced them as shooters were firing down range. Half of the platoons fired for a week while the other served in "the pits" as the bunker area was called. When it was my time to qualify, I didn't enjoy the sitting, kneeling, or standing positions. I was not a force to be reckoned with in the prone position. I could effectively hit the bullseye at 500 yards away. I graduated from boot camp with an Expert shooting rating.

At the Camp Pendleton training grounds, we also participated in land navigation courses and had our taste of CS Gas in the Gas Chamber. I didn't like the gas, but it was an important training activity that, like Combat Hitting Skills, was necessary for the Marine to be accustomed to the reality of war as best as the training could provide. Before we would end the final phase of training, we completed our final classes, physical fitness tests, and our final close-order drill. Then it was time for the Crucible.

Recruit Training- The Crucible

The Crucible is the finale to recruit training. It is notable that this idea was designed and put into practice only a year before I began recruit training. It was the dream of General Krulak and is a 54-hour rigorous field training activity. It is a wartime simulation with constant obstacles, phases of battle, forced marches, and deprivation of food and sleep. At first, it felt like a breeze, and I thought it was all just hype to get us anxious....then the hurt began. It seemed that all of the training we'd had up unto that point was given a jarhead steroid shot. Many of the obstacles that we had to overcome required teamwork and to think outside of the box. Once we completed a stage, we'd move on to the next, for hours and hours. At the end when our bodies and minds were completely worn, there was a forced march with all of our gear up a very steep hill simulating the iconic Iwo Jima climb during World War II. At the top, we were no longer considered recruits and the drill instructors recognized us as US Marines for the first time. In all my life, I hadn't heard such sweeter words expressed. There was a short ceremony where the drill instructors stepped in front of every new Marine and handed him an EGA (Eagle-Globe-Anchor) pin. I remember shedding a tear as did some of the others. Normally, the DIs would mock this reaction, but they knew what it meant, so in that company of men on that hilltop, tears were accepted and expected. It was complete. Mission accomplished.

When we returned to the squad bay, there was a grand feast awaiting us. It was called the "Warriors Breakfast." Anything and everything we ever wanted to eat for breakfast at any quantity we wanted was there. Like a grand feast to the victors of war. The only thing missing was scantily clad women to help us celebrate the cold war we'd just fought and won. But that would come in time on the shores of Thailand and Singapore.

I received a host of encouragement and motivation from family and friends from Monroe. A total of 53 cards and letters came during "Mail Call" including: Joslyn Wright (15), Tina Ross (2), Tiffany, Takevia and Taborrian James (1), Natalie Williams (2), Myron Dubose (1), Beverly Millikin (2), Omega James (1), Harolyn

Hall (2), Melanie James (2), Mildred James (5), Lanore Williams (1), Sadie Cornelius (1), Viola Hill (1), Jessie Stewart (2), Roosevelt Wright, III (1), Marteal Riley (1), Patrick and Janet Davis Family (1), Ahmad Smith (1), Ariel Blueford (1), Debra Ratcliff (2), Sgt. Jerry Antoine (My Recruiter) (1), Debra James (1), Robert and Pamela Tanzy (1), Debra Neal (1), Jolinda K. James (1), Anita Thomas (1), Toria Adams (1), and Santressa Evans (1).

"I want you to know that I am proud to have you as a God Son. You have always respected me, and I love you for that." John Joseph James, Sr. (My Godfather)

"I have tried to stay out of the personal affairs of all three of you (brothers). Decision making is your priority. It's part of the maturity process. I try to help you with all you want to do. I only hope that you learn to stick to a course once you have decided…..especially if it requires the involvement of others." Roosevelt Wright, Jr. (My Father)

Funny Episodes of Boot Camp

There were many funny episodes during my experience as a recruit. I would often write home to my mother to tell them, to her laughter at what I was experiencing. Drill Instructors can be very humorous, and it required an abundance of bearing to remain focused on commands while listening to their quirky comments and responses to our actions. Here are a few that I recall:

A drill instructor grew tired of a recruit asking him if he could take his pills. The DI finally told him "If you keep on you're gonna be taking them like suppositories."

A recruit farted during a class, and a drill instructor became irate and exclaimed: "Who's the fucking sick bastard."

A recruit was not moving at the required pace in the squad bay, and a DI told him "Hey, we don't move slow here, you'd better put some fire in your ass."

There are procedures for walking in the squad bay and on one instance, a recruit was walking down the wrong side of the bay. The DI caught him in his tracks and scolded him. "Hey I don't know where you buy the crack you smoke, but you need to take it back, because it's fucking you up. Are you out of your mind? Go back and go the right way," he harked.

A recruit couldn't answer a knowledge question, and a DI responded "Your IQ must be the same as the number of push-ups you can do...ZEEERRROOOO!"

The platoon was conducting rifle drill, and one recruit appeared scared of his weapon. The DI came up to him and said: "Stop being scared of that rifle, it ain't gonna kick your ass."

The platoon was turning into our racks one night, and a whole bunch of us were acting silly as if we were sick and coughing. The DI heard it and instantly fired back "Y'all better stop all that coughing. If I come over there next to you and you're doing all that I'm gonna turn the whole rack over with you in it."

During class one day, a recruit complained that he was missing a page in his book and that he needed another as a replacement. The DI, in the middle of his instruction, responded, "Ok, wait a minute and let me see if I can pull one out of my ass. Go sit down!"

I graduated from recruit training as a PFC instead of a Private because of my status as an Eagle Scout. The graduation ceremony was held on August 1, 1997. My father, mother, and brother Kita drove to California in their white Lincoln Town Car to be a part of the ceremony. We took turns driving back to Monroe for my two weeks of liberty before reporting back for infantry training school.

NINE

TERROR STORY: GUARDING THE USS COLE

"The instruments of war do have a role to play in preserving the peace. And yet this truth must coexist with another- that no matter how justifies, war promises human tragedy."
President Barack Obama

The Marines trained me for war, but I was never engaged in warfare. The closest I ever came to it was being activated to secure the $2 Billion Destroyer, the USS Cole.

On October 12, 2000, the USS Cole, under the command of Commander Kirk Lippold, set into Aden harbor for a routine fuel stop. The Cole completed mooring at 9:30 AM. Refueling started at 10:30 AM. Around 11:18 AM, a small craft approached the port side of the destroyer, and an explosion occurred, putting a 40-by-40-foot gash in the ship's port side, according to the memorial plate to those who lost their lives. According to former CIA intelligence officer Robert Finke, the blast appeared to be caused by explosives molded into a shaped charge against the hull of the boat. It was speculated at the time that over 1,000 pounds of explosive were used. The blast hit the ship's galley, where the crew was lining up for lunch. The crew fought flooding in the engineering spaces and had the damage under control by the evening. Divers inspected the hull and determined the keel was not damaged.

Seventeen sailors were killed, and thirty-nine others were injured in the blast. The injured sailors were taken to the United States Army's Landstuhl Regional Medical Center near Ramstein, Germany and later, back to the United States.

The attack was organized and directed by Osama bin Laden's al-Qaeda terrorist organization.

The USNS Catawba, USS Camden, Anchorage, Duluth, and Tarawa arrived in Aden some days later, providing watch relief crews, harbor security, damage control equipment, billeting, and food service for the crew of the Cole.

My company was housed on the USS Duluth and was activated to secure the ship, aiding the investigation. We provided a 24-hour security detail for a month until the ship could be removed from Yemen aboard a heavy lift salvage ship, the MV Blue Marlin. The ship arrived in Mississippi for repairs on December 24, 2000.

My initial thoughts as I looked at the ship were of horror. I'd seen nothing like it in real life and never thought in my life that someone could blast a hole that big in the side of a $2 Billion warship….and we were not at war as a result. The sights and smells of that ship will never be forgotten. The crew had to sleep outside on the helo deck because it was not safe or cool enough for them to sleep below decks in their berthing spaces. They were comforted as much as possible, but nothing could ease their emotions as 17 of their friends and crew members were just killed.

We spent three weeks in Yemen aboard the ship. Those were some very hot days. The temperature was in the 100s, and we were in full gear and mostly outside all day. My company stood 24-hour duty, and I served as Sergeant of the Guard when my unit was on the ship. We maintained our posts and kept an eye out for any possible threats. During the day, teams investigated the ship and prepared it for transit back to the States. We were fully armed and ready for action. For me, this was the closest I ever came to being in combat. It was an active incident scene, and it became a moment in US History in which I played a role. I've used my real-world experience in Geography and Social Studies classes as a teacher. It's one thing to talk about history and another to be a part of the story. I'm not an expert on everything that happened in those three weeks, but I am a credible witness to something that should never have happened to the United States of America.

In memory of those young souls who lost their lives in the incident, I pen their names here for reflection: Hull Maintenance Technician 2nd Class **Kenneth Eugene Clodfelter**, 21; Chief Electronics Technician **Richard Costelow**, 35; Mess Management Specialist Seaman **Lakeina Monique Francis**, 19; Information Systems Technician Seaman **Timothy Lee Gauna**, 21; Signalman Seaman Cherone **Louis Gunn**, 22; Seaman James **Rodrick McDaniels**, 19; Engineman 2nd Class **Marc Ian Nieto**, 24; Electronics Warfare Technician 2nd Class **Ronald Scott Owens**, 24; Seaman **Lakiba Nicole Palmer**, 22; Fireman **Joshua Langdon**

Parlett, 19; Fireman **Patrick Howard Roy**, 19; Electronic Warfare Technician 1st Class Kevin **Shawn Rux**, 30; Mess Management Specialist 3rd Class **Ronchester Manangan Santiago**, 22; Operations Specialist 2nd Class **Timothy Lamont Saunders**, 32; Fireman **Gary Graham Swenchonis Jr.**, 26; Ensign **Andrew Triplett**, 31; Seaman **Craig Bryan Wibberley**, 19

TEN

REPORTING THE NEWS: ARRESTED AT CITY HALL

"Our job is only to hold up the mirror-to tell and show the public what has happened."

Walter Cronkite

In 1969, in response to the social unrest in Northeast Louisiana, my father began the operation of a weekly news journal while a student at Northeast Louisiana University. It documented the struggle of the Ouachita Parish African-American community to achieve the American dream. It began as a fly sheet that was distributed to the local community to give information about the various sit-ins, boycott sites, and other information about the local Civil Rights protest. That original fly sheet was printed weekly on a mimeograph machine in the office of the Antioch Baptist Church. It was called the "Rapping Black." Over the years the name of that publication has changed to "Black Free Press" and to the present "Monroe Free Press." This was our family business.

I worked in the family business during my early school years. I worked in accounting, as a delivery paper boy, wrote articles as a youth reporter, learned and worked with word processing software, and took photographs at local events.

I was afforded the opportunity to work within many media formats through his family business experience. The Free Press was located on N.10th Street, downtown Monroe, in the Miller Roy Building. In the back of the building was a large format camera that was used to turn color photographs into PMT formatted images. PMT (Photo-Mechanical Transfer) was a trademark of 3M: used to refer to diffusion transfer techniques and to produce screened prints by exposing silver-based negative material and, after processing, transferring the image onto the receiving layer using diffusion. The family and workers would take a color photograph and attach inside a glass screen facing the large format camera. Though the family could not afford the expensive version, we used a vacuum cleaner, heated lamps, and a makeshift darkroom that exposed the negative Kodak paper. Then that negative paper would be added to the positive end, run through a photographic chemical solution, and allowed to dry out. This process took about 10 minutes per photograph. The photograph was then cut and pasted onto the page in which to be printed in the newspaper.

When I was in high school, my family moved the business to Winnsboro Road. Smaller offices were used, but the same paste-up publication sheets and the PMT Camera were used to capture images.

A few years later, around 1994, the Free Press was moved to its current location at 216 Collier, a large two-story metal framed building that was formerly a Fire Extinguisher distribution warehouse. Not long after they moved into the building, my father paid a few thousand dollars for the newest PMT camera on the market. Two months later, to his financial disgust, Adobe Photoshop was available on the market for $1,000. It changed the operation of media services, and no one was interested in buying the expensive, archaic PMT Camera. The Camera still rests in the building today, only used for a few months.

At the Free Press, I worked with many who found employment there including Sylvester Harris, Zelea Logan, Sylvia Campbell, Renarda Williams, Bridgette Hudson, Vontisha Wiley, Sallie Saulsberry, Marcus Allen, Chinasa Onyebueke, Shalivia Christopher, and Jacqueline Johnson.

A political change at the death of a mayor

Abe E. Pierce, III was elected as the first African-American mayor of the City of Monroe in 1994. He was a deacon at my church, and my father, veteran NAACP and civil rights activist was his campaign manager. His successor was Mayor Melvin Rambin, who was elected in 2000. In 2001, only a year later, a tragic event turned the tide of politics in Monroe even greater than the election of Pierce.

In May of 2001, after I returned home from the Marines, I began reporting for the paper. Two months later, my father was away at the annual convention of the National Baptist Congress, and I was managing the newspaper in his absence. The unthinkable happened. Melvin Rambin, the current mayor at the time, died from cancer leaving the mayor's office vacant. Rambin succeeded Pierce. I called my father and asked about the process of the continuance of government since this was a rare incident. He, being a walking government textbook, quoted the provisions of the Monroe City Charter from his head as it was written. He said that the city council had ten days to name an interim mayor and call a special election to fill the vacancy. Everything happened as he stated. Councilman Jamie Mayo, who was also a deacon at my church, was named Interim Mayor.

When my father returned, he busily began work to get Mayo elected as Mayor. That's when the rift between he and my father began, because this was an unusual call for him, giving the political history between he and Mayo.

The Press War with Mayor Jamie Mayo

My father became the campaign manager for Interim Mayor Jamie Mayo in his bid for election against State Farm executive Guy Barr. I believed that Guy Barr was the better candidate and that for years my father was a political opponent of Mayo. I decided to openly support Barr, even wearing Barr's campaign buttons on official press business. My father exclaimed that as long as I was in his employ as a reporter, I was to support whatever candidate I was told to support. I did not agree with that philosophy. So I quit working for the family newspaper as I considered something wrong with my father's decision to support Mayo. I proceeded to work as a sales associate at Structure, a clothing store in the Pecanland Mall.

Mayo won the election against Barr, but only a few months passed after the election that he and my father fell into a dispute over Mayo's reluctance to fulfill campaign promises. From my father's perspective, he put his political and social name on the line in supporting Mayo. The campaign promises were not being fulfilled, and my father kept pushing Mayo to fulfill them. He even wrote a book called *The Wise Prince* as a benign reminder to Mayo and others in the governance of their duties to the public. Mayo responded that the campaign promises were not his, but were my fathers and that he didn't like being pressured to do anything. His response prompted a virtual war between the newspaper and City Hall, a war that still exists today.

Then a year later, I found myself back at my reporting post when my brother, father, and I were issued a summons at City Hall, in the middle of a dispute with the same mayor, Jamie Mayo, who was the subject of the dispute the previous year. We received a tip that the news media and how the mayor's administration would interact with it was the subject of discussion at a meeting. The meeting would be held in the City Council Chambers at City Hall. Seeing this as a noteworthy meeting in a public meeting room, we decided to sit and observe. We arrived before anyone else arrived and waited patiently. As staff members reported and took their seats, the mayor finally showed up and was advised that members of the press were in the room. Reporters from the television station were also at City Hall. However, they remained in the lobby, while we were actually in the chambers.

After being briefed, the mayor sent his media coordinator, Rod Washington, over to tell us that the meeting was private and we'd have to vacate the room. I didn't know what was about to happen and was nervous about what was taking place. However, my father stood his ground and said that we were in a public room and had a right to be there. So quickly I assumed this was about to be another protest, similar to those that he was involved in that landed him in jail so many times in his earlier years. The mayor had the Assistant Chief of Police Zambie to approach us and give us one final warning. Zambie advised that if we did not comply that he would have to place us under arrest. "Mr. Wright, please just get up an leave. I don't want this trouble today. Can you just leave," Zambie pleaded? He asked were my brother and I with him. My father told him that we were grown and we could make our own decision. We chose to stay. So, after Zambie went back across the room to tell the mayor our response, he ordered him to remove us by arrest. Zambie came back over and said that we were under arrest and we were to follow him over to the police station. My father immediately stood up, and we followed suit.

It was an odd encounter that the Assistant Chief of Police had to go back and forth to deliver messages to the mayor who was once my Boy Scout leader and deacon at my church and he couldn't have just walked over to us and had the discussion. Nevertheless, he allowed the police to place us under arrest and walk us away to the police station. We pulled his card. He responded accordingly.

At the police station, officers went through about three books of ordinance codes to find something to charge us with, since we technically had not broken any laws and the meeting room was open to the public. They finally found one that was close to the encounter. The police department issued the three of us a summons for remaining on the premises. The mayor later had charges dropped against the family. This event automatically initiated my return to the press as a feud between the press and the mayor's office commenced. I remained as a reporter and manager until I moved to Shreveport, Louisiana in 2005.

Jump from the Front Page

With the use of the internet and network capabilities, I continued a connection with the newspaper and weekly conducted page layout from Shreveport. When I left Shreveport for Chicago, I continued the process of page layout even from the Windy City.

In January 2008, after my return from Chicago, I returned to the Free Press as Managing Editor. I signed checks, reported, managed the operations, and took photographs. I remained at the Free Press until November. Time had passed, and to me, old wounds needed to heal. So, I met with Mayor Mayo, and we discussed actions of the past. He still held that he never asked officers to arrest us. I kindly agreed to disagree and chose to move forward. Unfortunately, my family never approved of my association with City Hall or the photographic opportunity that was provided for me, regardless of the financial gain I enjoyed from it. Interestingly, I accepted the opportunity and was under the employ of the mayor's office at the same time that I was editor of the publication. My photography company was an independent contractor for the mayor's Public Relations department. It's highly possible that the two roles had biased persuasion on each other. It created much social and political pressure on me that constantly weighed me down. For on one end, I saw the inside operation of City Hall, but couldn't say too much about it in the press because I was getting a paycheck from both entities. This would last until 2012 when I submitted my resignation from the post with the Public Relations department.

My interrelations with City Hall were great lessons in Mass Communications. Of them, my father has often reminded me of my rights as a citizen and cautioned me not to relinquish them freely. One's freedom of the press and freedom of speech are eliminated once one takes money from the very institution that seemingly has the power to take away these rights. By working for the government in any form, my freedom of speech was controlled by a paycheck, regardless of its size. Likewise, those limits on speech ultimately result in limits on my exercise of a free press. Although I enjoyed having inside access to the halls of government, the ability to associate with people I would never have been given access to (with my city access badge) and as small paycheck on the side, I gave up my rights in the process. There was no way I could investigate government wrongdoing if I were to continue getting a check from it. If I was going to be an effective news publisher, I had to learn this lesson and side with that of journalism over financial perks from City Hall.

The troubles and future of journalism

In my time I've observed many technological changes in journalism and mass media. I'm fortunate to have been reared in the profession before the invent of the world wide web and Facebook. I have a greater appreciation for the news and the publication of it. My father told us even as children that there would come a day when the printed word would fade off the scene and one would be able to hold a gadget in one's hand. The news on that gadget would change as the news changed, as he said. Over three decades later, we found out that the road ahead was not a fantasy but a reality. The news changes so much that I think sometimes we were better off in our darkness. The more information we have access to, the more uninformed we get. Freedom of the Press may be one of the hallmarks of our American Democracy, but when everyone (educated and non-educated) has the means to create a blog or media site, the real news is diluted and unappreciated. Our craving for something new drives at us regardless of the validity of the content. Many times, we crave whatever satisfies our literary expectations, and that is a major problem for a democratic society.

I don't think humanity should ever get rid of the printed word. There is a connection to the paper that the internet cannot replicate. It's a human connection that has to be experienced in its natural form. The touch and smell of a fresh newspaper or a magazine that has never been opened has an exquisite quality that a computer screen can't replace. Books themselves have a quality that none other can replace, not a Kindle, a Nook, or even an E-book read on an iPad. I must have books. They hold a connection to other people that smart gadgets don't.

In my home, I have an autographed autobiography of the famous pianist Liberace. I never met Liberace, but the book that I bought at a book sale was thrown away as trash, an irrelevant creation. I had a moment of silence for humanity when I saw the inside cover signed by Liberace. Here was a book that was held by the great musician, with his signature affixed to a story about his life on Earth. In owning the book, I have a connection with Liberace that no blog or e-book can give me. That is the value of the printed word.

The printed word must continue to exist. Journalism must rekindle the fire from olden days of investigation, analysis, and strategically planned articles for readers. Most of what I know about the history of my hometown, I read in old papers. Modern journalism is fascinated with the ability to "get it out first," and in many attempts to be the first, the press often gets the story wrong. We don't take the time to accurately search for the sources or the full understanding of what we publish because news is time sensitive. Our response is to sell the paper today and print a retraction tomorrow. The printed edition is the record. I think the readers deserve better. I think history deserves better.

ELEVEN

PHOTOGRAPHY SCHOOL IN CHICAGO

"My first day in Chicago, September 4, 1983. I set foot in this city, and just walking down the street, it was like roots, like the motherland. I knew I belonged here."
Oprah Winfrey

I moved to Chicago, IL in August of 2006 to matriculate at Harrington College of Design in its Associates Degree in Digital Photography program.

I wasn't in the city but a day before I had to go and see downtown for myself. It was certainly a dream city. There was great architecture, skyscrapers, lots of traffic, and thousands of people moving to and from their destinations. I walked down Michigan Ave and took in the Buckingham Fountain near Lake Michigan, the massive silver Bean, Johnson Publishing Company (the home of Ebony Magazine), the Water Tower, and the many centers of shopping, museums, condominiums, and luxurious hotels. Chicago was a city that required one to look up, and looking up was something I did a lot in my first days in town. I was a traveler to a new land, this artist's lair that was home to a number of ethnicities and nationalities. Frank Sinatra had it right, Chicago was my kind of town.

There were cranes all over the city as new buildings were constantly being built. One of the major structures being built during my time was Trump International Hotel and Tower. Designed by architect Adrian Smith of Skidmore, Owings, and Merrill, the 98-story building is 1,389 feet, including its spire. Construction began in 2005, so when I arrived in Chicago in August of 2006, the structure was taking form. Daily I watched as floor after floor was constructed. It was such a notable place that a scene from the 2008 film "The

Dark Knight" was shot at the construction site. I also was fortunate to see the production of another movie while I was there. A scene featuring the crashing of a red sports car drew my attention one night when I was downtown. It would be the very scene from the movie "Wanted" starring James McAvoy, Angelina Jolie, and Morgan Freeman. I never saw the actors, but I had a better appreciation for the scene when I saw the movie. My time to be in the movies had not come just yet, but there would be a day in the distant future that I would have my time on a cold night shoot, being a part of a film production.

Mentoring from the Village of Black Women

I never met Oprah Winfrey, the most famous African-American woman in Chicago. However, I had the next best thing. Two African-American women from my hometown lived in the windy city and welcomed my move with open arms. They opened up their homes and mentored my professional life during my brief stay in the city. It is believed that "It takes a village to raise a child." Well, I was far from being a child, but Ingrid Larkin and Terisa Griffin were my village. They were home away from home, the support group that made Chicago possible for me.

For a month, I lived with Ingrid. She was a graduate of the Art Institute of Atlanta and was very proficient with graphic design. She had a small one bedroom apartment in town, and all that was available for me was her sofa sleeper in the living room. I was no stranger to altered living arrangements and accepted the sofa. I knew it would only be temporary, but I was there in Chicago, with a view of Lake Michigan. Larkin was the Art Director at Ebony Magazine, whose corporate office was located in downtown Chicago. Larkin advised me daily for a month on survival in the big city: how to dress, how to keep warm, how to get around, how to keep from getting sick, how to be frugal and most importantly how to be progressive, productive and get the best out of my art school education. I arrived in August, so the effects of the cold that I would face had not hit me like the hawk just yet. However, I would soon realize what she meant when she spoke about the "Hawk." Although she was a busy professional, she took considerable time in the evenings to evaluate my portfolio and advise me from an Art Director's point of view. She was impressed with some of the images. "That photo pops," she would say. On others that I considered memorable, Larkin would say "No! This doesn't say anything." She challenged me to go with a conceptual approach, rather than just taking random photographs that lacked a theme or any special meaning.

Larkin had met and been mentored by John H. Johnson, the founder of the company. She would often share photo collections of her time with Johnson and praise the gentle person that he was. Johnson was a member of Alpha Phi Alpha Fraternity and was a household name in Black America. He died in August of 2005, the previous year.

I was also mentored by another hometown friend, Terisa Griffin. She had lived in Chicago for over a decade. She also gave me her survival lessons on being productive and making the best out of my abilities in the city. She took me around Chicago and allowed me to work with her on her singing gigs. She introduced me to some of the notable people in Chicago, giving me an opportunity to network. She even arranged photography gigs for me with some of her friends.

Griffin is a recording artist and has performed on the Oprah Winfrey Show, sang backup for Diana Ross and has opened up for many singers like Isaac Hayes, Ashford and Simpson, Roberta Flack and Patti Labelle. She's worked in the studio with Lionel Richie and Chicago's own R. Kelly. She also sang at the funeral of Hollywood actor/comedian and Chicago native Bernie Mac. One of her great mentors is "The Iceman" Jerry Butler, who escorted her down the aisle at her wedding in 2012.

Larkin is a lady of Delta Sigma Theta Sorority, Inc., and Griffin-Kendall is a lady of Zeta Phi Beta Sorority, Inc. These two sisters were a great source of support and encouragement to me as I was seeking to take my talents to a higher level. They are two that I call big sisters and will always look up to them as they aren't just women from Monroe, but they are champions in their profession who sought to lift up a younger African-American male who sought transcendence. In Windy City Chicago, its difficult to find a genuine set of friends and supporters. It's not just cold because of its weather.

Larkin and Griffin were the radiators that helped me bear the cold, brave a new world and kept me going while I learned the lessons of professional photography.

School training at Harrington

I studied digital photography at the Harrington College of Design. The school is located in the Loop in the heart of downtown Chicago. There I learned photography fundamentals, theory, lighting for product photography and portrait lighting. I worked with the Mamiya 645 AFD Medium Format Camera system and learned the Macintosh Operating System. I bared freezing temperatures walking and riding the CTA (Chicago Transit Authority) to get to and from class every day. In my first semester at Harrington, I mastered all of my classes and maintained a 4.0 GPA.

Photography 101 was my first course taken at the design school. It comprised the fundamentals of digital photography. The course is one of my more memorable ones as it would be the very course to challenge my understanding of the medium I had been so used to for the previous four years. Peter Bosy taught it. The course familiarized us with digital cameras, exposure, capture, scanning, image manipulation, and presentation of prints. Mr. Bosy taught us how to recognize an original image from one that was manipulated in photoshop. He also taught us how to check the image metadata to determine whether a photographer used natural lighting or whether a strobe was used to light the image.

When I began the class, I was fresh from Monroe with a few photographs published in the JET Magazine. Certainly, I knew what I was doing and silently questioned the instructor's ability to teach me anything. I learned very quickly that, even though I was lucky enough to get my photos published, I was an amateur when it came to professional photography. I knew nothing about the theory of lighting or how to effectively use photographic equipment other than pointing and shooting. I knew how to frame images because I had an eye for it. However, there was much more to learn about photography. The techniques I learned in the course were speed, aperture, ISO, and troubleshooting maneuvers to manipulate ambient light for photographs in unpleasant weather conditions. These are things an amateur would never know.

In the course, we learned about notable photographers. An assignment required us to research the works of two famous photographers of our choosing. Mr. Bosy gave us a list of choices. I chose Herb Ritts and Richard Avedon. I also studied the works of James Van Der Zee, the famous photographer from the Harlem Renaissance. The lesson learned from this activity was that one couldn't become great without an appreciation for those who came before him. It was important to find a photographer's work that appealed to me, research the body of work, and submit an analysis of why the artist and his work was so significant. In Ritts, I relived the 80s. He was the photographer of photographers in Hollywood during my childhood. From Batman, Rocky, Superman, and many other superheroes featured in the movies, Ritts was the guy taking the photos used for publications and advertising. He also had a knack for black and white images. Though many of them were of nude content, his lighting control was spectacular to me. His beginning was also unique in that he was friends with the actor Richard Gere. On a road trip, their car was being serviced, and while they waited, Ritts took a photo of Gere that caught the attention of a magazine editor. The rest was history.

In the Tec 100 MAC course, I learned how to use the Apple Macintosh operating system. The instructor was Cassandra Sheffield, M.S. I was familiar with the Windows Operating System but had never used a Macintosh before, so the class was very beneficial. It was not a difficult transition, however many of the keyboard functions took a while to master. In the class, we also learned how to use Excel, Spreadsheet, and Microsoft Word. As part of the culture of the industry, one of our class assignments was to visit the Apple Store downtown Chicago. In the store, we traveled with our assignment sheet of an information scavenger hunt. We had to know the difference between an iPod Nano and the new iPod, Quicktime, iSight, types of software programs, the difference between the Macintosh computer systems, types of accessories, and the prices of these systems. We also had to create an original brochure and give a power point presentation on a photographer's work that interested us.

I took the Art 121 Design Foundations course under Kristy Yarbrough. The course was an introduction to the "basic elements and principles of design, the terminology of two-dimensional design and composition and the fundamentals of color theory." That we were in training to be photographers and graphic designers this course was an important foundation for our professions. We had to create an original color wheel, a grayscale, and a few more art creations to demonstrate competence of the course material. Having been in the Talented Art Program as an elementary school student, I had no difficulty mastering this course as the content was very similar. It was interesting that there I was an adult in an art class as if I were back in my elementary school class. However, it proved that a great photographer is an artist at heart. If one can't see the light, the fancy gear is pointless.

Tim Arroyo, a very talented graphic designer, taught the Digital Imaging 1 course. It was a continuation of Photography 101 and gave me not only a basic course in Adobe Photoshop CS2 but also introduced me to the professional art of digital printing. Emphasis was placed on color management and the techniques of enhancing, correcting and manipulating images. Some of the features of the class included adjusting color tones, image resolution, re-sizing, cropping, working with levels and curves, selection tools, retouching, brushes, framing, and the use of Photoshop automation processes. Arroyo taught us how to correctly print a photograph using the digital process, types of printing paper, and color management during the process.

At Harrington, I also took a studio lighting class in which we were introduced to product photography. We began with a basic gray box. We had to use the continuous lights in the studio labs to create different lighting captures of not people, but an ugly gray box. However, depending on how we arranged the lights, a different type of image could be produced. After the gray box assignment was completed, I was able to bring in some products. I shot a few beauty items including a bottle of Axe body wash and a tube of makeup. These were not easy setups for a few of them took hours of focus to make sure the light hit the product perfectly to get the desired effect. There were many hours of trial and error, but in the end, I learned why professional photographers in the field could make $10,000 for just one shot of a Rolex watch. If a company is paying $100,000 for a full-page ad in the Vanity Fair magazine, you'd better bet they made sure the photography was perfect....and this requires more than setting up a pop-up tent in someone's living room and using a cheap camera because it looked "okay" on a website.

Although I didn't complete the degree program at Harrington, the lessons learned would foster the quality of photographs I would produce in the future. I met many challenges in my professional work with solutions learned at Harrington. Knowing how to troubleshoot a situation is one of the major lessons learned at school. An amateur can go to Best Buy or the local camera store and buy a DSLR camera, print some business cards and begin accepting customers. Knowing how to frame the image, create a concept and know how to respond when the shoot does not go as planned are the lessons taught at school, and that knowledge is what separates the amateur from the professional photographer.

TWELVE

PHOTO SHOOT STORY: HURRICANE CHRIS

"When he was 10-years-old he was singing and probably before then."
Louisiana State Rep. Barbara Norton

Through an association with Hollyhood Bay Bay in Shreveport, Louisiana, I was introduced to a crowd of celebrity hopefuls. Shreveport is a booming town where money is gambled, crowds are entertained, movies are produced, and models and rappers are scouted. One such rapper is Chris Dooley, Jr. Dooley. In 2005, he was a student at Huntington High School and was an aspiring rapper. In August of that year, his cousin, a local rapper who went by the stage name "Three Feet," was in the limelight.

"Feet" entertained at the concerts, parties, and was introduced to the Shreveport audience on the airwaves. He contacted me one day and said that he required my services to obtain some photographs. The shoot was arranged, and we met up downtown Shreveport. Our shoot took place in an alley between Milam and Common Streets. During that time we shot some photographs in a few different outfits as "Feet" posed in XXL/Vibe hip-hop fashion. In the background was this young kid, who couldn't have been more than 16 or 17-years-old. As it turned out, his name was Chris, and he tagged along for the photo shoot with his cousin.

During outfit changes for the remainder of Feet's shoot, he began a cell phone conversation that lasted longer than normal for a typical temporary interruption. This was a shoot of which he was paying for my time. I assumed it didn't matter to him and he had the funds to cover the overlay. While Feet continued to talk on the phone, I asked Chris to come over to the shooting area in the vacant lot we shot in. He was dressed in a red jumpsuit that was styled with a black bandana, do-rag, and a black cap. Chris had a gold grille in his mouth and wore black Reebok sneakers and chains as accessories to his look. His hair was platted and braided.

Chris was a quiet character, unlike the person of which he would later develop into as "Hurricane Chris." I insisted that he pose with a fierce composure. One of the photos he is even posed with a brick as if to break down the barriers of his youthful existence. In only a few months that fantasy would come to life.

An entire photo shoot continued as "Feet" continued his phone conversation as if the world went on despite his involvement with whoever was on the other end of the conversation. Meanwhile, Chris was the subject of my camera's attention. Some months later, Chris, with the aid of Hollyhood Bay Bay, had begun recording in the studio and it was recognized that he would eventually break out of his Shreveport shell and on to higher levels in the hip-hop industry.

In April 2006, a second photo shoot with Chris was conducted in the parking lot of the Pierre Bossier Mall in Bossier City (across the Red River). This time Chris was not the sideline spectator. In fact, he had an entourage this time to include his cousin "Three Feet" who was in the background. Chris' attitude and composure were also modified by this time. His poses were no longer dictated as he was more confident and more extravagant with his wardrobe. A borrowed fully loaded Hummer was a prop on his scene in his rise to Hip-Hop fame. He wore a pair of red and white sneakers, jeans, and a T-Shirt with the Louisiana state outline in Red. Across the Louisiana state outline was the word Hurricane in bold black cursive. He donned black sunshades, a do-rag, a cross necklace, and a red New York Yankees baseball cap.

I didn't see Chris much after that photo session at Pierre Bossier Mall, but his success in the Hip Hop industry was very successful. He took the nightclub chant "A Bay Bay" and turned it into a hit song. His album "51/50 Ratchet" was released in 2007 not long after he dropped out of school to pursue his music career. In 2009, he released his second album "Unleashed" of which included the hit song "Halle Berry (She's Fine)." The song was so popular that a Shreveport State Representative, Barbara Norton, introduced him to the Louisiana State Legislature in Baton Rouge. During their regular session, Dooley performed the song in the House Chambers and was recognized for his success as an entertainer from Louisiana.

THIRTEEN

PHOTO SHOOT STORY: KATHERINE GOES TO VEGAS

"We pick politicians by how they look on TV and Miss America
where she stands on the issues.
Isn't that a little backward?

Jay Leno

In 2009, I began a photo journey that would culminate with a sendoff of Miss Louisiana Katherine Putnam to Las Vegas for the 2010 Miss America Pageant.

Putnam, an accomplished singer, and pianist competed at the 2009 Miss Louisiana Pageant at the Monroe Civic Center on June 20. I had the honor of being the official photographer for the Miss Louisiana Organization and took photographs during the pageant and the moments immediately following on stage. It was quite a night as the contest was very competitive, but Putnam pulled it off and took the crown. She competed as Miss Shreveport, with Dr. Ed Johnson as director. At 22, she played "The Hallelujah Chorus" on the Piano. I was amazed at her arrangement of the piece because it sounded similar to that of renowned pianist Dino Kartsonakis. I would later find out that Putnam had met and had lessons by Kartsonakis and her arrangement was produced by his production staff. A piano player myself, I met Kartsonakis once when he played at First Baptist Church in West Monroe in the 1990s. He signed an autograph for me, but never did I expect to meet someone else almost 20 years later who knew Kartsonakis and had lessons from him. I instantly became a fan of Katherine. She played her piece with all the splendor and majesty that the music demanded.

She and her family lodged at the Atrium Hotel. Early on the morning following the pageant, I designed a commemorative poster of photographs from the pageant, printed it, had it framed and rushed it over to the hotel. They were amazed at how quickly I'd produced such a presentation. I was amazed that she remembered my gesture of kindness while delivering her farewell speech the following year as she passed the crown to the next Miss Louisiana.

On October 8, 2009, Putnam served as the host for the Miss ULM Pageant. She didn't play the piano for entertainment at the pageant but surprised the audience with her voice. She was as much a spectacle with a microphone as she was with eighty-eight keys and a sustain pedal.

On January 9, 2010, I took photographs of Putnam's Trunk Show, which was held at the Biedenharn Recital Hall on the campus of ULM. This event was held to display the outfits that she would be wearing in Las Vegas at the Miss America Pageant, for which she would be shortly departing. She entertained the audience with a piano performance on ULM's Fazioli grand piano. Following the show, there was a private reception held at Bonaire, the President's Mansion. She met with university supporters and family and took photos with Dr. James Cofer, his wife, and other ULM students who were pageant titleholders.

Early on the morning of January 21, 2010, I arrived at the Monroe Regional Airport to take photographs of Katherine as she prepared to board her flight to Las Vegas. Others would be joining her there the following week. Members of the Miss Louisiana Organization, family, and friends were present to give her well wishes and to see her for the last time before she would hopefully be Miss America.

I too would be leaving for Vegas, as I later attended the 2010 competition at Planet Hollywood. It was my second time in Las Vegas, and I was thrilled to be there for my second Miss America Pageant experience. I wasn't there as a photographer, but as a pageant director, as I was the director of Miss Monroe Pageant at the time. The judges for the pageant were Vivica A. Fox, Katie Harman, Dave Koz, Shawn Johnson, Rush Limbaugh, and Paul Rodriguez. Miss Virginia Caressa Cameron, a 22-year-old from Fredericksburg, Virginia would become Miss America 2010. Putnam was 3rd Runner-up out of all of the contestants from around the country, a major accomplishment for her and the Miss Louisiana Organization.

I took final photos of Putnam at the 2010 Miss Louisiana Pageant on June 26, 2010, at the Monroe Civic Center, as she passed the crown to Kelsi Crain. What a year she had.

Coda.

FOURTEEN

PHOTO SHOOT STORY: KELSI GOES TO VEGAS

"There she is, Miss America, there she is, your ideal."
Bert Parks

I had the opportunity to photograph the journey of Kelsi Crain from her preliminary pageant win as Miss ULM until her sendoff to Las Vegas as Miss Louisiana from the Monroe Regional Airport two years later.

On October 8, 2009, I took photographs at the 57th Annual Miss ULM Pageant. Crain competed at Brown Auditorium for the title of Miss University of Louisiana at Monroe, a preliminary contest for Miss Louisiana and Miss America. She was a 19-year-old sophomore that year and competed on the platform "Heart for the Arts." Her talent was dance and she performed a Dance en Point. She won Talent and Swimsuit at the pageant and was named Advertisement Sales Winner. Her runner-ups included: Brandi Stout, Karmen Rubin, Lindsey Eickman, and Evan Lane. Dr. James E. Cofer, president of the university, was there to participate in the crowning ceremony.

On June 26, 2010, I had the privilege of being the official photographer for the Miss Louisiana Organization and had access to record the photographs of the pageant. Crain competed for the title of Miss Louisiana 2010 at the Monroe Civic Center. She was crowned Miss Louisiana by Katherine Putnam, Miss Louisiana 2009. Her runner-ups included: Miss Dixie Gem Peach Lauren Abshier, was first runner-up, and Miss Monroe Hope Anderson, was second runner-up.

Following the pageant, I took photographs at the reception, held in the B.D. Robinson Hall. Crain was escorted into the reception by Dr. Guthrie Jarrell, a long time friend and contributor of the Miss Louisiana Organization. She took photographs with former Miss

Louisiana title holders and with Louisiana State Senator Mike Walsworth.

Early on the morning of January 6, 2011, I arrived at the Monroe Regional Airport to photograph Kelsi's sendoff to Las Vegas for the Miss America Pageant. Members of the Miss Louisiana Organization including the director Dewanna Little were present. Her family and friends were also present. ULM President Nick Bruno even showed up to see her off to the big pageant. Although she didn't make the top 15, Crain still enjoyed a week of competition and fellowship in Las Vegas with the other winners of state titles from around the country. Teresa Scanlan, from Nebraska, would take the title of Miss America 2011.

FIFTEEN

PHOTO SHOOT STORY: SHE BECAME A 50 CENT STAR

"People often say I have so much energy, that I never stop; but that's what it takes to accomplish your goals."

50 Cent

I met model and movie star Jasmine Adams through my work with Grambling State University. I arranged a photo shoot with her at Lincoln Parish Park on November 4, 2003. Over the next three years, she and I would do another three photo shoots, with each presenting more of her photographic flare to my camera. Jasmine became very comfortable with posing for photos over the years and her talent and interest in modeling grew as well.

Standing at 5'8 with 34DD-22-37 measurements, Jasmine has appeared in music videos, hundreds of photo shoots, and her images have been used on dozens of marketing supplies for beauty products. A native of Thibodaux, Louisiana, she starred in the 2012 Lionsgate distributed film "Freelancers" with 50 Cent, Forrest Whitaker, and Robert DeNiro. I was viewing this movie before I knew she was featured in it and when she opened the door in her scene, my mouth dropped. Jasmine? She was unclothed showing all of her glorious 34DD blessings. "I know her. That's Jasmine from Grambling. I've taken photos of her," I exclaimed to myself. In the scene, 50 Cent (Curtis Jackson, III) and Forrest Whitaker's characters visit an apartment where working ladies of the night are serving their clients. All sorts of activity take place in the apartment. Jasmine walks over, hands 50 a beer and whispers something in his ear, then walks over to join the other ladies on the job.

In 2015, I shopped at a hair store on Winnsboro Rd., on Monroe's Southside, and saw a few hair items on a rack. The face used on the marketing material looked familiar. As I picked up the satin bonnet package, it became clear....that was Jasmine. She posed for photos with a number of items on that rack including satin bonnets, du-rags, and foam caps. They all had her face on them. She'd done it again. I wonder if anyone else knew who she was or that she was from Louisiana.

I have kept in touch with Jasmine and she still refers to me as her first photographer, the one that opened the door for her to chart her voyage into the world of modeling. She is now an SNBF-Supernatural Body Building and Fitness Pro and competes in many fitness competitions when she's not posing for the camera. If you google the name Jasmine Adams, she is sure to be the first images to come up, and she won't be mistaken for someone else.

SIXTEEN

PHOTO SHOOT STORY: MY PHOTO IN A MOVIE

"Whatever success I've had, I like to top it."
Bernie Mac

In 2008, my photo of Hollyhood Bay Bay (a Shreveport, LA radio personality) was featured in the major motion picture "Soul Men" starring Samuel L. Jackson and Bernie Mac. The shoot of which the photo originated took place on December 31, 2005. The main shot from the photo shoot was Hollyhood standing in front of his vintage blue convertible looking off camera. For many years, this was one of my favorite shots.

I didn't even know that the photo was used in the film until someone brought it to my attention that the poster that was displayed looked like the photo I shot of Bay Bay. When I sat and viewed the movie, it was. The poster that I printed and framed for Bay Bay found its way to a movie set. I was excited and confused at the same time. Where was my royalty check? It seemed that my photography arrived in a movie before I did.

It is seen in the scene of which Samuel L. Jackson and Bernie Mac are in the basement of his nephew's house. They're debating the merits of what is considered quality music when one of the young rappers points to the "Bay Bay" poster on the wall.

The movie was released on November 7, 2008. It was directed by Malcolm D. Lee and took in $12.3 million at the box office.

SEVENTEEN

PHOTO SHOOT STORY: SHOOTING O.J. & ARIEL

"The day you take complete responsibility for yourself, the day you stop making any excuses, that's the day you start to the top."

O.J. Simpson

I had an opportunity to meet two celebrities at once and photograph them at the Shreveport Airport on July 7, 2006. I met with Model Ariel Meredith and Heisman Trophy winner O.J. Simpson. Meredith is a celebrity model and a native of Shreveport. Simpson's maternal grandparents are from Louisiana, and those roots gave him his first name "Orenthal" because his aunt said it sounded like that of a French actor. He spent many boyhood summers in Caddo Parish at his grandparent's farm. Coincidentally, Meredith and O.J. Simpson were on the same flight to Shreveport, as they were coming to visit family. They spoke on the plane and became acquainted. I was there as a friend of Meredith's to take photos of her arrival and was afforded the additional opportunity to meet and capture Simpson.

At the airport, he walked through the gates with his famous stride and proceeded to baggage claim. While waiting, he and Meredith met up in a restaurant at the airport. Simpson signed a few autographs and took photos with people in the restaurant. I asked if he would take a photo with Meredith and he was more than willing. It is one of my more memorable photos. I remember Simpson's murder trial from 10 years earlier and yet here he was, in the flesh, a free man walking amongst us in Shreveport, Louisiana.

Meredith was a graduate of Huntington High School and had been modeling since she was 14. In 1998, she won a modeling competition against 500 other contestants and signed with modeling agencies in Dallas in New York. During her teen years, she appeared in Cosmopolitan, Seventeen, Teen Cosmopolitan and Teen magazines. She has posed for J. Crew, David's Bridal, Cover Girl,

110

Ann Taylor Loft, Fossil, Target, Roca Wear, Gap, and Victoria's Secret. She traveled the globe shooting with Sports Illustrated and appeared in the 2009, 2012, 2013, 2014, and 2015 editions of the Swimsuit Issue.

It was a great day for photography as I was in the right place, at the right time with two celebrities in their professions.....an NFL great and a fabulous celebrity model. What a walk in history.

EIGHTEEN

PHOTO SHOOT STORY: MY PHOTO ON A PHONE BOOK

"A man, as a general rule, owes very little to what he is born with — a man is what he makes of himself."
Alexander Graham Bell

The culmination of three years of work came to climax on May 3, 2012 when I received a text from the City of Monroe's Public Relations coordinator Rod Washington, who informed me that I needed to be present at a press conference. AT&T had chosen the Monroe Regional Airport Terminal photo to appear on the 2012 phone book. My photograph won the winning consideration. It was such an honor to have been given the opportunity to participate in the project. I worked as an independent contractor under Mayor Jamie Mayo's administration and was tasked through Washington to photo-document the entire airport construction project from groundbreaking to ribbon cutting. It was never in my imagination that my work would be on a telephone book.

The groundbreaking ceremony for the airport construction was held on July 17, 2009. A number of guests and politicians were present to usher in the $30 million project, paid for mostly through proceeds from the stimulus package of the Obama Administration. Speakers at the occasion included: Mayor Jamie Mayo, Councilman Jay Marx, Councilman Eddie Clark, Councilman Robert Red Stevens, Councilman Ben Katz, Airport Director Cleve Norrell, Chamber of Commerce President Sue Nicholson, and US Senator Mary Landrieu. Shortly after speeches, each of them and others took shovels and commenced breaking ground. Miss Monroe 2009 Raven Hollins was also among those breaking ground.

After the groundbreaking ceremony, the three-year-long photo project commenced. I made 13 visits documenting the process from the ground. I covered every inch of the complex as I was given all-access and a hard hat to document the process. Some of those experiences were not pleasant. Days were cold, scorching hot, and many were dusty. I had to replace a pair of shoes and buy boots for those muddy days in the aftermath of rain. It was quite interesting to witness how the designers and contractor planned the process. The new terminal was built on the same grounds as the old terminal. They began with the ticketing area building. Once that wing was complete, they began demolishing a portion of the old terminal. Once that was done, work began on the center lobby building. When that was complete, demolition began on the final portion of the previous complex. It took some time but the process was unique as the runway and tower were left intact, but the terminal was a fresh, well-needed upgrade for Monroe. I was proud to be a part of the process.

The grand opening ceremony was held on October 10, 2011, with comments made by Mayor Mayo and West Monroe Mayor Dave Norris. Others included Miss Louisiana 2011 Hope Anderson, who would be taking a flight soon to travel to Las Vegas for the Miss America Pageant, Councilman Authur Gilmore, Councilman Robert Red Stevens, Councilman Jay Marx and Councilwoman Gretchen Ezernack.

In the end, my perseverance would lead to me getting clearance from the Federal Aviation Administration the following year to come to the terminal tower and take an aerial photo of the main lobby and ticketing building that would eventually land on the cover of a telephone book. That was three years of work worth the struggle. I didn't get paid a fortune for the photography job, but the cover of the phone book was a nice reward for a job well done.

NINETEEN

PHOTO SHOOT STORY: MY PHOTOS AT CITY HALL

"When you start out, you're not really aware. I didn't have a sense of photographic history."

Herb Ritts

My photographs of Monroe elected officials hang on the wall of the Monroe City Council chamber in City Hall. I was afforded the opportunity to shoot these during my tenure as a contract photographer with the City of Monroe from 2008-2012.

There are only a few photographers who have had the honor of capturing the images of elected officials. In Monroe, these photographs are framed and remain on the wall of the council chamber indefinitely. There are black and white photographs that date back to the early 20th century, many taken by the same photographer.

Two photographers in Monroe's history have the most work featured in the council chamber....Durwood Griffin and Leonard Johnson.

Thomas Durwood Griffin was born the same year his father James Everett Griffin opened Griffin's Photography Studio in Monroe, in 1914. The shop was located at 318 DeSiard Street. His father died in 1932, the year of the Great Ouachita River Flood. Many of the photographs taken by the Griffins during the flood are archived by the University Of Louisiana at Monroe. The studio celebrated its 20th year anniversary in 1934 during the middle of the Great Depression. Durwood would later become a Master Photographer and President of the Professional Photographers of Louisiana from 1965-1966. He is the only photographer from Monroe to hold the position. In 1973, he was the national award recipient of the Professional Photographers of America. Durwood died in 1999.

The Griffin family contributed a number of photographs that are displayed in the council chamber including Councilmen: Will

Atkinson, D.A. Breard, Frank Cline, John P. Simmons, Luther Harper, Harlan Prestridge, Milton Moore, Tyson Bordelon, Charles Johnson, Gene Tarver, and Benny Ausberry. Monroe Mayors Ralph Troy and Robert Powell also sat for photographs with Griffin's Studio.

Mr. Leonard Johnson was well known in Monroe. I never met the man, but I knew of him by his work and the reputation it gained for him. He took a portrait of my grandfather, Roosevelt Wright, Sr. My grandfather was attracted to the status symbol that came from having a Johnson photo. If you wanted to feel important, you took a photo with Johnson, for people knew if you took a photo with him, you paid a great sum of money for it. Johnson, who operated his shop on Washington Street, had a window in the front of the building. His select photographs would be displayed in the main window, which would become a talking piece for people in the community.

Johnson was born in 1925 to Mary and Lloyd Johnson of Simsboro, Louisiana. He was one of 13 children. He attended college at Grambling State University where he learned the art of photography. He played an active role in the Monroe community through civic and pastoral service and was a business trailblazer as a photographer. In the mid 20th century, he founded Johnson Photography Studio, operating it for more than six decades. He leaves behind a long legacy of images and memories for thousands with school, portrait, and wedding photography clients for which he served. He operated throughout Louisiana, Arkansas, Mississippi and east Texas, winning awards from industry associations. Johnson died in 2015.

Johnson took several photographs that are displayed in the council chamber including Councilmen: James E. Mayo, Authur Gilmore, Robert E. Stevens, Robert Johnson and John Smith. He also took photographs of Mayors: Abe. E. Pierce, III, Melvin Rambin, and James E. Mayo.

When I became the city's photographer in 2008, I did not know I would have the honor of having my photographs displayed among the greats of the town. That year, the city needed new portraits of the council and mayor for the website. I photographed the entire council including Councilmen: Jay Marx, Ben Katz, Robert E. Stevens, Authur Gilmore, and Robert Johnson. We took these photographs in the chamber on June 10, 2008. None of these were used on the wall, just on the website. However, the photograph of Mayor Mayo was used on city presentations, brochures, and programs at events. It is still used on the digital sign at the Monroe Civic Center.

Later, the Council Clerk needed to get the new council members photographed for wall hanging. I was excited about the opportunity. I would photograph Interim Councilpersons: Rueben Oliver, Ellen Hill and Glenda Starr, and Elected councilpersons Eddie Clark and Gretchen Ezernack. Next time you visit City Hall, take a browse in the chamber and look up top on the Council photo side (left side). The top 5 are mine.

What an awesome experience and honor it was to work in that capacity and have my photography on display, knowing that it would still be on display for all that came behind me, for at least the next century, as is that of Durwood Griffin and Leonard Johnson, legends of photography in Monroe.

TWENTY

PHOTO SHOOT STORY: SIX BEAUTIES IN JET MAG

"To succeed, one must be creative and persistent."
John H. Johnson

In 1952, John H. Johnson's weekly magazine, JET, began a full-page feature promoting the beauty of African-American women. Published on page 43 of each issue was the "Beauty of the Week." The magazine had over a million subscribers weekly. In each issue, a photograph of an African-American woman in a swimsuit, along with her name, place of residence, profession, hobbies, and interests was printed. The women featured were not professional models. However, many of the women featured and their photographers made their mark on page 43. During the decades of its novelty, being featured in the JET magazine was a symbol of pride for African-Americans. Being featured as a JET Beauty of the Week was even more notable, for this was the only magazine available to African-Americans to display such beauty. I never thought it was possible for me to get my work included in the historic publication....until I stepped out on faith and tried.

Jacqueline Edwards- JET Beauty of the Week
November 1, 2004

On June 25, 2004, in my Monroe, Louisiana studio, I conducted a photo shoot with Shreveport native Jacqueline Edwards that would prove to later be a success on the national level. Little did we know that the photos we would take that night would become such a hit and achievement in my already growing photographic career. In fact, we went into the shoot not even envisioning submitting the photographs to a magazine. It was a normal fun shoot with one of my favorite female subjects from Shreveport.

Jacqueline, "Jackie" was very short and petite, but with the right curves and a pretty face to make "an old man wish for younger

117

days." She had recently graduated from high school and was attending Southern University in Baton Rouge, Louisiana. She and her friend Marchelle Carter from Shreveport traveled to Monroe for the shoot. The shoot included three outfit changes. One was a two-piece halter black swimsuit, one with a cute blouse and jeans with pumps, and the other was a floral printed two-piece swimsuit. Although we did a number of shots with the various outfits, it was the floral printed two-piece swimsuit that we later decided on giving a shot at submission to the JET Magazine.

The process was simple at the time. A photographer would send in two color photographs of a female in a swimsuit, and the editorial board would decide as to whether they wanted to feature the submitted print in one of their upcoming issues. So that is what we did.

I chose one of Jackie's poses in the floral print swimsuit and one in the black halter swimsuit, mailed a cover letter and waited for Ebony's response. To my surprise, in September, I received a letter in the mail from Johnson Publishing Company (the brown letter) stating that it was interested in using photographs of Jackie in one of its upcoming issues and that she was to sign the photo release form including biographical information that would be included in the feature. I was as shocked by the achievement as was Jackie and her agent Michelle Carter of Bronze & Gold Models in Shreveport.

Jackie's photos were published in the November 1, 2004 issue of the JET Magazine which hosted Jamie Foxx's role as Ray Charles in the upcoming movie "Ray" on the front cover. News coverage of the achievement was published in Monroe newspapers as well as in the Shreveport Sun-Times. It was a major achievement for Louisiana as well since only a few women from Louisiana in the history of JET Magazine had been featured as the Beauty of the Week.

Melissa Marshall- JET Beauty of the Week
February 6, 2006

It wasn't until June 28, 2005 that another shoot was conducted that images would be sent to JET Magazine that would be published in its magazine. The subject of the June 2005 shoot was Melissa Marshall, who was a model in another Shreveport model troupe headed by Tiffany "T-Shemise" Walker, a local clothing designer. Marshall's shoot was conducted at Cypress Lake in Benton, Louisiana. She wore a green two-piece swimsuit and posed in the sand at the lake's "Beach." The images were submitted to JET and as before, a return letter was sent stating Johnson Publishing Company's intent to use the photographs in its magazine. However, it wasn't until the following year before the photographs were published in the magazine. Marshall's photograph was featured in the February 6, 2006 issue of the JET Magazine that hosted Martin Lawrence on the cover for his movie "Big Momma's House 2."

Laquista Haywood/Ashleigh Anguiano- JET Beauties of the Week- April 3, 2006, April 10, 2006

With the notoriety of my national publication success, my Shreveport photography operations grew to the point of establishing a studio office on Youree Dr. In February 2006, almost immediately after the release of the Melissa Marshall JET issue, I had two interested females who wanted to pose with me for a chance at a JET spot. On February 21, 2006, in my Youree Drive studio, I conducted a shoot with Shreveport locals LaQuista Haywood and Ashleigh Anguiano.

The February 21 shoot was set up barnyard style. I went to a feed and seed store in town and purchased several bails of hay and had a friend who had access to some available weathered tin to make the background. These were set up in the studio and Laquista and Ashleigh posed for their shoot. Their shots were attractive and they captured the attention of Sylvia Flanagan, the editor of the JET Magazine who made the final decision on the ladies on Page 43. There was a unique twist to the prints that were sent to JET. The magazine decided to change the background on LaQuista's photo so as not to be identical to that of Ashleigh's. The result was a design in the background that one has to notice closely. The art director decided to sample a portion of Haywood's swimsuit and use as the background for her image. I was shocked by the presentation, but after I realized what they did, I thought it was very creative.

Ashleigh Angiano's photographs appeared in the April 3, 2006 issue of the JET Magazine, with Dionne Warwick on the cover. LaQuista Haywood's photographs appeared in the very next week's issue on April 10, 2006, with actress/comedian Monique gracing the cover.

Shanica Thompson- JET Beauty of the Week
September 11, 2006

Shanica Thompson, one of my most favorite subjects and friend that I'd worked with since she was senior at West Monroe High School was my next choice for a JET spot. I wanted to create a patriotic scene in which she would wear an American flag printed swimsuit and drape with my United States Marines uniform blouse and cover. I searched the internet for swimsuit sites until I located one that had the perfect patriotic swimsuit for her. It cost me about $75.00. I was operating out of Shreveport at the time. However, she was in Grambling at college and had to be transported to my studio. So I drove from Shreveport to Grambling (about 60 miles East) and picked her up for the shoot. When we returned to Shreveport to the studio, we tried out a number of different poses with the blouse, sword, and dress blue cover. They were all creative, but the one that made an impact was one in which I directed her to stand at attention with the cover on forming a salute. It was solid and was sent to JET. It was chosen and later appeared in the September 11, 2006 issue of the JET Magazine with LeToya on the cover.

Jennifer Hollingsworth- JET Beauty of the Week
July 3, 2006

On April 17, 2006, I selected another Shreveport native to pose for a JET spot. Southern University student Jennifer Hollingsworth and C.E. Byrd High School graduate, was the perfect candidate. She had a petite form, JET-type bust, with long lustrous hair, very beautiful and had a snappy attitude to go along with the set. We went to Dillard's in Shreveport's Mall St. Vincent to shop for a swimsuit. I paid about $90 for the two-piece swimsuit used in the shoot. We then went to Cypress Lake in Benton, which had become a usual shoot location for me. The swimsuit was a spaghetti strapped two-piece adorned with pink, green, yellow, brown, and green stripes. She accessorized her look with gold earrings and a pair of beach sandals and a green beach towel. In the shot that I sent to JET, she's sitting casually with legs folded and features her alter-ego…a big smile, which made the shot that more memorable. Her photograph was featured in the July 3, 2006 issue with singer India Arie on the cover.

There have been many actresses and entertainers to make their marks with a start as JET Beauty of the Week. In his book "Succeeding against the odds," Ebony Magazine founder John H. Johnson noted that in creating the magazine, he wanted to use black models in his marketing campaign. He noted that "Black people, like other people, respond more positively to ads featuring men and women they can identify with." And so in this medium began the careers of Lola Folana, Pam Grier, Diahann Carroll and many others. I am honored to be able to take a walk in history and be a part of this process, featured in such a historical publication.

TWENTY-ONE

PHOTO SHOOT STORY: SHOOTING GSU COVER GIRL

"The will to win, the desire to succeed, the urge to reach your full potential...these are the keys that will unlock the door to personal excellence."

Coach Eddie G. Robinson

In 2006, Mr. Terry Lilly, advisor to the Favrot Student Union Board at Grambling State University, chose my photography services for the union's annual pageant and calendar production. Every year, since 1969, the student union board publishes its activity calendar filled with campus events and dates of academic importance. The union holds a scholarship pageant to select a Cover Girl and twelve calendar month female students. Female students competing for Cover Girl compete in an interview, evening gown, swimsuit, daywear, talent, and they must present a platform of service. Calendar month contestants compete in the same phases of competition, but without the interview, platform, and talent.

The post as calendar photographer was once held by legendary television anchor for KNOE-TV's gospel show Earnie Miles. Miles was the university's photographer until 1992. I never met Mr. Miles, but when I look back on the many cover girl's he's photographed, I admire his commitment and willingness to maintain the opportunity for so many years.

I've been given the honor of photographing ten Cover Girls and over a hundred young ladies attending the university who were considered or chosen as calendar month winners. Along with Lilly, I've also worked closely with Casey Byrd, Dr. David Ponton, Sharon Perkins, Barbara Payne, and Kindrell Plains in coordination of photography and publication services.

Shanica Thompson

My first pageant as the official photographer was the 38th Annual Calendar Girl Scholarship Pageant. It was held on March 18, 2006 in the T.H. Harris Auditorium. Shanica Thompson, from West Monroe, LA, was crowned Miss Cover Girl 2006-2007. Natalia Stroman was the 1st Runner-Up and Chandri Morton was the 2nd Runner Up. Calendar month winners included: August 2006- Bayonne Gresham, September 2006- Whitney Moore-White, October 2006- LaTeryl Mason, November 2006- Ebony Perry, December 2006- Sirena Wilson, January 2007- Nicole Thompson, February 2007- Le'Ambrial Thomas, March 2007- Alexandria Jackson, April 2007-Ashley Bain, May 2007- Stephanie Gilyard, June 2007- Volonda Harris, and July 2007- Cierra Gardner. Miss Academic Excellence was Whitney Moore-White. Dr. Horace A. Judson was the university president and Pamela M. Payne was the Interim Vice President of Student Affairs.

Kourtni Mason

The 39th Annual Calendar Girl Scholarship Pageant was held on March 17, 2007. Kourtni Mason, from Monroe, LA was crowned Miss Cover Girl 2007-2008. Felecia Gibson was the 1st Runner-Up and Natasha Nzeakor was the 2nd Runner Up. Calendar month winners included: August 2007- Solange Robinson, September 2007- Passion Galbert, October 2007- Kristy Burrell, November 2007- Dominique Mayfield, December 2007- Ashley Warren, January 2008- Shamaya Floyd, February 2008- Jessica Harris, March 2008- Ahvery Thomas, April 2008- Denysha Hughes, May 2008- Erica Ward, June 2008- Marace Jones, and July 2008- Auctava Grant. Miss Academic Excellence was Khalilah Reed. The president of the university was Dr. Horace A. Judson and the Vice President of Student Affairs was Karen Martin, Ph.D.

Annia Jenkins

The 40th Annual Calendar Girl Scholarship Pageant was held on April 5, 2008. Annia Jenkins, from Shreveport, LA, was crowned Miss Cover Girl 2008-2009. Dawn Wilson was the 1st Runner-Up and Phairon Route was the 2nd Runner Up. Calendar month winners included: August 2008- Kayla Williams, September 2008- Whitney Henry, October 2008- Amyra Chapman, November 2008- Cemia Kahlek, December 2008- Amanda Henderson, January 2009- Keshia Thompson, February 2009- Bryana Brooks, March 2009- Patrice Brown, April 2009- Brittany Edwards, May 2009- Porsche Stillman, June 2009- Tiffany Wells, and July 2009- Shareena Fisher. Miss Academic Excellence was Whitney Henry. The president of the university was Dr. Horace A. Judson. The Vice President of Student Affairs was Stacey A. Duhon, Ph.D.

Krystle Cravens

The 41st Annual Calendar Girl Scholarship Pageant was held on March 28, 2009. Krystle Cravens, from Houston, TX, was crowned Miss Cover Girl 2009-2010. La'Nel Goshen was the 1st Runner-Up and Qwanelia Williams was the 2nd Runner Up. Calendar month winners included: September 2009- Solange Sayers, October 2009- Brittany Mitchell, November 2009- Shontae Austin, December 2009- Joy Rawls, January 2010- LaCresha Douresseaux, February 2010- Natasha Gaynor, March 2010- Crystal Watts, April 2010- Giorgio Green, May 2010- Bianca Harris, June 2010- Robyn Guillory, July 2010- Jessica Levi, and August 2010- Shakari Briggs. The university president was Dr. Horace A. Judson and the Vice President of Student Affairs was Dr. Stacy Duhon.

Brittney Brown

The 42nd Annual Calendar Girl Scholarship Pageant was held on March 20, 2010. Brittney Brown, a GSU Senior from Chicago, IL was crowned Miss Cover Girl 2010-2011. Julietta Gonzague was the 1st Runner-up and Courtney Mackey was the 2nd Runner Up. Calendar month winners included: September 2010- Hollye Williams, October 2010- Shay Synigal, November 2010- Chasity Williams, December 2010- My-Eisha Casmire, January 2011- Mambo Nadingwan, February 2011- Shanee' Kearns, March 2011- Cressida Montgomery, April 2011- Lauren Rock, May 2011- Terion Glenn, June 2011- Tiffanie Wiley, July 2011- Tonishea Mack, and August 2011- Courtney Nance. Miss Academic Excellence was Julietta

Gonzague. The university president was Dr. Frank G. Pogue and the Vice President for Student Affairs was Dr. Stacey Duhon.

Gerri Jackson

The 43rd Annual Calendar Girl Scholarship Pageant was held on March 26, 2011. Gerri Jackson, a GSU sophomore, was crowned Miss Cover Girl 2011-2012. Jouelle Young was the 1st Runner-Up and Deiona Frenche was the 2nd Runner Up. Calendar month winners included: September 2011- Demi Spencer, October 2012- Danielle Copeland, November 2011- Bethani Jackson, December 2011- Shimiyia McGlon, January 2012- Diamond Walker, February 2012- Ashley Giles, March 2012- Erina Love, April 2012- Courtney Parson, May 2012- Robyn Cole, June 2012- Ashley Baylor, July 2012- Raquel Brown, and August 2012- LaKetha Matthews. Miss Academic Excellence was Raquel Natasha Brown. The university president was Dr. Frank G. Pogue and the Vice President for Student Affairs was Dr. Stacey Duhon.

Ambra Brice

The 44th Annual Calendar Girl Scholarship Pageant was held on March 24, 2012. Ambra Brice, a GSU marketing major, was crowned Miss Cover Girl 2012-2013. Jamila Mamon was the 1st Runner-Up and Rashika Robinson was the 2nd Runner Up. Calendar month winners included: September 2012- Fredderka Anderson, October 2012- Alexandra Perry, November 2012- Jasmine Nash, December 2012- Micah Gholston, January 2013- Rachell Cartwright, February 2013- Quinsha Neal, March 2013- Desiree' Hardmon, April 2013- Kristanna Haynes, May 2013- Shyleice Mack, June 2013- Kenya Henderson, July 2013- Chelsea Smith, and August 2013- Shamyah Watts. Miss Academic Excellence was Charlene Corbette. The university president was Dr. Frank G. Pogue and the Vice President for Academic Affairs was Dr. Stacey Duhon.

I did not photograph the 45th Annual Calendar Girl Scholarship Pageant which was held on March 16, 2013.

Ciara Wilson

The 46th Annual Calendar Girl Scholarship Pageant was held on March 22, 2014. Ciara Wilson, a Sophomore native of Tulsa, Oklahoma, was crowned Miss Cover Girl 2014-2015. Elizabeth Eddy was the 1st Runner-Up and Yarica Charleston was the 2nd Runner Up. Calendar month winners included: September 2014- Briliante Osborne, October 2014- Oniesha Stevenson, November 2014- Amisha Jewitt, December 2014- Jacqueline Brown, January 2015- Kristen Jackson, February 2015- Ninfa Saavedra, March 2015- Keara Hughes, April 2015- Camika Price, May 2015- Kimberly Spikes, June 2015- Lyntoinette Jones, July 2015- Te'Leisha Johnson, and August 2015- Muridia Washington. Miss Academic Excellence was Muridia Washington. The university president was Dr. Frank G. Pogue and the Vice President of Student Affairs was Dr. Stacey Duhon.

Jo'Lavia Porter

The 47th Annual Calendar Girl Scholarship Pageant was held on March 21, 2015. Jo'Lavia Porter, a GSU Junior native of Dallas, Texas, was crowned Miss Cover Girl 2015-2016. Kristen Jackson was the 1st Runner-Up and Astra Watts was the 2nd Runner Up. Calendar month winners included: September 2015- Tiana Smith, October 2015- Taylor Roberson, November 2015- Genesis Williams, December 2015- D'Ashley Williams, January 2016- Kadija Hudson, February 2016- Diamond Nicholson, March 2016- Kayln Manning, April 2016- Angelica Woods, May 2016- Nofisat Shobawale, June 2016- Jakailya Strawder, July 2016- Danielle Dickinson, and August 2016- Angelique Stewart. Miss Academic Excellence was Jimmitriv Roberson. The university president was Willie D. Larkin, Ph.D. and the Vice President of Student Affairs was Dr. Stacey Duhon.

Due to extreme weather conditions and rain damage throughout the state of Louisiana in March of 2016, I was not able to make the 2016 pageant.

JaMariea Davis-Miller

The 49th Annual Calendar Girl Scholarship Pageant was held on March 18, 2017. The theme of the pageant was "Like Diamonds in the Sky." JaMariea Davis-Miller, a Junior native of Monroe, LA, was crowned Miss Cover Girl 2017-2018. Raven Carrington was the 1st Runner-Up and JoAja Wilson was the 2nd Runner. Calendar month winners included: September 2017- Lanhia Young, October 2017- Rachael Moten, November 2017- Dazmeiah Turner, December 2017- Charly Gay, January 2018- Raegan Nation, February 2018- Joynae Renter, March 2018- Asia Walker, April 2018- Kaniya Dudley, May 2018- Morgan Gainous, June 2018- Taylor Robinson, July 2018- Abrielle Chester, and August 2018- Kira Whitaker. Miss Academic Excellence was Ms. Raegan Nation. The university president was Mr. Richard J. Gallot, Jr. Esq. and the Vice President of Student Affairs was Dr. David C. Ponton, Jr.

TWENTY-TWO

PHOTO SHOOT STORY: THE WEDDING PHOTOGRAPHER

"It has to be a true partnership, and you have to really, really like and respect the person you're married to because it is a hard road."
Michelle Obama

I have had the honor of being the photographer for over forty weddings. I began as a wedding photographer during my teen years. I bought my first car in the summer of my junior year of high school from photography profits. I was shooting with a film camera in the mid-1990s. However, my photography pursuits came to an end after one bad wedding job. I opened up the back of my camera and exposed the film before it completed the rewind process. The bride came to pick up her prints and to her horror, she learned that there were no images. I was devastated and it was a huge burden on the shoulders of a teenager. I told myself I would never pick up a camera again.

In 2000, digital cameras hit the market and my first one was a Sony Mavica 1000. It came with a CD, no more film. With this, I thought, I could not make the same mistakes that I made with film. I began a professional pursuit two years later but didn't shoot my first wedding as a digital photographer until the end of 2004. It has been quite an experience since and I've been selected dozens of times to document the moments of newlyweds. Many are still married today and my photos are probably somewhere in their homes on a wall.

Here is the record of my wedding photography experience since 2004:

Shonda and Marcus Franklin

Shonda and Marcus Franklin were married on December 11, 2004 at the Divine Guidance Christian Church in Shreveport, LA.

Dometa and Sam Moore

Dometa Griffin was married to Sam Moore on January 16, 2005 at the Mt. Olivet Baptist Church in Monroe, LA. Rev. Oliver W. Billups was the officiating minister. The Matron of Honor was Devina Griffin-Harris. The Maid of Honor was Johnia Jackson. The Best Men were Anthony Neal and Gregory Smith. The Bridesmaids included: Deidra Nichols, Joyce Johnson, Robbyn Griffin, Keisha Neal, and Daphne Tolliver. The Groomsmen included: Vincent Landrum, Autrey Clatyon, Kimball Tate, Patrick Taylor, and Marquette Marshall. The Ring Bearer was Luke Harris, Jr. The flower girls were Amber Landrum, Daphnee Walters, and Michiah Liddell.

Daphne and Desmond Dorsey

Daphne Tolliver was married to Desmond Dorsey on April 23, 2005 at the United Baptist Church in Cleveland, MS. Rev. Sammie Rush was the officiating minister. The Maids of Honor were Janie Haynes and Alicia Lawrence. The Matron of Honor was Tamara Bonney. The Best Man was Jonathan Grant. The Bridesmaids included: Latoya Tubbs, LaDreka Dorsey, Monique Fuller, Johnia Jackson, Dometa Moore, Menyetta Tolliver, and Rhonda James. The Groomsmen included: Tony Tolliver, Brandon Mack, Devonne Mack, Akeem Lasisi, Jimmy Dorsey, Phillip Irvin, and Akela Bickham. The Miniature Bride was Kennedi Richardson. The Ring Bearer was Charles Bonney.

Jamekia and Willie Hunter

Jamekia Dial was married to Willie Hunter, III on June 25, 2005 at the Monroe Civic Center in Monroe, LA. Larry S. Burrell, Sr. was the officiating minister. The Matron of Honor was Julia Smith-Winston. The Maid of Honor was Jessica Dial. The Best Men were Daniel Hunter and Marcus Hunter. The Bridesmaids included: Ebony Hunter, Natasha Hunter, Shemeka Coleman-Lowens, Elisha McNeal, Shelia Simon, Cynthia Reed, and LaSonja Willis. The Groomsmen included: Robert Clark, Jr., Marcus Lewis, Demaine Riley, Kendrick Downs, and Omar Turner. The flower girls included

Jiya Dial and Jamya McNeal. The ring bearer was Kevyone Smith-Winston.

Deidra and Lewey Mims

Deidra Zimmerman was married to Lewey Mims on August 27, 2005 at the Parkview Church of Christ in Monroe, LA. The Maid of Honor was Kurston Dean. The Matron of Honor was Dawn Stewart. The Best Men were Benard Harris and Delbert Warner. The Bridesmaids included: Tiffany Beckwith, Desiree Cotton, Christina Cox, Jannica Cox, Ebony Grey, Jennifer Logan, Tiffany Riley, Trinesha Robertson, and Jennifer Thomas. The Groomsmen included: Damien Allen, Andrick Harris, Jabari Dailey, Demond Jefferson, Shawn Shell, Jason Stewart, Roger Robinson, Harrington Watson, III, and Jesse Watson. The Miniature Bride and Groom were Reyna Robertson and DeMaine Riley, Jr. The Flower Girls included Kayla Hopkins, Kennedy Robinson, and JaKayla Jones.

Zanetta and Cory Lamar

Zanetta Stewart was married to Cory Lamar on September 3, 2005 at the First Assembly of God in West Monroe, LA. Rev. Gordon Ford was the officiating minister. The Matron of Honor was Tamika Cherry. The Maid of Honor was Kimberly Wright. The Best Men were Calvin Lamar and Christopher Lamar. The Bridesmaids included: Taketa Clark, Dachan James, Chache Franklin, Kimberly Perkins, and Joylene Thomas. The Groomsmen included: Jerome Byam, Bennie Clark, Jonathan McGhee and Keith Perkins. The Flower Girls included Tia Ford and Asaria Thomas. The Junior Bride and Groom were Jo'Mereckle Ellis and Darrius Lewis.

Sabrina and Jerry Scott

Sabrina Malone was married to Jerry Scott on October 29, 2005 at the New Elizabeth Missionary Baptist Church in Shreveport, LA.

Benedra and Derrick Williams

Benedra Hester was married to Derrick Williams on December 3, 2005 at the Zion Traveler Baptist Church in Monroe, LA. Rev. Dr. Tracy Dewitt was the officiant. The Maids of Honor included Wanda Coulter and Karen Jack. The Best Man was Barry Jones. The Bridesmaids included: Nicole Buckley, Crystal Covington, Casey Nesbit, and Jennifer Williams. The Groomsmen included: Michael Chatman, Frank Crowder, George Reeves, Ahmon Thomas, and Marlon Wade. The Ring Bearer was Derrick Williams, Jr. The Bell Ringer was Jayelle Lockett.

Shellina and Johnathan Murphy

Shellina Jackson was married to Johnathan Murphy on April 20, 2006 at their residence in Springhill, LA.

Cherie and Theodis Douglas

Cherie Brazil was married to Theodis Douglas on May 5, 2006 at the Church of the Living God in Shreveport, LA.

Kimberly and Phillip Rivers

Kimberly Wright was married to Phillip Rivers on May 27, 2006 at the Liberty Christian Center in Monroe, LA.

Gia and Gerald Wright

Gia White was married to Gerald Wright on June 3, 2006 at the RCA Convention Center in Indianapolis, IN.

Stephanie and Cory Broussard

Stephanie Broadnax was married to Cory Broussard on June 10, 2006 at the New Tabernacle Baptist Church in Monroe, LA.

Yolanda and Antonio Riser

Yolanda Robinson was married to Antonio Riser on July 9, 2006 at the St. Joseph Baptist Church in West Monroe, LA.

LaTonya and Jotavius Jones

LaTonya Credit was married to Jotavius Jones on March 8, 2008 at the Parkview Church of Christ in Monroe, LA.

Alecia and Alvin Francis

Alecia Taylor was married to Alvin Francis on June 14, 2008 at the New Light Baptist Church in Monroe, LA.

Courtney and Jorge Alvernia

Courtney Bryant was married to Jorge Alvernia on December 27, 2008 at the First United Methodist Church in Monroe, LA.

Jeremeka and Anthony Reese

Jeremeka Bradley was married to Anthony Reese on April 11, 2009 at the Living Waters Church of God in Shreveport, LA. Superintendent Stephen Bradley and Pastor Clarence Reese were the officiating ministers. The Matron of Honor was Desiree Johnson-Reese. The Maid of Honor was Brittany Autrey. The Best Man was Steven King. The Bridesmaids included: Alexis Bradley, Courtney Cummings, Rebecca Price and Wendy Price. The Groomsmen included Kevin Creagh, Micah Reese, Leon Reese, and Rodrick Stevenson. The Ringbearer was Jeremiah Reese. The Flower Girl was Kyndal Reese.

Britney and Darren Hammond

Britney Lindsey was married to Darren Hammond on April 17, 2009 at Sam's Town Casino in Shreveport, LA. Pastor Vincent Webb was the officiant. The Maid of Honor was Shreka Johnikin.

The Best Man was Wayne Harley. The Bridesmaid was Rekesha Harrell and the Groomsmen were Eric Bonner and Juan Hall.

Valarie and Louis Brown

Valarie West was married to Louis Brown on June 27, 2009 at the Zion Springs Baptist Church in Monroe, LA.

Tenesha and Clyde Lain

Tenesha Jones was married to Clyde Lain on August 1, 2009 at the Monroe Civic Center in Monroe, LA.

Tiffany and Jonathan Gales

Tiffany McGhee was married to Johnathan Gales on August 22, 2009 at the Atrium Hotel in Monroe, LA.

Keisha and Marlon Rolland

Keisha and Marlon Rolland were married on January 1, 2010 at the New Tabernacle Baptist Church in Monroe, LA.

LaTasha and Tavares Wiley

LaTasha and Tavares Wiley were married on March 14, 2010 at the New Tabernacle Baptist Church in Monroe, LA.

Felicia and Carlos Stephens

Felicia Lee and Carlos Stephens were married on August 28, 2010 at the Feazel Chapel in West Monroe, LA.

Rasheeda and Terrance Simmons

Rahseeda Joseph was married to Terrance Simmons on September 4, 2010 at the Scottish Rite Temple in Shreveport, LA.

Alexis and Brandon Robinson

Alexis Smith was married to Brandon Robinson on September 25, 2010 at the Mary Evergreen Baptist Church in Shreveport, LA. Pastor Willie Giles, Jr. was the officiant. The Matron of Honor was RaShawna Anderson. The Maids of Honor were Commanisha Smith, Sha'Corie Smith, and Charity Robinson. The Best Men were Michael Washington, Reginald Mims, Jr., Jessie Scott, III, and Gary Parks. The Bridesmaids included: La'Chatsia Robinson, Brandi Graham, Sha'Tamia Fleming, La'Delia Woodard, and Markeisha Smith. The Groomsmen included: Dennis Robinson, II, Tyrone King, LaTari Fleming, DeMarcus Robinson, and Ta'Varius Hines.

Tamara and Brandon Gultery

Tamara Byrd was married to Brandon Gultery on April 23, 2011 at the Starlight Baptist Church in Swartz, LA.

Rosa and Kinscem Danzie

Rosa Rojas was married to Kinscem Danzie on July 2, 2011 at the Triumph Baptist Church in Monroe, LA. Rev. Lewey Mims, Sr. and Pastor Eddie Stewart, Sr. were the officiants. The Matron of Honor was Cassandra Webb. The Best Man was Terence Danzie. The Bridesmaids included: Mildretta Dade, Zebie Grayson, Kayla Hopkins, Osna Horne, Deidra Moy, and Monica White. The Groomsmen included: Roy Harrison, Y'Wante James, Lewey Mims, Jr., Adrian Robinson, Joseph Suero, and Gerald Whatley. The flower girl was Madison Leonard and the keeper of rings was Joshua Hopkins.

Kajuana and Dion Armstrong

Kajuana Bias was married to Dion Armstrong on September 18, 2011 at the Student Center at the University of Louisiana at Monroe. Pastor Bakari Beckwith was the officiant. The Matron of Honor was Metoq'ua Anderson. The Best Man was LenDarius Armstrong. The bridesmaids included: Dorene Bell, Ro'Quintessa

Givens, Misty Andrews, Ashley Bynum, Franchester Wilson, and Kourtni Mason. The Groomsmen included: Miguel Reed, Wilfred Smith, Antonio Dennis, Rodney Stewart, Dameial Armstrong, and Damario Armstrong. The junior bride was Jmoni Wright and the junior groom was Deavion Armstrong.

Venesia and Jason Heyward

Venesia Sims was married to Jason Heyward on November 26, 2011 at Mt. Zion Baptist Church in Monroe, LA. Pastor Ike Byrd was the officiant. The Maid of Honor was Chevalia Winters. The Matron of Honor was Lakesha Price. The Best Men were Damon Jackson and Jerry Simmons. The Bridesmaids included: Kelli Collins, Danielle Cole, Trenica Gray, Tiasha Wade, and Jo Woods. The Groomsmen included: Adrien Anderson, Zimbalist Chalk, Damon Heyward, Jesiim James, and Lance Williams. The flower girl was Jaylynn Johnson and the ring bearer was Berry Crosby.

Brittani and Robert Powell

Brittani Collins was married to Robert Powell, III on May 12, 2012 in New Iberia, LA.

Anitra and Irwin McCall

Anitra Robinson was married to Irwin McCall on June 23, 2012 at the Monroe Civic Center in Monroe, LA. Rev. Charles Stevenson was the officiant. The Matrons of Honor were Johnia Henderson and Kimberly Robinson. The miniature bride was Daylin Bosley. The flower girls were Alaiya McNeal and Aniyah Collier. The Bridesmaids included: Chastity Collier, Anitra Hunter, Angel Joshua, Cora Lewis, and Lecole White. The Best Man was Russell McCall. The miniature groom was Hunter Fields. The ring bearer was Sebastian Wells. The Groomsmen included: Harold McCall, Michael McCall, James McCall, Kevin McCall, and Derrick Robinson.

Tiffany and Jodie Bradley

Tiffany Mitchell was married to Jodie Bradley on July 7, 2012 at the Monroe Civic Center in Monroe, LA.

Terisa and John Kendall

Terisa Griffin was married to John Kendall on November 24, 2012 at the Beloved Community Church in Chicago, IL.

Christal and Juantarion Wheeler

Christal Winfield was married to Juantarion "Trae" Wheeler on May 17, 2014 at the Monroe Civic Center in Monroe, LA. Pastor Gilbert Wilson was the officiant. The Maid of Honor was Jimeka Winfield. The Matron of Honor was Brittany Williams. The Best Men were Quentin Wheeler and Marcus England. The Bridesmaids included: Johnnette Hicks, Briana Graham, Amechea Turner, Shenetha Caldwell, Mariah Hall, and Jasmine Williams. The Groomsmen included: Chardrick Turner, Jeffrey Seay, Monturios Howard, Andre Williams, Joshua Smith, Jimmy Winfield, III, and Nathan Roberts, II. The Flower Girl was Ashlei Ellis.

Bythnia and Dario Trice

Bythnia Ross was married to Dario Trice on March 21, 2015 at the Peter Rock Baptist Church in Monroe, LA.

Brittney and Courtney Sutton

Brittney Stevenson was married to Courtney Sutton on May 23, 2015 at the Venetian Room in Atlanta, GA. Bishop Dreyfus Smith was the officiant. The Matron of Honor was Dawnette Carter. The Maids of Honor were Shassity Stevenson and Brittany Beal. The Best man was Byron Williams. The Bridesmaids included: Robbin Robbins, Nicole Banks, Freda Todd, Jasmin Lewis, Jameslynn Owens, Kyler Robinson, Jaelynn Ballard, and Ikia Thomas. The Groomsmen included: John Herring III, Ronnie Colbert, Jr., Freddrick Britton, Jr., Joshua Stevenson, Eric Williams, Shondell

Ultsev, and Lewis Carter, II. The ring bearer was Caden Sutton. The broom bearer was Chase Ballard and the bride announcer was Paris Branch.

Chasity and Damian Harris

Chasity Davis was married to Damian Harris on June 27, 2015 at the Downtown Riverfront in Monroe, LA. Bishop Michael Douglas was the officiant. The Matron of Honor was Sharon Bethea. The Best Man was Ed Hunter, Jr. The Bridesmaids included Jacqueline Blackman and Iesha Davis. The Groomsmen included Kendall Harris and Jerome Caldwell.

Jerica and Jino Moran

Jerica Washington was married to Jino Moran on May 21, 2016 at Elegant Affairs in Gonzales, LA.

Marvita and Rodney Johnson

Marvita James was married to Rodney Johnson on June 25, 2016 at the Greystone Country Club in Denham Springs, LA. Rev. Fred Smith was the officiant. The Groomsmen included Robert Johnson, Rodney Johnson, Jr., Keith Johnson, Keanon Johnson, and Kevin Johnson. The Bridesmaids included: Sharon Bethea, Jacqueline Blackman, Tyrelle Maxon, Demetrice James and Courtnei Simmons.

Mary and Calvin Hunter

Mary Williams was married to Calvin Hunter on April 15, 2017 at the First Baptist Church in Monroe, LA.

Victoria and Trey George

Victoria Alford was married to Trey George on June 10, 2017 at the First United Methodist Church in West Monroe, LA.

Natasha and Charles Williams

Natasha Robertson was married to Charles Williams on July 3, 2017 at KM Designs in Monroe, LA.

TWENTY-THREE

PHOTO SHOOT STORY: SHE BECAME A ROCKETTE

"I know that I'm talented, and I know that I'm not in American Ballet Theater because I'm black- I'm here because I'm a gifted dancer."

Misty Copeland

In 2007, I had the privilege of being the school photographer for Neville High School and had the chance to photograph Jacie Scott being crowned Homecoming Queen. Scott would later become an NFL spectacle as one of the dancers with the Dallas Cowboys.

Born in New Orleans and raised in Monroe, La., Jacie Veronica Scott developed an appreciation for dancing at an early age, having trained in ballet, tap, jazz, modern, and hip-hop since age 6. While at Neville High School, she trained under Jessica Smith with the school's dance line the Bengal Belles. She was not only elected the Homecoming Queen of her senior year, but she was also elected as Miss Neville High School by the senior class. As a freshman, she served as Co-Captain of the Freshman Cheerleaders, and for three years she was selected as an All-Star Dancer. With that honor, she was asked to dance in Hawaii, Rome, and the Capital One Bowl Halftime Show. She also danced with the Twin City Ballet Senior Company and Linda Lavendar School of Dance.

At the homecoming game, on October 5, 2007, I photographed Jacie as she was crowned by principal Brent Vidrine. With her were the other maids of the court including Mary Frances Bratton, Karrington Lewis, Caroline Scott, Kelsi Siudy, and Chauncey McCoy (who would one day become a dancer for the New Orleans Pelicans Dance Team).

Later that year, on December 28, 2007, Jacie was presented to society as a debutante at a cotillion hosted by the Zeta Phi Omega Chapter of Alpha Kappa Alpha Sorority, Inc. I took the official photographs at that event and captured her being ushered onto the floor by her father Charles and Cathy Scott, then escorted by her cotillion escort for the night.

Graduation day came for Jacie on May 15, 2008 and I had the honor of taking the official photo of her receiving her diploma from Principal Vidrine. It was the culmination of a year of success for her and a door opened for great things to come in her immediate future.

In 2008, she headed to Louisiana State University to study journalism and dance with the LSU Tiger Girls, who were crowned the 2010 Universal Cheerleading Association Hip-Hop National Champions. As graduation loomed, Scott searched for her next adventure. A fellow Tiger Girl, who was planning to audition for the DCC, encouraged Scott to do so also. After a recruiter also reached out to her, Scott decided to go for it – despite her initial hesitance.

In 2012, Jacie became a dancer with the Dallas Cowboys Cheerleaders. In 2015, the D Magazine named Jacie as one of the ten most beautiful women in Dallas, TX. Off the field, she is a full-time fitness instructor. It would seem that the little girl who danced ballet as a child would end up doing that very thing as an adult, living out her dream, and teaching others to enjoy it.

Exciting news came in the summer of 2017. Jacie auditioned and was hired to be a Rockette. The Rockettes is a precision dance company at Radio City Music Hall in Manhattan, New York.

It is a privilege to have known her and to have been able to be at the right place at the right time to capture moments of her high school days.

TWENTY-FOUR

PHOTO SHOOT STORY: SHOOTING A DANCING DOLL

"You've got big dreams? You want fame?...Well, fame costs. And right here is where you start paying.
With sweat."
Debbie Allen

I've been fortunate to take photos of one of the most impressive dancers. She is one of the famed "Dancing Dolls" of Southern University's "Human Jukebox" Marching Band. A native of Chicago, Melody Byrd represents the legacy of Dr. Greggs and Ms. Gracie Perkins. She has style, flare, and when it came time to shoot, she required no direction, as if Perkins or Greggs were silently guiding her along the way. I guess that's what should have been expected when I asked a doll to shoot for me.

In 1969, Dr. Isaac Greggs left a job at the Southern University Lab School to take a post as the director for the University's marching band. Greggs didn't come alone. He not only brought with him the dance director (Perkins) but eight of the dancers from the school to form the "Dancing Dolls." The first eight dolls included: Niehma (Betty) McDonald Lowe, Gail Leggins Gaines, Sarah Moody Thomas, Lois McFarland Gattis, Theta Batiste Augustus, Linda Watson Mitchell, Brenda Mack, and Mauretta Wailes Hurst. They, along with the direction of Greggs and Perkins, began a legacy and a tradition of professionalism and precision showmanship that has lasted for 49 years.

Many who dance on their high school dance team dream of going to Southern University with aspirations of becoming a doll. It is not easy auditioning for the title nor is it easy maintaining the position. The dolls are protected and are held to strict rules. As public spectacles, they have not only traditions to uphold, but a high level of sophistication comes with the title they bear. Long hours of practice and even longer hours of performance, bus rides, traveling nationally and internationally, go into making the name that they all strive to uphold. They've marched in parades, danced on highly sacred football fields and even performed at events as popular as the Superbowl.

I've taken photos at many Bayou Classic games in New Orleans at the Superdome where the Grambling Tigers compete against the Southern Jaguars. The halftime show features the performances of the Grambling and Southern Bands on the field. The dancing dolls are a feature of this segment of the televised rivalry. It has always been a photographic career goal to have a photo session with a doll. They were a sight to see, and as I would learn, were a joy to work with on a photo shoot.

Byrd was selected as a Doll in August of 2015 along with four other successful candidates including Jacqueline York, Tailyn Smith, Jordan Ezell, and Alyx Harris. Their audition process was not a cake walk, as they had to demonstrate mastery of tap, jazz, modern dance, and ballet. Byrd passed the test and has been successful in her performance routines for the past three years.

My first shoot with Ms. Byrd was on May 27, 2017 in Morgan City, Louisiana. I made the four-hour voyage from Monroe to south Louisiana. We shot at Lake End Park. The weather was lovely and we shot on the beach sandbar with cypress trees as a backdrop. She did not require direction, for being a doll, she knew how to pose for a camera. Some of her poses and stances were evidence that she was a doll, for they were a living signature of her training and performances. It was worth the trip down.

I kept in touch with her and six months later she drove up to Monroe for a shoot in my studio on December 29, 2017. During her brief visit, she modeled a number of pieces in my studio's wardrobe collection. Again, she shot without direction. All she needed was the cue that it was time, then she went to work. We captured some fabulous images and some of the items in the collection became favorites of hers, for they were just her size. I think she enjoyed herself and it was worth the trip up to Monroe.

I don't know if she knows, but she is walking history, for the legacy that Dr. Greggs and Ms. Perkins began in 1969 was there with her...and it made it all the way to Monroe in my studio. I was one honored photographer.

TWENTY-FIVE

AN ACTOR'S STORY: OLIVIA, MELLIE, & FITZ

"Happiness comes from living as you need to, as you want to. As your inner voice tells you to. Happiness comes from being who you actually are instead of who you think you are supposed to be."
Shonda Rhimes

As a Hollywood Actor, I was thrilled to work on the set of ABC's "Scandal." I did not believe it when Extras Management, my booking agency, emailed me and informed me that I'd been cast for a feature background role on the show. This meant that I would be near the principal characters and my face would be seen on camera. I didn't have a speaking role. However, I would only be on the scene as part of the characters in a church scene and a White House reception room scene. I was a fan of the show and they were making me a character. It was so surreal. We shot the scenes for the episode entitled "Whiskey Tango Foxtrot" on January 24, 2013. It aired on February 14, 2013 on ABC with 8.02 million viewers. One scene was filmed in a church. The other scene was shot in the White House set.

The television drama takes place in Washington, D.C. It focuses on Olivia Pope & Associates (team of D.C. crisis management professionals) as well as the White House political scene. The show also features Tony Goldwyn as Fitzgerald Grant III, the president and Olivia's main love interest. It's a political thriller and high drama series, with the screenplay written by Shonda Rhimes.

As we arrived and were put in place inside the church, in walked Dan Bucatinsky (the character James Novak) and Bellamy Young (the character First Lady "Mellie" Grant). They were preparing for the christening scene of Baby Ella. Bucatinsky and Young were cordial and engaged in conversation with the few background actors on set; something principals don't normally do. As the rest of the crew and cast came on the scene, Kerry Washington entered in her light green dress. As I lived and breathed…..Olivia

143

Pope in the flesh was on the scene. I had to contain myself. I wasn't just a character in the show....I was a fan on the other side of the TV screen playing a character in the show. Jeff Perry (Cyrus Beene) and Tony Goldwyn (President Fitzgerald Grant) finally arrived and the filming commenced.

In the scene I shot in, the adopted daughter of Cyrus Beene and James Novak (Baby Ella) was being baptized and President Grant was becoming the godfather. After the church scene completed, the crew and background were transported to complete the final scene, which occurred in the studio White House.

I think I suffer from a slight PTSD when I watch Scandal. It's very weird being on the opposite side of the camera as a cast member only a few feet from Kerry Washington and Tony Goldwyn, then having to return to being a viewer of the show on the outside of the television screen. It's a total mind job. However, it was a memorable experience that for many background or principal actors, only seldom comes. Not only was Goldwyn President Grant, but I'd remembered him from the hit movie Ghost starring himself, Patrick Swayze, and Demi Moore. Of course Kerry Washington, to me, was a star by which to be mesmerized as she played in memorable movies such as Django Unchained, She Hate Me, Save the Last Dance, Ray, The Last King of Scotland, and A Thousand Words.

To be there on set with them was memorable and I'll never look at Scandal the way I looked at it before I was a character on set.

TWENTY-SIX

AN ACTOR'S STORY: ARRESTING FRANKLIN & BASH

"I want to keep a mysterious side to me. I want to keep a mysterious side to me."

Mark-Paul Gosselaar

In March of 2013, I worked on the set of the TV Show "Franklin and Bash." The series focuses on two longtime friends that are law partners. They are very unconventional and are often arrested in court because of their antics. It's a comedy-drama series produced by TNT starring Breckin Meyer and Mark-Paul Gosselaar. The show premiered in 2011 and was retired only three years later in 2014.

This filming was one of my favorites. I had an opportunity to work with an actor whose television shows I grew up watching after school. I worked on set with Mark-Paul Gosselaar (who starred as Zack Morris on NBC's Saved by the Bell), Breckin Meyer, Eddie Jemison, Currie Graham, and Courtney Pauroso. I'd been a fan of Jemison from his roles in the movies Ocean's Eleven and the Punisher. Meyer was also a notable star of whom I'd seen in the movies "Ghosts of Girlfriends Past," "Blue State," "Rebound," "Kate and Leopold" and "Road Trip"….all good movies. We filmed this episode on March 25, 2013.

The episode entitled "Freck" aired on July 17, 2013 to an audience of 1.96 million viewers. In this episode, I have a feature background role as a courtroom bailiff. In the scene, the judge orders me and my co-bailiff to arrest one of the lawyers. I had an opportunity to put the handcuffs on Breckin Meyer and walk him out of the courtroom. On the set, when the director cuts the filming a bell would go off signifying filming was halted. We had a set time to get out of the courtroom before the bell would usually sound. On one particular take, we made it out of the courtroom before the bell sounded and I mouthed off "Saved by the bell." To my surprise, Mark-Paul turned around and gave me a smirk. It was surreal. I was on a TV set with Zach Morris. HA!

TWENTY-SEVEN

AN ACTOR'S STORY: ARRESTING MICHAEL NOURI

"When you give up your dream, you die."
Michael Nouri (as Nick Hurley)

I was cast as a Los Angeles Police officer in the Lifetime movie "Hunt for the Labyrinth Killer." It starred Coby McLaughlin, Amanda Schull, and Michael Nouri.

In my scene, Nouri plays a judge suspected of murder. I assist a detective, played by McLaughlin, in arresting Nouri's character and placing him in the patrol car. I had brief conversations with Nouri. I remembered him from the 1983 movie "Flashdance." He told me to not be too easy on him and to rough him up a bit while handcuffing him. "I'm going to tug and get rough, so go along with it," he told me. I went along with him and the scene looked awesome.

It was cool getting to ride around in the police cruisers, turning on the lights and driving off the scene. There was another scene where we drove up in a convoy of police cars arriving on the scene. That was pretty intense, but nothing like having a known principal character tell you to get rough with him. To me, I was more than background on this particular set; if only they allowed me to speak.

The movie, directed by Hanelle Culpepper, released on DVD in August of 2013.

TWENTY-EIGHT

AN ACTOR'S STORY: ON SET WITH CCH POUNDER

"I don't have a problem with recognition…It's very, very rarely about who I am, it's always 'I love your work.'"

C.C.H. Pounder

During a brief stay in New Orleans, I was registered with Central Casting of New Orleans. I was cast in a featured background role on an episode of NCIS: New Orleans. Episode 2-11 was filmed on November 4, 2015. The show is a military/police procedural drama that is produced by CBS. It focuses on a team of criminal investigative agents stationed out of New Orleans, Louisiana.

The episode entitled "Blue Christmas" aired on CBS on December 15, 2015 to an audience of 12.09 million viewers. I worked on set with actors Scott Bakula, CCH Pounder, and Christopher Meyer. CCH Pounder (Carol Christine Hilaria) is a veteran actress and has had roles in movies such as Avatar, End of Days, Face/Off, and RoboCop 3. Scott Bakula has been in such films as Major League, American Beauty, and Necessary Roughness.

I suspected that something good would come out of this opportunity when I received an email that the director of the episode wanted to see me personally. This is not a general practice for a regular background actor. If the director wanted to see me, it was obvious I was going to be in the scene. So, I put on my best suit and appeared to be looked over. The director took one look at me and said: "yes, he's good." That was it. The production assistant said, "Well, he likes you, so we'll see you in a few days for the shooting." When I worked on the set, I had a guy checking my wardrobe and applying light makeup for the camera. I was even allowed to sit with the principal characters in their waiting area instead of waiting in the tent outside with the other background actors. That was a good place to be and I was honored.

In the scene I appear in, I play the role of Meyer's character's lawyer. He's being interrogated by detectives played by Bakula and Pounder. As the scene commenced, Pounder looks at me then back to Meyer. She says "It's okay Danny." Meyer looks at me for approval to give the detectives information. I give him a light head nod of approval. The camera focuses on me and my classic head nod. It was magic. What made it even more magical was that my head nod was not in the script. It came at the suggestion of Pounder. She asked the director if I could add life to the scene instead of just sitting there motionless. It was questionable because usually, the directors don't like to add to the script. However, he gave it a go and it worked. I will never forget Ms. Pounder for her consideration in making that moment live for me.

TWENTY-NINE

BUNK'D: THE PAINTING HORSE

"We keep moving forward, opening new doors, and doing new things, because we're curious and curiosity keeps leading us down new paths."
Walt Disney

I had many reviews from friends and family about my appearance on Scandal. However, the show that I get more views than Scandal is the episode in which I appeared in Disney's "Bunk'd." This episode filmed on June 29, 2016.

The episode was centered around kids at a summer camp. The camp was called Camp Kikiwaka and the campers were engaged in an art auction. I played one of the townspeople there to attend the auction. In the scene, one of the actors is speaking to me and two other background actors about a horse that could draw. He later engages in conversation with friends and we go off to see the items for sale by the campers. The scene ends with the horse, Wildfire, tripping over a paint can and the paint gets all over the actors.

It was a fairly short scene. However, it took a while to shoot it. The colt would participate, then it wouldn't. It was a great challenge to keep the paintbrush on the canvas and it was even more challenging to set up for the paint toss at the end.

The main stars in the production were Karan Brar and Nathan Arenas. The episode named "Zuri Weasels Out," Season 2 Episode 4 aired on August 26, 2016 on the Disney Channel to an audience of 1.54 million viewers.

When I became an elementary school teacher, the kids would go crazy over the fact that their teacher was a Disney star. "He played on Bunk'd" and "My teacher is a celebrity" they would say. Although I only had a small role in the episode, that was one of their favorite shows and they were delighted to have physical contact with someone who was on the show with their favorite characters walking around in their presence every day. I guess I was not the only one walking in history…they were too.

THIRTY

AN ACTOR'S STORY: A MATTER OF BLACK LIVES

"People, I just want to say, can we all get along?"
Rodney King

In 2013, in response to the killing of seventeen-year-old Trayvon Martin by George Zimmerman in Sanford, Florida, a group of African-American radicals formed the organization, Black Lives Matter. Within three years, the organization became a hashtag and rallying cry for countless losses of life and liberty of people of color in the United States at the hands of law enforcement officials including Mike Brown, Tamir Rice, and Sandra Bland. The summer of 2016 was a very hot time in the United States, and not because of the weather.

On August 1, 2016 at the headquarters of the Los Angeles Police Department downtown, I had an encounter with "Black Lives Matter" protesters during the filming of an episode of the TV Show "Bosch." I was booked as a police academy graduation guest. There had to have been over 100 background actors on this particular job. It was a hot day and the ceremony was held outside.

We were set in our chairs as family and friends of the recruits who were graduating. The main actor on the set, Lance Reddick, was portraying the role of the Police Chief Irvin Irving. He made short remarks and welcomed the recruits into the department. I thought his performance was moving. It had evidence of adequate thought, rehearsal and preparation. Reddick is popular for his roles in the John Wick movies and the movie "White House Down."

What made this experience so memorable was what happened during the takes. As we were in the middle of the scene, a group of 5 teenagers appeared with poster signs and a bullhorn shouting "Black Lives Matter." I assume they thought we were the police and wanted to disrupt the ceremony. The production crew attempted to persuade them to move away from the scene, as we were actors and not real police. It didn't matter to the protesters. They still wanted to fire away. Some of the background actors thought the protesters were part of the scene until they were told, "No, they are the real deal." The irony of that statement, as the numbers were mighty low for a full protest being "the real deal."

So on one take, the director had to halt the roll because the protesters were standing in the shot and wouldn't move. Then they started to move up the side and started with the bullhorn. "We don't give a fuck about your movie because black people are dying in the streets." Now, keep in mind, it's still about 90 degrees outside and we are in full suits and ladies had on sweaters. So we were baking in the sun and these protesters were making this experience very uncomfortable. I couldn't take it anymore. I jumped up out of my seat and yelled at her "Hey, my life matters too, we're working here." The female with the bullhorn fired back at me "Fuck you too; you're a part of the system that is killing us." I wasn't too worried about her comment. I was more worried, after the fact, that I'd be reprimanded by the director for speaking out during the take when I, of all people, was not cast with a speaking role and could have instigated a much more complex incident with the protesters. No one said anything though. I like to think they were glad that somebody said something in defense of the production and from a black person. Maybe not. I don't know. But they soon went about their business and the scene was completed.

This episode was Season 3 Episode 1 entitled "The Smog Cutter." It aired on April 21, 2017 on Amazon.

THIRTY-ONE

AN ACTOR'S STORY: SETTING IT OFF, HITTING THE FLOOR

"Unfortunately, when you're an actor,
you're like 'ah, if they only knew."
Kimberly Elise

I had the opportunity to work on the set with two of Hollywood's biggest stars on the show "Hit the Floor." This was one of those semi-cattle call productions with a large background crew. The scenes we were cast in were mostly for gala events. The show is about the scandalous events within an NBA cheerleading team in Los Angeles. The scenes I filmed on mostly required wearing a tuxedo, as the cheerleaders and the NBA players in their lives frequented red carpet events. So there was much toasting, clapping, and smiling at all of the festivities.

On the episode I filmed, entitled "Rebound," I can be seen sitting at the bar drinking a drink and later dancing with the lovely Didi Tospon. Tospon and I became good friends throughout the filming and we still are today. We shot the scene on February 25 and 26, 2013. On the set were principal actors Katherine Bailess, Logan Browning, Dean Cain, Kimberly Elise, McKinley Freeman, Taylour Paige, Robert Christopher Riley, and Jonathan 'Lil J' McDaniel. During one take, the director needed someone to stand-in for Jonathan 'Lil J,' and my height and complexion matched his. So I received a pay bump for standing in for the main actor. Standing-in is a process of allowing the principal to leave the set while the production crew arranged the set for the next take. They would get their lighting sequence coordinated and get their cameras situated, such that the principal actors could walk on set and do their job.

It was a treat to work so close to Kimberly Elise. Kimberly Elise? She played the character Tisean 'T.T" in the movie Set it Off. I also remember her from the movies John Q., For Colored Girls, and

Tyler Perry's "Diary of a Mad Black Woman." I was almost as delighted as I was to see Kerry Washington earlier in the month while shooting on Scandal. But there she was in the flesh….setting it off. Of course, it was an even greater treat to be on the set with Mr. Clark Kent…er…Superman himself, Mr. Dean Cain. My dancing lady and I danced right behind him on the episode on which I filmed.

The episode aired on June 17, 2013 to an audience of 2.16 million viewers.

THIRTY-TWO

SHAMELESS: BEING ON SET WITH FIONA & NIP

"I am whatever I need to be at the time I need to be it."
William H. Macy (As Frank Gallagher)

I appeared on the TV Show "Shameless" in 2016. It is one of my favorite shows and I was very excited to work on this project. I'd watched four seasons, missed Season 5 and 6 but there I was working on Season 7. Seeing the real characters on set was amazing. Shameless, a Showtime production, is a comedy/drama set in Chicago, IL. It features a struggling family of mixed-aged children trying to maintain themselves in the absence of a mother and their alcoholic father. Every episode is filled with some wild escapade of surviving in the city, with Fiona (the oldest sister) Gallagher trying to keep the family together, despite her constant longing to simply be a young adult.

We filmed this episode on July 8, 2016. The scene we filmed was at the Patsy's Pie diner that is featured on the show. The main actress, Emmy Rossum, played in this scene as her character, Fionna. Rossum was also remembered playing one of the lead roles in the doomsday blockbuster feature film "Day after Tomorrow." Jeremy Allen White, who plays as her brother Nip, also worked in the scene as a busboy. The scene centered around the hiring and firing of a café waitress of whom Fionna was seeking to fire. She interviewed one and fired the black waitress. The black waitress told her that she would sue her because she was the only black waitress there, then another black girl walks in looking for employment.

I shot in three scenes on this episode. One eating cake at a table right across from Rossum's activity, once at the counter where Rossum was working, and at a back table next to the restroom, of which Rossum goes to get a young boy from holding up the line.

It was interesting to watch Rossum get in character before the takes. There she was, Fionna in the flesh. Like my Scandal experience, I would soon have to return to being a fan on the other side of the television. For that day, I thought, I'd live out the fantasy. The episode I filmed on was Season 7 Episode 2. It aired on October 9, 2016 to an audience of 1.11 million.

THIRTY-THREE

DRIVING DENNIS RODMAN IN AN UBER

"We see our customers as invited guests to a party, and we are the hosts. It's our job to make the customer experience a little bit better."
Jeff Bezos

In the 1940s, my grandfather, Roosevelt Wright, Sr. and a man named Ansley Reed opened the Courtesy Cab Company in Monroe, Louisiana. It was one of the first cab companies to have two-way radios in its nine brand new Ford Sedans. Along with the transportation service, he also operated a fruit stand and an ice market. He specialized in customer service and wanted to be known as the cab that provided luxury services. Of course, I wasn't around to see his operation in its heyday, but I did get a glimpse of the elder Wright with what was left of the cab station on DeSiard Street when I was younger. Never in my life would I have considered driving a cab…that's until Uber came on the scene.

Since becoming a rider with Uber's services, I developed a fancy for its operation and wondered what it would be like to be an Uber driver. I'd heard so many stories from friends who were drivers and how much money they made just driving people in their cars. Either I was not in the right area or my car was not current enough for the job, I was not able to take part in the operation. However, on August 19, 2016, Uber approved me to be a driver on its platform. Soon after, I entertained an advertisement on Craigslist of a Los Angeles company that provided vehicles looking for driver-partners. It was just what I was looking for, or so I thought. So I met with the manager of the operation, a guy by the name of Georges, a Frenchman, who had been driving for the company a while. We met at a Starbucks at the corner of Sunset and LaBrea to discuss the details of the operation. After our meeting, I was ready to drive the next day.

During my first week, I had many interesting riders in my Black Chevrolet Suburban. Here are a few crazy and unbelievable stories from my nights as a driver:

1. A couple was in the car and one kept sneezing in response to an allergy. The partner said "God bless you" once and the other one kept sneezing. He became irate when his lover didn't continue to say "God bless you." His lover responded, "Oh you think I'm going to keep saying God bless you?" The other one said, "Apparently not." The other responded, "God, get your allergies under control."

2. On a Thursday night, I picked up a couple from a restaurant. They must have kissed and kissed away for the entire 30-minute ride to their mansion in the hills.

3. I picked up two businessmen in Santa Monica who were headed to Redondo Beach. It was a lengthy drive. However, the guy who ordered the services immediately started making 5-Star demands. "I need water and a phone charger now thank you." I had to comply because he paid top dollar for the ride.

4. I picked up a group of ladies at a hotel and took them to a hair salon in Beverly Hills. After I saw one of them with a white veil on her head, I realized it was a wedding party. I had to be extra careful with that ride. I certainly didn't need anything happening to a bride and her bridesmaids the day before her wedding.

5. On August 28, 2016 I picked up a woman and a guy from a hotel in West Hollywood. I took them to a restaurant and the gentleman wanted me to return to pick them up. He inquired about hiring me for private transportation services. I went back to pick them up and they gave me directions to a

mansion about 25 minutes away. As they were talking, buzzwords began to flow, like Beyonce, TMZ, Kanye West, performing at a concert. I became interested, for I didn't' know who these people were. So as I was outside waiting for them at her mansion, I texted her assistant and inquired about who she was. He replied "Pepa from Salt-N-Pepa." I was too embarrassed. Maybe I should have known who she was. I didn't. I listened to her music in my teen years but never paid attention to her looks. I had to Google her, and to my amazement, there she was, Jamaican born Sandra Denton...Pepa. There I was, riding around and talking to a Grammy Award-winning rapper...and didn't know it.

6.   One night, I picked up a group of men at the Abbey on N. Robertson. One of the gentlemen was a very tall black guy. I noticed the tattoos all over his arms and there was a piercing in his nose. It occurred to me....that's Dennis Rodman. Sure enough, there he was in the flesh. Rodman, the celebrity NBA player was riding in my Uber SUV. I wish I would have met him in more sober conditions, for he was not the celebrity that I saw on TV, or was he? His speech was slurred and he was uncontrolled. As he and his friends were chatting he started tapping me on my shoulder. His friends told him "Dennis let the man drive." Rodman was persistent. He asked "Say bruh, how many bitches am I going to fuck tonight?" I was shocked. This celebrity was in my Uber drunk asking me this type of question. So I gave him back the answer I assumed he wanted. "As many as you want." He started yelling "YES! That's my nigga there. I like this guy." I was totally outdone by this experience.

Driving for Uber would be my first experience providing luxury services to the rich and fabulous of Hollywood and Beverly Hills. One would question why a millionaire living in Beverly Hills would be riding in an Uber. They didn't get to be rich by not controlling their spending habits, and the expense of having a personal driver on the payroll is one budget item worth eliminating. Call an Uber when you want a Mercedes or a luxury SUV to take you and your guests to a party in town. That's the service I provided.

I practiced the art of being seen and not heard. I didn't talk to my passengers unless they spoke to me. I gave them an introductory hello, informed them of the amenities available, and highlighted the controls to the air and lights in their section of the vehicle. From there, I let the GPS navigator guide the way and they listened to smooth jazz through my vehicle's sound system. Many of them appreciated the sounds of John Coltrane, Sarah Vaughan, and Billie Holliday. They often complimented the atmosphere that I created for them. I would often receive $10-20 tips on top of the rate they were paying for Uber Black/SUV. I always wore a black suit, white shirt, and black tie, the preferred wardrobe for an Uber Black driver. When I arrived, I always stood outside the door and waited for the passengers as they made their way to the vehicle. I had two clothes hangers available for suit coats, water, gum, mints, and the latest "People" and "Vanity Fair" magazines available. It was a premier luxury ride that I took pride in hosting.

After a few weeks of driving with Uber, it became financially taxing on my budget, as I saw many of my profits used to rent the SUV I drove. Uber has a policy in major cities where they put a limit on the number of drivers who can drive Uber Black/Uber SUV (the top tier drivers). This is to keep the competition low and allow those drivers a chance to profit. Although it seems fair, what it creates is relatively not. Because the licenses are limited to those companies that already have them, they rent out their vehicles (limousines, SUVs, luxury sedans) to drivers who can't get SUV/Black distinction on their own. The rental fee is generally around $500-600 a week, plus the expense for gas and cleaning. Many of these partner companies will advertise on Craigslist that they are looking for people who want to drive Uber and make up to $1800 a week. It seems very profitable at face value. However, once a driver starts reeling in the money and notices that $500 is automatically deducted (whether he makes 500 or not) for rent, an SUV runs on about $50 per night on gas ($300) and daily cleaning, a driver is at around $800 a week in expenses.

I drove 8-10 hours, six days a week in the SUV I rented. It became a full time job for me. However, the competition was out there and it was difficult to maintain a steady $1,000 a week, for some weeks, the rides were low, and yet I was still required to pay the rent plus gas. I had one bad week which forced me out. I drove my third week and didn't make but $500. I could not face another week like that. So I stopped driving for Uber and went with Lyft, the other popular rideshare service in Los Angeles.

When I began driving for Lyft, the ride experience for the customers was similar to that of which I provided for Uber Black customers. Although the fee for riding had decreased, I still offered them a well dressed driver, a clean vehicle, water, gum, mints, magazines, clothes hangers, and smooth jazz on the radio. I even stocked the SUV with my iPad and hosted Spotify and Pandora options so that the riders could control their own music if they preferred. I also allowed the passengers to use the wifi from my cell phone's hotspot. The first rider I had was so thrilled to be able to get on wifi in the vehicle, she called her friend and exclaimed "Girl, this Lyft has wifi." Lyft's system allowed riders to give tips though the app, so I would often receive sizeable tips for my service. My extra services were not necessary, but I took my job seriously and wanted good ratings to let future customers know of my driving experience.

Lyft provided me with a vehicle, a Chevy Trax. It was a small SUV that seated four. The profits from Lyft were not as lucrative as Uber SUV/Black. However, there were steady rides. The rental on their vehicle was around $134 a week. However, if I serviced 75 rides or more in a week, the rent was free. Again, on the surface this seemed glorious. However, for me there was a catch. I lived about 30 miles from the heart of Los Angeles. In Lyft's contract, I was not charged for mileage on the vehicle as long as I was online and in driver mode on the app. When the app was turned off and the vehicle was moving, I was assessed .25 cents per mile. It seemed reasonable at first but when I had to factor in the reality that at some point I was going to have to turn off the app to get home, those miles were going to add up....and they did. I was taxed around $100 a week for mileage, which cancelled any hopes of not having that expense for car rental. With profits around $600 a week and around

$200 per week for fuel, I was only bringing in around $400 a week for sometimes 12 hours of driving every day for six days. Again, this was a huge burden and taxing on the body. So I ceased this operation and ended the chapter on rideshare driving.

Overall, it was a very interesting adventure because it was not in my plans when I moved to California. If only my grandfather could have seen me then, me…a cab driver. Who would have thought? Not me.

THIRTY-FOUR

VOLUNTEERING WITH THE
MISS AMERICA ORGANIZATION

"Success is the sweetest revenge!"
Vanessa Williams

The Miss America Organization, which began in Atlantic City in 1921, is the world's largest competitive scholarship program for young women, and one of the nation's leading achievement programs. Margaret Gorman, Miss District of Columbia, was declared "The Most Beautiful Bathing Girl in America" in 1921 at the age of 16. Since then, annually there are over 13,000 contestants who compete for local and state pageant crowns in the fifty states, US Virgin Islands, the District of Columbia and Puerto Rico. It has evolved from a mere beauty contest of young ladies in bathing suits to a more professional and more competitive experience with an emphasis on public speaking, community service, and educational achievement. The Miss Louisiana Organization is based in Monroe and hosts a fabulous extravaganza for an entire week in the City of Monroe at the Monroe Civic Center. Contestants from around the state assemble in town for the week for preliminary activities and remain until the Saturday night final competition, which is aired on a live television broadcast.

In 2008, my association with the structure of pageants had taken form when a close friend of mine, Karmen Rubin, took an interest in competing in the Miss ULM Pageant (a preliminary contest for Miss America). I helped her develop a platform title and we discussed direction into her entry. The idea came to me to take the knowledge I had about pageants to develop a new pageant in Monroe. There was a limited opportunity that existed for young ladies in the area, as Miss ULM was the only major preliminary

162

contest in Monroe to get to the state competition, which was held in Monroe. One had to be a student at ULM to compete, so there were many who had no chance of competing.

I went to work contacting Dewanna Little, the Executive Director of the Miss Louisiana Organization, on procedures of getting a franchise. I had letters written on my behalf from Monroe Mayor Jamie Mayo and Sue Nicholson, the President of the Monroe Chamber of Commerce. In September 2008, I received a call that the Miss Louisiana Organization Board had approved my request for a franchise and the Miss Monroe Pageant was approved for operation.

I formed an LLC and a board of young professionals with previous pageant experience including Jeremeka Bradley, Gaundi Hays (Kline), Comedian Robert Powell, and Natalie Williams (Stevenson). In January 2009, I directed the first Miss Monroe Pageant affiliated with the Miss America Organization. The Monroe City Council approved a $10,000 Economic Development Grant to help fund the pageant.

Miss Monroe's Outstanding Teen 2009 Pageant was held on Saturday, January 10, 2009 at Neville High School. The contestants in the pageant included: Cheyenne Little (West Monroe), Zia Gordon (Monroe), T'Angela Jackson (Monroe), Kelly Bernard (Hammond), Sacorya Williams (Bastrop), Kaitlin McKinley (West Monroe), and Rachel Causey (Monroe). The Host of the pageant was Miss Louisiana 2008 Blair Abene. Kelly Bernard was crowned as Miss Monroe's Outstanding Teen 2009.

The Miss Monroe 2009 Pageant was held on Saturday, January 17 at the Monroe Civic Center. The contestants competing in the pageant included: Rebecca Price (Bossier City), Raven Hollins (Bastrop), Kandice Williams (Monroe), Jennifer Free (Rayville), Kimberly Rusley (Bossier City), Desiree Cotton (Monroe), Tiffany Terrell (West Monroe), Christa McCann (Benton), Shantira Prowell (Monroe), Kimberlee Ross (Monroe), and Brandy Hotard (Port Allen). The show was hosted by KNOE Anchorman John Denison and featured special guest singer Terisa Griffin. Raven Hollins was crowned Miss Monroe 2009.

We created a year-long list of activities and engagements for Miss Monroe as she would be the signature crown of the city. We wanted the name to be recognized, as the program received a considerable amount of funding from the Mayor and City Council. She would be a host at the annual City of Monroe's Martin Luther King Day program, participate in the annual Christmas Tree lighting ceremony, lead the pledge at city council meetings, ride in the parades, have a seat at the head table at the annual Monroe Chamber of Commerce's dinner, cut ribbons at openings of businesses and public buildings, and shovel dirt at groundbreaking ceremonies. There would be many opportunities for her to speak and make public appearances, so if anyone ever asked her about Monroe, she would be well prepared to speak with confidence. Today, Miss Monroe is still active in many of these programs.

I attended the 88th Miss America Pageant in January 2009 at the Planet Hollywood Casino and Resort in Las Vegas, NV. At the pageant, Katie Stam (Miss Indiana) was crowned Miss America 2009.

During our first year of operation, my teen titleholder, Kelly Bernard (of Hammond, LA), won the state competition as Miss Louisiana's Outstanding Teen 2009. Through my efforts and with the help of the board, in my first year as director of the Miss Monroe Pageant, $11,000 was raised and offered for scholarships to young women aged 13-24.

In 2009, I served as a judge at three pageants throughout the state. I judged the Miss Minden Pageant, the Miss Black Louisiana Pageant (held in Shreveport) and was selected to judge the ULM Alpha Phi Alpha Fraternity's Miss Black and Gold Pageant in October 2009.

The second Miss Monroe Pageant was held on Saturday, November 14, 2009. The event was held in the Neville High School Auditorium and another $18,000 was raised for the pageant. The Miss Contestants included: Tiffany Terrell, Kandice Williams, Kellye Armstard, and Hope Anderson. The Teen Contestants included: Taylor Woods, Cheyenne Little, Brittany Branch, and Rae'ven Jones. Hope Anderson, a student at the University of Louisiana was crowned Miss Monroe 2010. Cheyenne Little, a student at West Monroe High School, was crowned Miss Monroe's Outstanding Teen 2010.

In January 2010, I traveled with Anderson and Little to Las Vegas for the 89th Miss America Pageant. There at Planet Hollywood, Caressa Cameron (Miss Virginia) was crowned Miss America 2010. The judges of the 2010 pageant were a panel of star-studded celebrities including Vivica A. Fox, Katie Harman (Miss America 2002), Dave Koz, Shawn Johnson (The 2008 Olympic Gold Medalist), Rush Limbaugh and Paul Rodriguez.

Hope Anderson and Cheyenne Little both participated in the Miss Louisiana Pageant in the summer of 2010. Cheyenne participated in the teen pageant preliminaries on Sunday, June 20, 2010. She did not place in the finals and did not compete in the finale pageant. Hope participated in preliminary competitions on Thursday and Friday of the same week. She, however, was chosen as a top ten semi-finalist and a top five finalist. She was very long with her on-stage question response, which I believe led to her being named 2nd Runner-Up to Miss Louisiana 2010. Kelsi Crain (Miss ULM) was crowned Miss Louisiana 2010.

In 2010, I was given the opportunity by the Miss Louisiana Organization to serve as the official photographer for the pageant. During pageant week, the contestants assembled for the annual meetup at the home of Dr. Guthrie Jarrell. He had been a major sponsor and contributor of the Miss Louisiana Pageant for decades. He also made annual pilgrimages to Atlantic City and Las Vegas for the Miss America Pageant. He was given a treat this year as a Miss America visited his Monroe home. Ericka Dunlap, Miss America 2004, was a judge at the 2010 pageant. All the judges attended the meeting at Dr. Jarrell's home. I took photos of Miss and "Mr. America." I even got a chance to take photos of them on stage at the Civic Center as a royal salute to him was organized by the Miss Louisiana Organization. Dunlap came out on stage in a sparking red dress, sang to Jarrell, and he was presented with a Miss America trophy for all of his hard work and tireless efforts to support the Miss America program.

The Miss Monroe 2011 Pageant was held on Saturday, November 13, 2010 at the Monroe Civic Center in the Bayou Room of the Convention Center. Lauren Vizza was crowned Miss Monroe 2011 and Dailey Joy Foster was crowned Miss Monroe's Outstanding

Teen. Sydney Andrews was crowned Little Miss Monroe 2011 and Tyeece Robinson was crowned Miss Monroe Princess 2011.

In January 2011, I traveled with Vizza and Foster to Las Vegas for the 90th Miss America Pageant. There at Planet Hollywood, Teresa Scanlan (Miss Nebraska) was crowned Miss America 2011. Scanlan, 17 at the time of crowning, was the youngest Miss America since 1937, or historically Margaret Gorman, who was only 16 in 1921. The judges at the 2011 pageant included Joy Behar, Debbye Turner Bell (who was Miss America 1990), Marc Cherry, Tony Dovolani, Marilu Henner, Taryn Rose, and Mark Wills.

Later that month, I served as a judge for the Miss Tech University Pageant. There were 16 contestants in this competition. The top five were: Tori Close, Meagan Lee, Elizabeth Whitford, Jessica Hill, and Mallory Cox. Elizabeth Whitford was the winner in the pageant.

I met Miss America Judge's Chairman/Oklahoma State Senator Rick Brinkley at the 2011 Miss Louisiana State Meeting. Brinkley was the keynote speaker at the banquet. His message to the Miss Louisiana gathering was "You don't know what you're doing." He challenged mothers to stop living out their dreams through their daughters, directors and volunteers to support the girls and not tear down their spirits, and he challenged the contestants to seek more than a crown and a t-shirt. He told the group that their ability to affect the lives of others was the true meaning of being Miss America and that if they didn't grasp the concept…."they didn't know what they were doing."

In July 2011, I submitted my resignation as Director of the Miss Monroe Pageant. On August 8, 2011, the Miss Louisiana Organization Board of Directors met and named Gaundhi Hays-Kline my successor. Since Kline took over as director, I have remained a supporter of the pageant by working as a volunteer at the annual pageant moving pianos and bringing out microphones, taking care of the website hosting every year, and providing complimentary photography.

The Miss Monroe Pageant continues to receive financial contributions from the City of Monroe and continues to provide local young ladies with an avenue to Atlantic City. Since it began in

2008, the Miss Monroe Pageant has provided thousands of dollars in scholarships to young ladies 13-24. Two of the Miss Monroe title holders since 2008 have been crowned Miss Louisiana and traveled to Las Vegas, not as guests...but as participants. Lauren Vizza and Hope Anderson...the two I traveled with in previous years to Vegas...were Miss America contestants. Kelly Bernard, whose first experience in a pageant was in our Miss Monroe's Outstanding Teen Pageant at Neville High School in 2009, went on later to win Miss Louisiana's Outstanding Teen pageant and traveled to Orlando, Florida to compete in the national event.

It's an honor to have been a part of the process to create such an avenue and see it continue to be an asset to the city and a contribution to so many lives.

THIRTY-FIVE

BEING AN ALPHA MAN

"Darkness cannot drive out darkness; only light can do that. Hate cannot drive out hate; only love can do that."
Dr. Martin Luther King, Jr.

When I returned to the University of Louisiana at Monroe in 2009 as a Freshman, I wanted to join a fraternity. I attended the Informational meetup hosted by the university's Pan-Hellenic Council. Female students went to the various sorority groups and the male students moved to and from the various fraternities and received information on those groups. I and another freshman, Quentin Stubblefield, whom I met while working as the photographer at his high school, dreamed of becoming Alphas. We spoke about it on many occasions. However, when I realized that I was already considered the old guy on campus, I did not need a crew of 19 and 20-year-olds running me around campus doing all sorts of crazy things. So I put off that pursuit. Stubblefield went on to become an Alpha Man. So after I graduated and was a working professional, I decided to take up the interest again and follow through with the desire to become an Alpha Man.

The Fraternity was founded as a literary club in 1906 when seven college men at Cornell University in Ithaca, New York needed a brotherhood in segregated New York. We recognize them as the Jewels of Alpha: Henry Arthur Callis, Charles Henry Chapman, Eugene Kinckle Jones, George Biddle Kelley, Nathaniel Allison Murray, Robert Harold Ogle, and Vertner Woodson Tandy. Callis was a physician and Howard University professor. Chapman was a professor of Agriculture at Florida A&M University. Jones was the first Executive Secretary of the National Urban League and organized the fraternity's first three chapters. Kelley was the first African-American engineer registered in the state of New York. Murray was a teacher in Washington, D.C. public schools. Ogle worked on Capitol Hill as a staff member of the United States Senate Committee on

Appropriations. Tandy was New York's first registered black architect and designed the home of Madam C.J. Walker, America's first female millionaire.

Why Alpha? Many of the men I knew as community leaders, men of conviction and public stature were Alphas. Two deacons at my church, of which one was the former mayor of the city, Abe E. Pierce III, was an Alpha Man. I also knew city council members, judges, lawyers, doctors and educators in town that were Alpha Men. They were professional men who were active in community service and social uplift. As I researched, I found out that nationally, many of the leaders of African-American experience were Alphas like Dr. Martin Luther King, Dick Gregory, Maynard Jackson (former mayor of Atlanta), John H. Johnson (the publisher of Ebony Magazine), Ernest Morial (first African-American mayor of New Orleans), Roland Martin, Olympian Jesse Owens, Congressman Charles Rangel, Supreme Court Justice Thurgood Marshall, Professor Cornell West, Andrew Young (UN Ambassador), Coach Eddie Robinson, Singers Donnie Hathaway, Jerry Butler, and Lionel Richie, Historian John Hope Franklin, Duke Ellington, Pastor T. J. Jemison, Isaac Greggs (the long-time band director for Southern University), Actors Tim Reid, Joseph Phillips, and Keenan Ivory Wayans.

It wasn't all about the black and gold colors and the letters to wear on cool wardrobe, but it was a call to service and one of being a member of an organization with a national platform. I'd been involved in community service since my early boy scouting days, so naturally, I was compelled to continue as an adult and being a member of this group could allow me to do bigger and better things for my fellow countrymen.

Initial Membership Development Process into the Alpha Phi Alpha Fraternity, Inc. for me began on Friday, October 17, 2014. I proceeded through the intake process with eight other men to become members of the Eta Delta Lambda Chapter. There were 20 other young men from the undergraduate chapters at the University of Louisiana at Monroe and Louisiana Tech University participating in the process as well. The Chief Deans of the process were Brother Rodney Welch, Brother Alvin Williams, and Brother Christopher Jackson. Welch was an insurance agent with State Farm, Williams was the Principal at Martin Luther King, Jr. Middle School and Jackson was the principal of a school in Shreveport, Louisiana. Seven other alumni candidates, who would be the new brothers in the Eta Delta Lambda Chapter including Dezmun Payne, Rickey Jones, David Jones, Robert Coleman, Tommie Nelson, John Ford, and Anthony James, became my line brothers for life. My candidate sponsor was Dr. Richard Smith.

Even though I was a working professional, coming up with the funds for the initial fees was challenging. A generous African-American woman would step in to assist me in this effort. I'd been working with ladies in the Alpha Kappa Alpha Sorority for years as a photographer. Alpha Phi Alpha Fraternity and Alpha Kappa Alpha Sorority are synonymous when it comes to greek life and the tie that binds us is often referred to as PhirstPham. Hence the two were the first two organizations of the Divine Nine and a member of one married a woman who helped form the other. A lady of Alpha Kappa Alpha Sorority, Mrs. Dorothy Minor, of the Zeta Phi Omega Chapter in Monroe, was very instrumental in my becoming an Alpha Man. She loaned me the funds to make it happen and I would not be the Alpha Man today had it not been for her generosity in that effort. I find no embarrassment in documenting this act of kindness, for anyone in greek life knows how hard it is to fund an initiation. As far as it concerns me, Mrs. Dorothy, a veteran health professional, is the epitome of "PhirstPham" and is a woman with a great heart for sisterhood and public service.

Ironically, the very type of college guys I attempted to avoid in 2009 was there during the intake process, ushering me into the fraternity. It seemed that I should have gone through the process during college after all.

I hope by reading this section of my story you didn't expect me to go into detail about the process. That can never be revealed to the public. I will say that all men can apply, but not all men will qualify, and all men won't have what it takes to complete the process. It's Alpha Phi Alpha. The first African-American group for college students, fraternity or sorority. The others of the 'Divine Nine' all originated with Alpha. So, naturally, obtaining that title would come with a challenge, and not an easy one. I crossed at 11:02 PM on

November 8, 2014. The probate and the official announcement of the Fall 2014 line took place at ULM Coliseum on Wednesday, November 12, 2014.

I attended my first meeting with the Eta Delta Lambda Chapter on Thursday, November 13, 2014. Brother Dyrick Saulsberry served as the President of the Chapter during the first meeting. I was named as the chapter's reporter for the Fraternity's Sphinx Magazine.

I attended the 69th Annual Southwestern Regional Convention in Dallas, Texas April 9-12, 2015 as a neophyte. The theme was "Alpha Impact: Impacting the Community." At the conference, I met with the General President Mark S. Tillman.

In April 2016, I received my official ballot for the election of the 35th General President of the fraternity. The two choices for the post were Aaron Crutison, Sr. and Everett B. Ward. On April 30, 2016, I cast my vote online for Brother Ward.

On Saturday, May 7, 2016, I attended the 21st Scholarship Banquet, hosted by my chapter's Educational Foundation. Dr. Richard Smith was the committee chair for the foundation. It was held at the Monroe Civic Center. I invited six of my former male students to join me at my table. The speaker for the event was Brother William Gipson. Gipson, at the time, was the Associate Vice Provost for Equity and Access at the University of Pennsylvania. There were seven young men being saluted and presented awards including: Lorenzo Price (Ouachita Parish High School), Terricus Aubrey (West Monroe High School), Jae'Veric Bradley (West Monroe High School), Larry Wright (Wossman High School), Dalen Alexander (Neville High School), and Boris Allen (Carroll High School).

On July 22, 2016 in New Orleans, the fraternity made its official announcement that Bro. Everett B. Ward had been elected as the 35th General President and would assume the office on January 1, 2017. It was a good feeling knowing that he was my first fraternity presidential vote, and he won.

When I moved back to Monroe in October of 2016, I reconnected with Eta Delta Lambda and was immediately put back to work in service. On Saturday, October 22, 2016, I traveled with a few of the brothers to chaperone 30 local youth to the Grambling State University homecoming game. We traveled to Grambling on a school bus and we merely provided the experience for the little guys. They enjoyed the good clean fun and a chance to be in the midst of the HBCU experience at no expense.

On Sunday, December 4, 2016, the Eta Delta Lambda Chapter hosted its Founder's Day program. I joined the brothers and attended morning worship services at Lone Wa Worship Center, where Rev. James Garland Smith is pastor. After worship service, we met in the church's fellowship hall for our program. At the program, I recited the poem "Invictus" by William Ernest Henley. The menu included roast beef, baked chicken, green beans, scalloped potatoes, dinner roll, and peach cobbler. The speaker for the event was Judge Alvin Sharp. He spoke from the subject "You don't want to be in a chapter with four members." He said that in such a group "there is an important job to be done and Everybody is sure that Somebody will do it. Anybody could do it, but Nobody will do it." Brother Anthony Turner received the Brother of the Year Award.

On Friday, December 16, 2016, my chapter sponsored a Christmas shopping spree to nine local boys. We met at Target and each young boy was assigned to a brother and was taken around the store to spend his allotment of Christmas funds. They procured everything from clothes to video games. I was amused at how long it took them to spend someone else's money. The two young guys I chaperoned were very decisive and one even broke out in a sweat, not knowing what to get after I told him he was reaching his limit. They were fed and given gifts bags and an additional gift card. Afterward, the brothers took photos with the happy group of boys. It was a memorable occasion for them.

On Saturday, January 28, 2017, I attended the Louisiana District meeting. It was held at Sam's Town in Shreveport. This was my first experience at a District Conference.

On Friday, April 21st through April 22, 2017, I attended the Southwestern Regional Conference in New Orleans, Louisiana. The convention was held downtown at the Hyatt Regency Hotel. I represented my chapter as a delegate and was charged with voting for the new regional Vice-President and Assistant Vice-President. It would be my first opportunity to vote as a delegate in the fraternity. At the conference, I met many brothers from Louisiana, Arkansas, Oklahoma, and Texas. I even met and took photographs with the General President Everett Ward, who attended the event.

In July 2017, the Eta Delta Lambda Chapter voted me in as Secretary. As an office holder for the chapter, my duties would include taking notes at the meeting, recording and storing the official meeting minutes.

In January of 2018, I attended the Louisiana District Conference. It was held at the Regency in Baton Rouge, LA. I was there as a brother and as a vendor as I provided photography service as a vendor in the exhibition hall. At the conference, Bro. Keith Dillon was re-elected as Louisiana District President.

The men I serve with in the Eta Delta Lambda chapter include: Alcide Baker, DeQuincy Bingham, Johnny Braden, Robert Bradford, Garren Bunton, Robert Coleman, Cedric Crossley, Steven Davis, Adrian Fisher, John Ford, Alfred Garrison, Oscar Hamilton, James Hill, Ralph D. Holley, Ralph Holley, Jr., Gary Jackson, Jarreau Jackson, Leon Jackson, Anthony James, Benjamin Jones, Charles Jones, Davis Jones, Fred Jones, Tavell Kindall, Larry Marshall, Phillip McClain, Lindsay Moorehead, Tommie Nelson, Dezmun Payne, Abe E. Pierce III, James Ratcliff, Dyrick D. Saulsberry, Charles Scott, Kerry Scott, Derek Smith, Richard Smith, Anthony Turner, Craig Turner, Eric Washington, Jimmy Washington, Rodney Welch, Alvin Williams, Maquista Williams, and Mark Wilson

I'm often asked by men in the community what it's like being an Alpha or why did I choose this fraternity over the others. A lot of Alpha is seen in our public works. However, the best thing about being an Alpha can't be spoken. One must know it in his mind, in his own heart, and that is not something I can describe. It must be experienced by each Alpha Man. My advice is to inquire, apply, complete the process and make the transcendence. At that moment, you'll know the meaning of what I have explained.

THIRTY-SIX

WORKING WITH THE LADIES IN PINK AND GREEN

"Anytime women come together with a collective intention, it's a powerful thing...magic happens."
Phylicia Rashad

As a youth, I was surrounded by sorority women in my church, school, and in the community. There was a woman at my church who would plant a divine seed during my youth that wouldn't grow until a few decades later. Her name was Doris Jean Welch. She was the church clerk, an educator, graduate of Southern University and A&M College, and was a lady of Alpha Kappa Alpha Sorority, Inc. She was a life member of the Zeta Phi Omega Chapter.

I was a youth musician and had taken lessons to read music. Welch told me that she wanted me to learn to play the Greek Medley and gave me the sheet music to learn. At the time, many of the hymns were complicated and it was a task that was difficult for me. However, over several decades I would finally learn all nine of them. It was as if her spirit was still speaking to me long after she died... "learn those hymns Robert." So I not only learned them but made a recording of them, allowing others to use them in their social programs. This was a tribute to not only the Divine Nine but also to Mrs. Welch.

When I became a photographer, I worked closely with the local chapters of Alpha Kappa Alpha Sorority, Inc. There are two in my local area, the Zeta Phi Omega Chapter and the Omicron Iota Omega Chapter. It has been a rewarding experience working with so many ladies over the years. They are teachers, school principals, lawyers, doctors, nurses, elected officials, and serve in so many other capacities.

The sorority was founded on January 15, 1908 on the campus of Howard University in Washington, D.C. Since then, there have been scores of women who have taken up the task of service to mankind and maintaining a sisterhood that extends the borders of the continental United States. There are many notable Americans who have earned a place in the celebrated sisterhood including: Vanessa Bell Calloway, Loretta Devine, Tanisha Lynn Eanes, NASA mathematicians Katherine Johnson and Dorothy Vaughan, Star Jones, Bernice King, Toni Morrison, US Presidential Secretaries Azie Morton and Hazel O'Leary, Regina Taylor, Wanda Sykes, Cassandra Wilson, Phylicia Rashad, Roxie Roker, Rupert F. Richardson, and Miss America 1991 Marjorie Vincent.

With the Omicron Iota Omega chapter, I worked under the leadership of Elizabeth Pierre, Laura Spencer, Jackie Slack, Alvina Thomas, Raven Owens, and Dr. Naomi Smith. With the Zeta Phi Omega Chapter, I've worked under the leadership of Renita Bryant, Greta Wiley, Angela Claxton, Shirley Burch, Dr. Sharilynn Loche. I have been the photographer for the Founder's Day Program, Debutante Tea and Debutante Cotillion for these chapters since 2004. During my brief residence in Shreveport, Louisiana, I also worked with the Sigma Rho Omega Chapter, photographing their debutante tea and cotillion.

Capturing the Cinderellas

In 1959, the Zeta Phi Omega Chapter of Alpha Kappa Alpha Sorority, Inc. organized the Cinderella Guidance Clinic. It was presented to the chapter by Mrs. Emily P. Robinson. The clinic focuses on good grooming, social graces, aesthetic and social dancing, music appreciation and drama, and the appreciation of literature.

The debutante tea is the informal presentation of senior high school girls to society. Each debutante performs a talent and introduces themselves and light refreshments are served to the public. At the cotillion, a few months later, the debutantes dress in white ball gowns and are officially presented. They are escorted by young males in a tuxedo and after they take their bows and make their walk, the event includes a period of waltzes and dances with the debutante and their escorts. It's a very authentic and regal event and one of the photographic highlights of my years.

I've photographed dozens of Cinderella debutantes since 2004 including: **(2004)** Cortney Bibby, Chanda Hunter, Courtney

Jacobs, Chastity Johnson, Jarika Johnson, Ashley Mayo, Takia Richard, Jasmine Ross, and Ashley Smith; **(2005)** Ariel Blueford, Kaneeka Burks, Camille Bryant, Erika Chisley, Janai Davis, Ursula Douglas, Kirsten Gix, Ashley Gray, Ora Greely, Alexis Griffin, Shalyse Jackson, Monique Reese, Candace Robinson, Doneshai Robinson, Summer Tate, Margie Vernon, and Sabrina Whitney; **(2007)** Grejikia Abram, RaNeiqua Bailey, DiTesha Hamilton, Brianna Marbles, Chauncey McCoy, Andre'ana McDonald, Kiara Montgomery, Jasmine Moore, Teelah Rawls, Alease Scott, Jacie Scott, Angela Webb, and Tiffanie Wiley; **(2009)** Angel Chafford, Deidre Dade, Ingrid Gilbert, Raven Jackson, T'Era Jones, Ashley Jordan, Tyler Malone, Nathayai Moore, and Kenya Ross; **(2010)** Brittany Branch, Kara Brown, Chauncei Croom, Shan Delaphous, Naomi God, Alexandra Green, Kamari Green, Ke'Andria Henry, Amisha Jewitt, Cashea Jones, Jessica Jones, Alexcia Lewis, Brittany Long, Shaterrica Sampson, LaKesisha Smith, Tiffany Smith, Ebony Whitfield; **(2011)** Kadedra Carter, Taeler Coleman, Marnesha Davis, Trinity Davis, Brittany Gibbs, Zia Gordon, Kadijha Hudson, Danielle Linkford, Kadijah Neal, Orlean Patterson, Chastity Price, Monohn Prud'homme, Morgan Scott, Breonda Simmons, Anteenee Thomas, Jayla Thompson, Taylor Woods, and Chelsea Wyatt; **(2013)** Heather Arthur, Melissa Blackson, Jakira Gibson, Shantevia Goins, Alexis Horne, Raleshia Johnson, Ce'Layra McClodden, Erin Minor, Kandace Moss, Tyra Page, and Maya Turner; **(2014)** RaMari Bailey, Gladys Bridges, Destiny Coleman, Kalliyah Gardner, Lesa Hall, Alexis Hogg, Kierra Horne, Jada Mack, Shila Morgan, Karman Moss, Tomarisha Slack, Zakkirra Smith, Carliya Trotter, Briana Washington, Aja Winslow, and Courtney Wyatt; **(2015)** Ma'Kira Cooper, Destini Davis, Angel Dixon, Millicent McFarland, Raegan Nation, Allison Payne, Jaylin Potter, Kyla Roland, Gabby Williams; **(2016)** Tae'lor Arnold, Alexis Baker, Brandi Bell, Brielle Johnson, Martianna Jones, Diandra Lewis, Miya Reed, TyTiana Roy, and Caitlin Wade; **(2017)** YaTierra Brown, Falon Butler, Dominque Carmouche, Ebony Crawford, Sydney Gant, Faith Johnson, Arielle Lain, Jalissa Loyd, Malissa Loyd, Briyana Powell, Cedrica Sims, Lenecia Turner, and Kennedy Boston-Woods.

The Precious Pearls

The Omicron Iota Omega Chapter of Alpha Kappa Alpha Sorority, Inc. has a similar guidance clinic for the young ladies it services. Its program is the Precious Pearls Guidance Clinic. Their senior girls are presented in the Spring.

I've photographed dozens of Precious Pearl debutantes since 2005 including: **(2005)** Kellye Armstard, Brandye Fobbs, Nakia Gray, Martresaca Jackson, Devon Pierre, and Brittney Stevenson; **(2006)** Kalicia Bates, Desiree Cotton, Gabrielle Griffin, LaToya McLemore, Gabbriel Smoot, Jessica Taylor, and Whitney Triplet; **(2008)** Raven Belton, Jametria Flowers, Takhira Gardner, Tyeasha McLemore, Bianca Teats, Cleotha Thomas, Ashley Williams, and Stephanie Wright; **(2009)** Patrice Bell, Jamillah Canada, Chelsea Fobbs, Philicia Jackson, Kenyatta Johnson, and Deidra Williams; **(2011)** Quenisha Givens, DeAndrea Harris, Caprice Lee, Anitria Lawrence, Ericka Robertson, Briana Spivey, Johnise Thomas, and Bryanna Williams; **(2014)** Shetocquie Burks, La'Tesha Dowles, Demecia Foy, Arial George, Kimberly Johnson, Faith Jones, Deja Pierre, Danielle Potter, and Gabriella Wiley; **(2016)** Nia Brooks, Gurs'thangel Cotton, Kayla Fenison, Tamia Hamilton, Jasmine Hunter, Myesha Williams, and Courtney Wright; **(2017)** Ikeyja Brown, Marshalla Cherry, Emoni Davis, Diamond Knox-Jackson, Ja'Mya McNeal, Precious Richardson, and Bethany Spencer.

As I've worked with the sorority for so many years, it is sentimental when the ladies gather in a great circle to sing their national hymn. The spirit of Doris Jean Welch hits me and although I wouldn't dare sing along with them, I know the words to the song, for she insisted that I know them. I enjoy working with these ladies that wear pink and green, for they do things that are worthwhile and you can always find them doing those things with a smile.

THIRTY-SEVEN

CROSSING THE EDMUND PETTUS BRIDGE

"I believe race is too heavy a burden to carry into the 21ˢᵗ century. It's time to lay it down. We all came here in different ships, but now we're all in the same boat."

US Congressman John Lewis

On May 26, 2015, I crossed the Edmund Pettus Bridge in Selma, Alabama. On a school trip, the bridge was temporarily closed for our historic walk to teach the students a history lesson and allow them to walk in the textbook. The bridge was the site of a historic event in the Civil Rights Movement in the United States.

The bridge, which crosses the Alabama River, is named in honor of Edmund Winston Pettus, a Confederate general during the American Civil War, former US Senator and Grand Dragon of the Ku Klux Klan. On March 7, 1965, the bridge was the stage of Bloody Sunday. Civil rights demonstrators led by Dr. Martin Luther King and the SCLC planned to cross the bridge from Selma on their march to Montgomery, the capital city of Alabama. There they planned to protest the violent social climate in Alabama in the fight for justice. On Bloody Sunday, armed police officers brutally attacked the demonstrators, a scene that was televised on national TV. It would be one of the scenes that changed the minds of Washington and the course for the changes sought by those willing to put themselves in harm's way for a greater cause.

In Selma, the students from Excellence Academy Charter School received a brief overview of the events of Bloody Sunday before we walked in locked arms across the bridge, escorted by Selma Police. At the foot of the other side of the bridge was the National Voting Rights Museum of which we visited. There were many displays and exhibits to view and behold including the Bloody Sunday displays and a Ku Klux Klan figure in full costume. This frightened some of the students, but it was there in there face, outside of the textbook.

Three months before we made our historic walk, I watched the 50th Anniversary of Bloody Sunday on television. Presidents Barack Obama and George W. Bush, along with John Lewis (who was a participant and demonstrator in Bloody Sunday) were there to make remarks. President Obama gave one of his most memorable speeches at the gathering, with the bridge as a backdrop.

This was another exciting moment in my life for its one thing to read the history book and another to walk in history. Certainly, I was walking in history as this was the same concrete of which Dr. Martin Luther King and John Lewis walked on that historic day in 1965.

THIRTY-EIGHT

MEETING THREE
LOUISIANA GOVERNORS

"I'm often introduced as the governor of the great state of Louisiana.
But you know what makes our state great? It's you…the people."
Louisiana Governor John Bel Edwards

I've had the pleasure of meeting and shaking hands with three governors of the State of Louisiana. I'm naturally excited about the Oval Office but meeting the state's governor is almost as fascinating.

In 1990, on a Boy Scout trip to Baton Rouge, Louisiana, I had the opportunity to meet Governor Charles "Buddy" Roemer III. During our visit, arrangements were made to visit him at the Governor's Mansion. We had light refreshments and Roemer spoke to us. Roemer served as a US Congressman for the 4th Congressional District from 1981-1988. He was elected governor in 1988 and served until 1992. He was preceded and succeeded by Louisiana Governor Edwin Edwards.

In 2012, I met Louisiana Governor Bobby Jindal on several occasions, while as a photographer during news conferences and local events. As a teacher at Excellence Academy, I took several of my students to meet him when he came to town to give the State of the State Address. He met with the students, shook their hands, gave them a motivational pitch and took a photo with them. I had the opportunity of photographing Jindal's inauguration in January 2012. The ceremony took place on the grounds of the Old State Capitol Building in Baton Rouge. Jindal served as the Assistant Secretary of Health and Human Services from 2001-2003 during President George W. Bush's administration. He made an unsuccessful run for governor in 2003 but lost to Kathleen Blanco. In that void, he won a seat in Congress as Louisiana's 1st District Representative from 2005-2008. He came back an won an election against challengers Walter Boassco, Foster Campbell, and John Georges. He was governor for two terms, ending in 2016 with the election of Democrat John Bel Edwards.

In 2017, I met and shook hands with Louisiana Governor John Bel Edwards. I was initially not a fan of Edwards and voted for his opponent in the 2015 election. Since the election, I would say that he wasn't a bad guy for the job and when he came to town, I was delighted to meet him and hear him speak. Edwards was a graduate of West Point and served in the US Army before becoming a lawyer. He later served in the Louisiana Legislature as a representative from 2008 until 2015 when led a successful campaign against challenger David Vitter.

I've had many people who didn't like Governor Jindal to question my excitement about meeting him. "How could you shake hands with him. He messed up Louisiana," they'd say. Regardless of my personal political views, when the governor comes to town, and it's possible to meet him, one should take up the opportunity. For me, it was a walk in history. Afterall, he was the governor of the state, and that has importance.

THIRTY-NINE

TEACHING LOUISIANA HISTORY AT EXCELLENCE ACADEMY

"Treat them just the same as anybody else, give them an opportunity to make a living, and to get an education."
Louisiana Governor Huey P. Long

If ever there was a public school that exposed middle school students to the politics, geography, economics, and history of Louisiana, it was the Excellence Academy Charter School in Monroe. I taught at the school for two of the four years it operated. Although its tenure with the Monroe City School District was brief, the students and faculty of the institution were greatly impacted by the experience.

The school's curriculum was totally internet-technology based. There were no textbooks and the instructional model used iPads and Laptops. At any given time, almost 200 electrical devices were operating simultaneously on WiFi from the school's powerful network housing room. Through that system, I was able to prepare authentic and original Louisiana History Lessons. Not only did I have a digital copy of the textbook for students to read documents, but I also made original video footage for them to view. In every chapter of the textbook, I found videos or prepared original ones that were content-based. The chapter on Louisiana Government required the students not only to understand how the federal government worked but how the state and local governments worked. Through my connections with the local municipal government and state officials, I created video interviews in my classroom for the students to view through their ILP (Individualized Lesson Plans). With my iPad, I interviewed the Mayor of the City of Monroe, Jamie Mayo; Ouachita Parish Police Juror Pat Moore, and Louisiana State Representative Katrina Jackson. Each of these officials introduced themselves and talked about the nature of government and the role in which they played. When students watched the videos, they were somewhat familiar with the officials, but I ultimately had them teaching their lesson instead of simply relying on the textbook. This was the magic of Excellence Academy.

Visiting New Orleans and Baton Rouge

On June 10, 2014, the school took over 100 students on a "Learn-Fun" trip from Monroe on a journey to New Orleans and Baton Rouge. It took four school buses and a travel bus to accommodate the staff and the students who would get the ultimate learning experience outside of the classroom. They would eventually step into the textbook and be able to relate much better to it than a student who simply sat in a classroom. I, as the 8th Grade Louisiana History teacher at the school, had a plan in my head to spark their interest in the subject, and the school assisted me in making that happen. Not only did I want to make sure they saw Louisiana History, but I also wanted to create the classroom in such a way that they were a part of the atmosphere. It was to be the best presentation of the subject…and in no other educational institution could this be done in than at Excellence.

On June 11, the students visited the Audubon Zoo in New Orleans. There they toured the various exhibits and took a train ride around the campus. After the visit to the zoo, the students took a streetcar ride to the French Quarters. They spent an afternoon of eating and shopping at the Canal Place Mall.

On June 12, the school traveled to Baton Rouge to tour the Louisiana State Capitol building. It was at the capitol building that I was able to collect the most material to create my new classroom theme. I took photos of the students who would be taking the 8th Grade Louisiana History Course in the 2014-2015 school year standing in the lobby next to the statues of Governor William C. Claiborne (the first non-colonial governor of Louisiana) and Bienville (the four-time governor of French Louisiana). The photos I took of them were later enlarged to 11×14 prints, framed and displayed in the classroom. When the students came to school in September, they were amazed to see that this was THEIR room. There weren't just illustrations on the wall, but there were photos of them at the Capitol

Building standing next to a statue of the Governor on the wall. I also took photos of them and with them in the chambers of the Louisiana House of Representatives.

A one-of-a-kind Louisiana themed classroom

Over the summer of 2014, I completed the preparations in the classroom in expectation of my new 8th graders. The desks were numbered in French numbers from Une to Vingt. The centerpiece of the classroom was the photo I took of the empty Louisiana House of Representatives Chamber. I had it enlarged and printed on a 9ft by 12 ft vinyl banner. On both sides of the banner hung flags. One was the American Flag and the other was an official Louisiana State Flag. Both flags were presented to me compliments of Louisiana State Representative Marcus Hunter. They both flew over the capitol building and it was quite sentimental to have them in the classroom. I had original posters of which I designed hanging on the walls. There were posters that displayed the governors of Louisiana, movies produced in the state, the Bayou Classic, nationally known businesses that were based in Louisiana, and celebrities who were natives of Louisiana.

A visit to City Hall, meeting with the Mayor

On October 23, 2014, I arranged for a trip for my entire 8th-grade class to the Monroe City Hall as we discussed Louisiana State and Local Government in the lesson. The students had a chance to meet Mayor Jamie Mayo, Police Chief Quentin Holmes, and other city officials. The mayor invited the students to his office and allowed one of them to be the mayor for 5 minutes, sitting at his desk. The students learned a great lesson about state and local politics from a simple visit to city hall. After the meeting in the mayor's office, I arranged for the students to have a demonstration from the Fire Department and the Monroe Police Department. The students were given an opportunity to wear a fireman's outfit and feel its weight, they sat in the firetruck and even had a chance to sit in the driver's seat of one of the police department's newest patrol cars. The seeds planted in this experience were sure to be there for a lifetime.

Popeyes: A Lesson on Louisiana Business

Economics is one of the four strands of social studies. I tried to emphasize the study of Louisiana businesses that had national prominence, but either originated or were based in the state. One of the businesses and Louisiana celebrities we focused on was Al Copeland. Copeland was the New Orleans native who founded Popeye's Chicken & Biscuits in 1972. The company he created is also the corporate holder of the famous restaurant Copeland's of New Orleans, with franchises all over the state. On October 31, 2014, I showed the students a documentary on Copeland and we discussed his impact not only on Louisiana economics but cuisine that extends beyond the state boundaries. After our lesson, I ordered two big boxes of Popeye's Chicken and the class enjoyed a tasty treat along with a memorable lesson.

The Chennault Aviation Museum Visit

On November 11, 2014, we visited the Chennault Aviation Museum for Veteran's Day. This trip was very beneficial for we had lessons on Louisiana's involvement with World War II. General Chennault was a military aviator with the United States Army Air Corps. He is best known for his command over a volunteer group of aviators, the "Flying Tigers." The museum, located at Selman Field (Monroe Regional Airport) is dedicated to him and the war. It has many artifacts of which my students could again…walk around in the textbook. A month later, one of our lessons was on the Higgins Boats, which were instrumental in the US Navy's battle campaigns. The boats were made in New Orleans. There were models of the boats at the Chennault Museum. It was a good thing they'd seen these, for they understood the lesson much better because of the visit.

Classroom Mardi Gras

In February of 2015, it was time for Mardi Gras. Although we did not get out of school for the holiday, I could not let the holiday pass and not include it in the classroom. So there were decorations set and I came in festive attire with a purple, gold and green hat and long tie to celebrate. I bought a King Cake for every class period and after watching a video on the history of Mardi Gras, the students enjoyed a small party in class.

Visiting the site of Fort Miro

One of the many lessons of the Louisiana History course was the topic of Fort Miro. In 1790, Jean Filhiol served as a commandant to Louisiana's Spanish Governor Estiban Miro. Filhiol had the duty of gathering the inhabitants into settlements, preventing English and American settlers from coming into Spanish territory. The City of Monroe began as a stockade, or fort, named to honor the Spanish Governor. What grew out of the fort and the village around it became Monroe. It was important that my students know this piece of Louisiana History. It was not a major section in the textbook, but being that we were only a few blocks from the site of the original stockade, I ensured that my students saw the marker. So, on May 6, 2015, we walked downtown Monroe to the site of the Fort Miro marker. We read its inscriptions and took photos as a group. We later walked to the Monroe City Hall. In the lobby of City Hall is a painting that depicts Fort Miro as it sat on the banks of the Ouachita River. We took photos around the painting. Following our visit, we walked back to the school. It was a high day for seed planting, for many residents of the city are not even aware of the origins of the town.

Attending a City Council Meeting

A few of my students attended the May 12, 2015 meeting of the Monroe City Council. I designed an assignment to accompany the meeting. They were tasked to listen to the proceedings and answer questions about what they witnessed. Following the meeting, each student was assigned to meet with a city councilman and ask them questions. They met with Councilman Eddie Clark, Councilwoman Betty Blakes, and Councilman Dr. Ray Armstrong. It was a great experience for them and it went well for their understanding of Louisiana politics.

A final farewell in my Napoleon Bonaparte costume

At the conclusion of the 2014-2015 school year, I awarded my students as promised earlier in the year, for making good grades in the class. My top award was an X-Box gaming system. The students didn't believe that I would follow through with my promise. When it was time to purchase the game in Wal-Mart, I was hesitant. However, I do not believe in making promises to students and then falling back on those promises. So I paid the $195 for the X-Box game system. Mary Goins, a graduating 8th-grade student, took that award. The next 17 best performing students in the class received a gift card to Cinemark Theaters. To seal the surprise at graduation, I gave the class a parting gift of me dressed in costume to present the award. No other costume would have celebrated a year of Louisiana History than that of Napoleon Bonaparte, the French Emperor who sold the Louisiana Territory to the United States in 1803 for $15 million. I walked out on stage in that outfit to "oohs, aahs and big eyes" of excitement. Again…this was the magic of Excellence Academy.

During my tenure at the school, I served under Principal Shandra Smith. There were 97 8th grade students in the 2014-2015 year. They included: Jeremiah Allen, Micah Allen, Desmond Barber, Takema Barber, Jeremiah Bennett, Ronquez Bethley, Kenshauna Blade, Keyara Boatwright, Ronald Brown, Tylor Brown, Mynesha Burrell, Amber Butler, Walter Bynum, Lonell Cage, Tatyana Caldwell, Dakevia Charleston, Rayland Coleman, Devonta Crump, Maxwell Davis, Aloria Dickson, Deja Dorsey, Transel Dunn, Devin Edwards, DeEdrick Ellis, Joshua Ellis, Lachandra Ellis, Emya Fields, Kiara Fields, Anthony Garrison, Corey Givens, McKell Gix, Mary Goins, Aaliyah Goodin, Jacarius Gooden, Antonio Grace, Christian-Paris Griffin, Daisha Hall, Mya Hamilton, Nekesia Hamilton, Lashanta Hardwell, Diamond Harris, Destiny Hawkins, Ekaria Hollis, Shemeka Holloman, Mercedes Holmes, Laadrian Hoston, Wylis Houston, Jamartavia Jackson, Kendrix Jackson, Kyle Jackson, Tyana Jefferson,

Octavia Johnson, Ja'Onna Jones, Mackeyana Jones, Martez Jones, Nicholas Kirkendoff, William Latchinson, Johann Leonard, Kewaski Mack, Hermiya McMiller, Jada Mims, Keldrick Minnieweather, Jakerstien Minor, Taylor Moore, Ezekiel Moy, Bryaneisha Newton, Rashad Newton, Ricki Newton, Tahir O'Steen, Jalen Page, Michael Perry, Jacobi Rice, Raniesha Riley, Jaylond Roberson, Markese Robinson, Alexis Smith, Gary Smith, Kevyone Smith, Zaria Smith, Keana Starr, Kobe Sutton, Laushenia Thibideaux, Kiara Thomas, Nan'Derryia Thomas, Jordan Turner, Donaess Wade, Charles Walker, LaShay Walker, Xyavier Walker, Ja'Kyra White, Jaevynne Williams-Taylor, Lorean Williams, Tayla Williams, India Woods, and Thomas Woods. They will graduate from high school in the Class of 2019.

I believe as I did then, that they are excellent, and extraordinary by far. Regardless of the politics that surrounded the operation of the school around them, they were taught, tested, and exposed to economics, history, politics and the geography of Louisiana, the best that money could provide. Soon, the world will see, through the works of those students, what took place within the walls of the most controversial educational establishments in the city. Soon the world will see what those students have in them, a touch of magic from the place once known as Excellence Academy.

FORTY

TEACHING HIGH SCHOOL IN NEW ORLEANS

"Respect-Commit-Succeed"
Lake Area New Tech High School Motto

In July 2015, I was hired by Kelly Educational Services of Jefferson Parish to serve as a substitute teacher in middle and high schools in Jefferson Parish, Louisiana. I worked in a number of schools including West Jefferson High School, Livudais Middle School, Riverdale Middle School, Alfred Bonnabel High School, Grace King High School, and Henry Ford Middle School. The last substitute job I would take would be my final substitute job.

In November of 2015, I took a substitute position at Lake Area New Tech Early College High School in New Orleans. The school is located near the campus of the University of New Orleans, of which campus rests on Lake Pontchartrain. What began as a temporary substitute pursuit would ultimately result in full time employment. There was a vacancy and I in time proved to the school's administration that I was capable of filling the position.

As a substitute, every morning for three weeks I would report to Mrs. Lotten, the school's secretary, to receive student attendance rosters. I was not the permanent teacher, so I didn't have access to computers or official records. Substitutes are not given keys to the room, so I had to constantly get someone to open the door to the classroom. The room key and a lanyard around one's neck with the building entry card, as I would learn, was an authentic sign to students that you were the real teacher and not a substitute. I'd learned many lessons from other jobs of what to do and what not to do as a substitute. One thing you dared not do was teach. When I learned that the World Geography course teaching position was available and I had the degree to teach it, I only made matters worse for myself...for many of those students were not eager to learn from a substitute. I expressed my interest in the position and was brought in for an interview. I met with Mrs. Nicole Cooper (the assistant principal) and Mrs. Schwan Sceau (the faculty's instructional coach) and they were impressed and quite interested. I was given a conditional stay as a substitute while they initiated the hiring process.

Officially Hired

On December 2, 2015, I was officially hired as a teacher with the New Beginnings School Foundation. I was assigned as a 9th Grade World Geography teacher at Lake Area. The principal at Lake Area upon hire was Darren Lewis. He and Mrs. Cooper were my general supervisors. However, my immediate supervisor was Mrs. Latosha Prevost-Scott, who was the 9th Grade Administrative Team Leader. Scott was a no-nonsense kind of administrator. She carried a big stick and was not afraid of any teacher or student at the school, as tough as they believed they were.

My co-workers at Lake Area included: Dr. Christina Albers (English), Donyea Allen (Social Studies), Diane Anderson (Science), Brenda Barabino (Physical Education), Duane Bell (JROTC), Frank Buckley (Math), Harry Cass (Art), Kipp Chopin (Social Studies), Debra Davis-Freeman (Special Education), William Elder (English), Natalie Franklin (English), Rahmel Fuller (Science), Cobren Greer (Science), Joseph Guyton (Physical Education), Keyontae Hamilton (Drama), Jessica Harvey (Choir), Rickey Henry (Art), Eva Hingle (Spanish), Dr. Kyle Hubbard (Science), Jessica Hudson (Science), Lindsey Hutchins (English), Wanda Johnson (Math), Christopher Labee (Special Education), Michelle Marquez-Williams (Business), JaMichael McCants (Math), Danielle McFadden (Math), Robert McGriff (English), Lynett Morrisette (Business), Jeremy Roussel (Instructional Coach), Victoria Roussel (English), Jordan Sanchez (Special Education), Edmund Sangel (Special Education), Keith Thomas (Band), Virgil Tiller (Science), Ida Wilson (Special Education), Bing Zhang (Social Studies). Other staff members included: Meatrice Bealer (Admin Assistant), Essie Blanchard (Administrative Assistant), Cheerie Brooks (Parent Liaison), Nira Cooper (Data Manager), Shontell Dolliole (Counselor), Diane Evans-Sams (Administrative Assistant), Marcel Fisher (Behavioral Intervention), Tonja Jackson (Social Worker), Dwight Jarrett (Academic Assistant), Keisha Jones (Administrative Assistant), Derrick Lewis (Academic Assistant), Paulette Lotten (Secretary),

Harold Nunnery (Academic Assistant), Farah Parker (College Counselor), Julie Pertuit (Librarian), Kenneth Thomas (Behavioral Intervention), Dale Valdery (Administrative Assistant), Arthur Williams (Dean of Students), and Debra Woods (Academic Assistant).

With only a few weeks before the Christmas/New Year holiday break, I had the task of completing the semester course and bringing up the students who had been without a consistent instructor for the entire semester. So many teachers had come and gone within a few months. The students were irritated and I felt their adolescent agitation during the process but attempted to guide them as best as possible. Many of them took my approach seriously, others still looked at me as a substitute and paid me no attention. To those who were willing to stick it out and finish the course, I offered them rewards for an A average. Six of my students scored 90 and above on their overall grade in the class. I gave them each a certificate of achievement. It was signed by myself and Principal Lewis. In addition to the certificate, they received $10 in cash and a gift card to AMC Theaters. There were a few who exclaimed, "Well we didn't know you were the real teacher." I don't know how much more real I could have been.

In my Fall 2015 term, I instructed 85 students including: Briana Abdull-Rahmaan, Miguel Alix, Jaron Barra, Keywan Brass, Christopher Brown, Vintrell Cheavious, Devinnell Clark, Garian Gibson, Kenneth Grant, Denisha Hartford, Joseph Hill, Cire' Johnson, Raymond Joseph, Jermaine Kelley, Moesha King, Tatyana Shelton, Tyronique Smith, Ceto Strowder, Jolla Terroll, Tyvis Wilson, Jazhmine Addison, Akil Allen, Richard Boutain, Anderson Cayette, Ken Green, Terrance Harris, Hillary Hawkins, Glenn Jackson, Dalijah James, Ranesha Johnson, Bailey Jones, Ty'jon Jones, Atraiena Kelley, Corey Labeaud, Bruce Lawrence, Dejone Lawson, Perriane Luque, Abdul Madison, Precious Major, Angela McCoy, Darnyell McDaniel, Osbreanna Mendoza, Wysheka Nicholson, Albert Odds, Tory Perrette, Jayce Perry, Treyanna Perry, Francisco Pierre, Chrishell Robertson, Dwayne Sentino, Hakeem Shawl, Troy Spencer, Quinton Stockman, Kalin Thomas, Jimmiel Walters, Kimani Williams, Traviann Williams, Semaj Allen, Tyeast Bannister, Janiya Barnett, Ilene Barton, Nia Bernard, Steven Brumfield, Asada Bryant, Coreyell Celestine, Jamyra Craft, Christopher Craig, Leyonce' Davis,

Jayda Doyle, DrewKayla, Kayla Falkins, Jazzmyn Falls, Jaylin Franklin, Charlie Ginn, Ayanna Harris, Diamond Joseph, Da'Mahari London, Aviere Masters, Shane Minor, Hasan Mitchell, La'Ron Moore, Kolby Navarre, Ayriahna Purvis, Essence Rainey, Brian Washington, and A'Lesia Williams.

A new classroom design

I took the time during the holiday break to design a classroom environment. From my previous experience working at a charter school, a teacher is often given ample free reign in a classroom to experiment with whatever works. There was not any funding for classroom lagniappe, but that was never an issue for me. On January 2, I came to the school to set up the new scene. The centerpiece was a large 9×12 vinyl photo of a kid holding the globe in her hands with the continent of Africa displayed. This being a world geography class, I planned to expose them to as much of the world outside of New Orleans as I could. I made original 8×10 photo displays of 20 major cities of the world. These prints were posted around the room. So every day, they would be surrounded by the sights of the Eiffel Tower, the Great Wall of China, the Empire State Building, the Taj Mahal, the Burj Khalifa and over a dozen more prominent world sites.

On January 18, 2016, we watched the movie Ice Age: Continental Drift. Although this is an animated film, I was surprised that many of the teenagers found the movie enjoyable. The movie was used to complement a study on plate tectonics and continental drift. They were tasked to watch the film and complete a comparison and contrast graphic chart. The lesson proved to be a success.

Focus on Literacy with Malcolm X

On January 20, I began a weekly literary exercise with the students. I checked out a classroom set of "The Autobiography of Malcolm X" from the school's library. The activity required students to read to me individually. I believe that students who refuse to read in class do so out of fear or embarrassment. However, this approach worked because the other students in the class were not paying attention to the reader who was only reading out loud to me. As they read pages from the book, I corrected incorrect words and kept a weekly journal of their progress. In a short amount of time, students began pronouncing words with accuracy, a skill with which they previously had difficulty. I chose this book for the first half of the semester for its focus on geography and the study of Islam, both lessons which we would cover in the course.

In February, I began voluntary unpaid after-school tutoring for my students. These would be opportunities for them to complete homework assignments, get interventions, or complete weekly reading assignments. I held the sessions at Domino's Pizza, which was within a mile from the school. Only three students attended the first session, held on February 2. They ate pizza, read books, and completed assignments. The second session was held on March 3. Four students came to this session. It was only one more than the first, but one was an improvement, I thought. The next sessions were held at the school. I would order in and the pizza was delivered.

The weather lady from the news comes to class

On February 3, 2016, I invited the local meteorologist Kweilyn Murphy to speak to my class. Murphy received her journalism degree from Ohio University. She worked on the weather team in Greenville, North Carolina before moving to join the weather team at WDSU News in New Orleans. She was a very fashionable, knowledgeable, and energetic speaker for my class. She spoke about her profession and taught a little about the weather. In class, we were engaged in the unit on the Coriolis Effect. So I brought her in to put a face to it, as she deals with the subject on a daily basis. They asked questions and she answered them. She asked them questions and was pleased that they could answer them back. In the end, the students took photos with her and she gave them advice about being successful in school and launching a career in journalism should they find interest.

Kente design activity

In April, I conducted a country study on Ghana. On April 15, the students watched a video and we discussed African culture. In the video, they saw Africans, old and young, weaving kente cloths. As an activity to complement the lesson on African culture, the students were tasked to design their Kente pattern. I had poster board cut into rectangular pieces and passed out crayons and markers. I showed them samples of Kente patterns and they went to work constructing their own. After all of the students submitted their work, I displayed them on the board.

The world turned Purple when Prince died

On April 21, 2016, pop icon Prince died at the age of 57 at his Paisley Park recording studio in Minnesota. The world went purple and from the images I saw of Paris, London, New York City and other places, I could not let the moment pass without making it relevant to world geography. I immediately began to design a lesson that I could use to not only focus on the historical impact of Prince to the world but also to teach a geography lesson. The activity was entitled "The World Geography of Prince." Some of the questions on the assignment included: "In 2009, Prince performed at the Montreux Jazz Festival in Switzerland. What is the absolute location of Montreux, Switzerland?" and "The following are cities of which Prince visited on his 20Ten Tour. Match the cities with their corresponding countries." I took one of my tables, draped it with purple paper and put a purple book cover over the class textbook, making a memorial for the fallen pop star. The world rained purple and so did my world geography classroom.

A trip to the National World War II Museum

On Saturday, April 23, 2016, I sponsored a trip to the National World War II Museum in New Orleans. The opportunity was available for all of my students. However, only seven of them made the trip. I bought entrance tickets for six of the seven, as the last student came late. We toured the many exhibits and I had a chance to use the visual media in the exhibits to teach world history and geography lessons as we moved through the museum. Following the museum tour, I treated them to ice cream at the museum's Soda Pop Café. The museum opened in 2000, the 56th anniversary of D-Day. At its inception, it was named the National D-Day Museum. It was designated by the U.S. Congress in 2003 as the nation's official National World War II Museum.

The Karate Kid and Fried Rice Activity

In May, during the last month of the semester, we discussed the country of China. There were two activities that the students enjoyed during this unit: a movie and free food. We watched the movie "The Karate Kid" starring Jaden Smith and Jackie Chan. The movie took place in Beijing and displayed much of Chinese culture and the scenes of the country. We watched the first half of the movie on May 10 and the remainder on May 12. After the movie on May 12, I taught the students how to eat with chopsticks. I bought 100 chopsticks the previous day from a Chinese restaurant in Metairie. I also ordered fried rice for all three class periods. One of the students' grandmother, Mrs. Ella Wilson, even came out to help prepare and serve fried rice during the class period of which her granddaughter was involved. I will always remember Mrs. Wilson. She was a retired educator and was raising her granddaughter. She thanked me often for my commitment and hard work. Her contributions to the class are commendable and I hope God has a special place in heaven for her.

Final goodbye

The last day for students at Lake Area was May 20, 2016. I promised my students at the beginning of the semester (as I'd done in my previous school) that if they made the grades, I'd reward them. The student with the highest grades would get a $200 cash award; then the second and third highest would receive $50 gift cards. Only one of the students with the highest grade came to school. He picked up his certificate and $50 card. The student with the highest grade didn't get her reward. She's never claimed, but it is always available to her, should I ever see her again. A promise is a promise.

Teaching at Lake Area

Teaching at a charter school was not new territory for me, as I'd taught at Excellence Academy in Monroe for two years. Lake

Area operated in a similar fashion. However, there were more students and a much bigger campus in which to operate. Many teachers found difficulty teaching at the school. There were some things that were annoying (like weekly professional development sessions) and having to climb three flights of stairs everyday to get to my classroom. You won't find too many teachers who like mandatory training workshops. Other than those, I really found working at the school quite pleasant. The pay was good and the working hours were acceptable. There were long 90-minute class periods, however each teacher had a 90-minute preparation period and duty-free lunch. This is unheard of in many schools. So, I counted my blessings over the few flaws in the mix. And as annoying as they may have been, the professional development meetings with Mrs. Sceau and Dr. Jeremy Roussel, were informative. I would agree that I learned a thing or two from them. Roussel was so energetic and motivated about his job. He was a valuable resource for teaching strategies. He later would become the 11th and 12th Grade Academy Principal at Edna Karr High School in New Orleans.

We would be somewhat reluctant to say it but, the staff enjoyed a certain spirit. Although we may have dragged into meetings and workshops, it didn't take us long to come together and enjoy each other's fellowship. There were plenty of outings, parties, and activities that fostered teamwork and team building. We had faculty cookouts and a talent show at the end of the year. Retention was a big problem at Lake Area. So Principal Lewis and Assistant Principal Cooper took strides to make life bearable and rewarding while working at Lake Area. However, they would always remind the staff "If you're not here to teach, then this is not the place for you." Mrs. Cooper was soft-spoken, but she surprised me during one faculty meeting. I assume she did walk-throughs on a day when many of the teachers were a bit lackadaisical. She came to the emergency meeting screaming mad, threatening dire consequences. She proved that she might have been a nice lady, but was not a force with which to be reckoned.

The Class of 2019

During the Spring semester of 2016, I instructed 95 students including: Antoine Adams, Coreione Alexander, Saki Armour,

Varinyka Atkins, Travis Briggs, Amber Brown, Ta-Janae Bush, Dajuan Carrie, Aaron Delgado, Curtis Dyer, Alexus Hatcher, Ma'Kia Hayes, Jamocha Heno, Mickel Hill, Keithen Hunter, Secret James, Byron Jiles, Derrick Jones, Kiante Jones, Samara Jones-Metz, Zukuri Magee, Skyel Moore, Dayton Peters, Lorenz Robert, Malik Simms, Michelle Smith, Ronald Smith, Leary Sterling, Kirmisha Watson, Ja'Milla Wilson, Dorian Barnett, Jim Brown, Bria Butler, Laneisha Cloud, Troydell Craige, Jamyra Davis, Trinae Duplessis, Tyren Fields, Arman Hausey, Emanuel Henry, Paola Hernandez, Ronneka Hill, Daishanae Jackson, Semaj Jenkins, Keiana Johnson, Ariane Jones, Jada Kaufman, Jasmine Kaufman, Kendrall Kirkpatrick, Kelsey Lash, Lyndell Lewis, Jerry Marshall, Braione Martin, Ikia Mayes, Arrionja Morgan, Troy Petite, Caleb Ridgley, Herbert Riley, Cubionne Smith, Kennide Smith, Nia Smith, Chassity Sutton, Tamyria Thornton, Ke'wuan Whittaker, Ta'Janique Alphonse, Brianton Bagneris, Jovian Baker, Kenyatta Brown, Mia Burns, Tyran Chambers, Kalen Duncan, Christopher Forstall, Willie Francis, Roshonda Francois, Robert Franklin, Kolby Green, Raheem Marshall, Anacia McKinney, John Mosley, Jasmine Richards, Michael Shelton, Austin Smith, Jyla Smith, Raniya Studyviant, Darrius Thornsberry, Kristiana Tillman, Carlton Williams, Chad Williams, Tanoah Wright, and Jessica Young. I also taught an all-girls advisory class for the 2015-2016 year including: Kalifa Broussard, Jamyra Davis, Donna Gibbs, Zana Hall, Mya Harris, Denisha Hartford, Dwynisha Harvey, Ma'Kia Hayes, Monae Henderson, Jamoca Heno, Paola Hernandez, Mickel Hill, Robin Holmes, Eboni Howard, Kayla Humble, Cheryl Hurst, Tyreyanna Irby, Jimani Jackson, Madison Jacque, Amyari James, Secret James, Taylor Jiles, Ariane Jones, Reign Jones, Diamond Joseph, and Ikia Waters.

The school motto at Lake Area was Respect, Commit, Succeed. This message was shared over the intercom on a daily basis. The students I taught will graduate with the Class of 2019. I hope that they will commit to being successful in life. Such a choice is very respectable.

FORTY-ONE

TEACHING 5TH GRADE AT MINNIE RUFFIN ELEMENTARY

"Civic education and civic responsibility should be taught in elementary school."

Donna Brazile

On August 7, 2017, I was hired as a 5th Grade Social Studies teacher at Minnie Ruffin Elementary School. I attended the new teacher orientation at Carroll Junior High School. During the orientation, we were greeted by a few administrators from the district office. However, none would be as inspiring as that of the superintendent, Dr. Brent Vidrine. I'd known the superintendent for over a decade. I worked as the school photographer at Neville High School when he was the principal. I remember the first time I took photos at his school's prom and I attempted to give him a personal commission from prom profits. This was often an understood procedure in other places, so I assumed he wanted his cut as well. Vidrine quickly shook his head and refused the offer. "You make that payment to Neville High School. I don't do that," he told me. I've always remembered him for that response and after a decade of a professional working relationship, there he was standing before me welcoming me as a teacher in one of his schools.

I worked under the supervision of Principal Sylvia Brass and Assistant Principal Jenett Hunter. My fellow 5th-grade teachers were Nicholas Harrison (ELA), Eashell Salsberry (Math), an MiSha Jackson (Science). The school is named for Minnie Ruffin, the former principal of Monroe City High School.

Fifth Grade social studies content consists of American History from the civilization of the natives until the French and Indian War. I chose as a class theme "CSI: Colonial Scene Investigators." There was a large photo of Fort Miro on my wall, as it was similar to the makeup of Jamestown, Virginia. Fort Miro is the original Monroe, Louisiana on the banks of the Ouachita River. The name of the city changed to the present name when a steamboat called the "James Monroe" sailed downstream. The townspeople were amazed and decided to change the name from Fort Miro to Monroe. This was a lesson I included in my curriculum. It would not be evaluated on the state test in April, but I thought it was important.

I never wanted to teach at this level. However, I found that it wasn't as bad as I imagined. There were some differences in routine as I was used to older students having more independence in their hourly movements. At the elementary level, there is little freedom for the students or teachers, as we had to be with them all day long. They traveled to the bathroom, cafeteria, library, and PE together, normally accompanied by their homeroom teacher. I didn't get a lunch break, for I had to sit and eat with my students. I often received a 45-minute break two days out of the week while students were in PE or at the library. Other than those two days, the students were in my presence from 8:00 AM until dismissal at 3:15 PM. It was a work situation with which I had to become familiar.

The emphasis during the year was on reading and understanding documents. Solving DBQs (Document Based Questions) was the priority task and the main skill of which they would need to be successful at the end of the year on state tests. Daily they wore badges wearing the CSI logo. As they progressed through the lesson, they investigated the documents and evidence that earlier Americans left behind, hence the phrase "Colonial Scene Investigators." I taught them and advised that document-based questions were the easiest ones, because as the questions were based on the document, so were the answers. The only catch was that they would have to sit silently and read to find the answer. This was the hard part.

On August 31, I treated my students to the first of many PBIS (Positive Behavior Intervention Strategies) events. This was a bonus for students who had good behavior for August. They were treated to Johnny's Pizza. Over a dozen students were invited and they, along with their parents attended the gathering. It was a two-fold success, as not only did the students learn that I make good on my promises, but I was able to meet some of their parents for the first time. It was a good parent-teacher meetup.

On September 30, I invited over a dozen students who qualified for the month's behavior gift to meet me at the Ark-La-Miss Fair. Only two students showed up for the gathering, so both of them were given a $20 sheet of tickets. Their eyes lit up with excitement and they quickly were on their way for fun at the fair.

I incorporated CNN 10 News into their daily curriculum as a bell ringer activity. The principal wanted the teachers to ensure that students were well rounded and could not only learn the lesson but be mindful of what was happening in the world around them. The news series, hosted by CNN's Carl Azuz included all the elements of social studies- economics, geography, history, and civics. The daily activity also helped foster Accelerated Learning. Students read daily with the online Renaissance learning program. I made it a point that they learn how to sit still and pay attention for 10 minutes during the CNN episodes. If they could do this and take a brief quiz, it would do wonders for their AR (Accelerated Reader) performance. So many seeds are planted during the CNN 10 News segments that aren't seen today and may not be seen for years, but their eyes were opened and they were exposed to the world daily, just as I was when I was a grade school student.

On October 4, I taught the lesson on the "Columbian Exchange." I thought it would be great to give a visual demonstration of the exchange. So, before I traveled to the school, I went to Wal-Mart and bought $70.00 worth of groceries, the things that were a symbol of the exchange of goods from the Old World to the New World. I set up a table in the middle of my classroom and donned an apron. On one side of the table, I had food items that came from the Old World and on the other side, food items that came from the New World. Some of the items the students had never seen or touched with their own eyes. However, the next time they read about a pineapple, squash or pumpkin, they would have a visual reminder in their heads.

On October 29, over a dozen students were invited to Skatetown for maintaining good behavior. Unlike the other trips, this event was well attended. They were given free skates and pizza. The whole trip cost well over $150.00. However, it was promised and for those who were invited, that was 20 less behavioral problems in the classroom.

I designed a social studies vocabulary game in their curriculum. It was modeled after a scene in the movie "Lean on Me" starring Morgan Freeman. During my class, the students were given new words to write in their notebooks. We'd discuss the spelling and meaning of the words. They'd have a few moments to review them; then I split the class into teams of two. I drew a line dividing the whiteboard and each team had their side upon which to write. I'd set the timer for seven minutes and then I'd call out a word. The students were in line at the back of the class and had to race to the board to spell the word. The student who was the first to spell it correctly won the point for his or her team. The game would continue for the duration of time, allowing all team members to participate.

On November 29, I treated two of my students to the movies. A number of them were invited, but as I was learning, only the same ones were showing up to claim their award. So the two that came were treated to see the movie "Wonder" at Tinseltown Cinemark Theaters. "Wonder" is the movie featuring Jacob Tremblay, Julia Roberts, and Owen Wilson and tells the story of a 5th-grade boy dealing with a physical deformity in an era of chronic bullying.

On December 23, three students showed up for my December PBIS treat. I bought tickets and snack boxes for them to see the movie "Jumanji: Welcome to the Jungle" starring Dwayne Johnson and Kevin Hart.

On January 8, 2018, the students played an original game of which I designed to reinforce their understanding of the Characteristics of Civilization. I set up two tables in the front of the class and had the 9 Characteristics placed of which they had to put the descriptions in the right area. I pulled up a looped video of Jeopardy game music on YouTube through the classroom's Smartboard and played it during the game. It was timed and there were game prizes for the winning team. So, the competitive element was added to the class as they became engaged in learning the characteristics.

On January 11, 2018, I traveled with a number of my students to the Monroe Civic Center for the City of Monroe's annual salute to Dr. Martin Luther King, Jr. The speaker for the event was Rick Gallot, Esq., the president of Grambling State University. After the event, the students were given lunch and we traveled back to the school.

In January of 2018, I introduced Google Classroom to the students. I'd been using my own Word Press website since August and did not want to use Google's platform. However, after I was shown how it could make the classroom experience more efficient, I was sold on the idea and put it to use. It was a great transition and it became the main tool for classroom delivery. I put up daily lesson plans, objectives, links, and their tests, which were all accessible to the students and their parents.

It was a joy to work with 10-year-olds at this level. I hope that I made an impact on their lives and exposed them to something that will be beneficial to them in the future. Every day in class I had them to recite the class chant from a quote made by the salesman and motivational speaker Zig Ziglar: "If I'm not willing to learn, no one can help me. If I'm determined to learn, no one can stop me." They sometimes screamed it at the top of their lungs, but I hope that they understood what they were saying. Maybe in time, they will. I expect great things from them and as they go forward in their lives. I hope that they will heed the words of Principal Brass that they should strive to be boldly beautiful, regal, astute, stupendous, and shine they must....everyday!

FORTY-TWO

GOING FISHING: MEETING WILLIE ROBERTSON

"You don't set off in life to be mediocre.
At least, I don't."
Willie Robertson

I had an opportunity to meet the CEO of Duck Commander at a book signing event at Books-A-Million, in Monroe, Louisiana. Willie Robertson held a book signing event to market his new book "American Fisherman" on Saturday, December 17, 2016. I saw the announcement posted in the store a few weeks ahead of the date and had to get me a copy signed.

When he arrived, he looked just like the photo on the book cover…a shirt, jeans, long hair, beard and an American Flag bandana wrapped around his forehead. He came in the store and went to the table greeting customers who were there for the signing. I was the first in line. He signed my book "Robert, all the best Willie Robertson."

It was cool getting a piece of American History signed by one of the players who shaped it. His family is known for their work in the outdoors, fishing and hunting. Their reality show "Duck Dynasty" aired on A&E from 2012 until 2017. It portrayed their lives and how they made a million-dollar business making products for duck hunters in the Monroe/West Monroe area. The show, produced by Gurney Productions and distributed by A&E and Lionsgate, was narrated by Willie Robertson.

His book "The American Fisherman: How our nation's anglers founded, fed, financed, and forever shaped the USA" was a history book indeed. I didn't grow up with an appreciation for fishing or hunting, so I was naturally mystified by Robertson's accounts. However, I was also educated at how important and popular fishing was to the American landscape. In the book, Robertson begins with the Vikings and continues with a number of episodes in American history where fishing was involved including the Pilgrims, colonial America and even the role fishing played in winning the American Revolution. Certainly, it didn't make me want to be a fisherman, but it was enlightening and educational. I think it even made me hungry for a plate of fish.

FORTY-THREE

THE PRESIDENTIAL LIBRARY TOURS

"Oh, that lovely title, ex-president."
President Dwight D. Eisenhower

In April 2013, I made my first visit to a Presidential Library. That would spark an interest which would carry me across the country on an adventurous scavenger hunt for the others. Although there have been 44 presidents (Grover Cleveland served two non-consecutive terms), not all of them have libraries and museums. Of those that do, only 13 of them are sponsored and maintained by the government. I found these facilities to be fascinating and after visiting the Reagan Library in Simi Valley, California, I was ready for more. I wanted to see them all. So I began. At the writing of this book, I have visited nine such libraries and museums.

In 1955, Congress passed the Presidential Libraries Act which established a system of privately constructed and federally maintained facilities. It encouraged presidents to donate their historical materials of which the government pledged to maintain. The National Archives and Records Administration manages the Presidential Libraries and Museums. It is an independent agency of the government that is charged with preserving governmental and historical records. Those that it manages include: Herbert Hoover, Franklin D. Roosevelt, Harry S. Truman, Dwight D. Eisenhower, Lyndon B. Johnson, Richard Nixon, Gerald R. Ford, Jimmy Carter, Ronald Reagan, George H.W. Bush, William J. Clinton, and George W. Bush. There are many other museums in operation throughout the country. However, they are mostly operated by private foundations and organizations.

The President Ronald Reagan Library Visit

On November 4, 1991, the Ronald Reagan Presidential Library was dedicated in Simi Valley, California. Construction began on the 153,000 square foot facility in November of 1988. The total cost of the facility, designed by Hugh Stubbins and Associates, was $60 million. At the dedication ceremony, Presidents Gerald Ford, Jimmy Carter, Richard Nixon, and George HW Bush were in attendance, the first time in US History that five presidents were assembled at the same time. In his remarks, President Gerald Ford said that "old presidents don't just fade away." President Jimmy Carter brought those in attendance to laughter when he joked about the overwhelming presence of Republicans, as he was a Democrat. "Mr. President, I have to say, though, by looking over the program, I had one concern. I noticed that the Republican representation has four times as much time on the program as the Democratic (applause and laughter). You have another advantage over me. At least all of you have met a Democratic President. I've never had that honor yet," Carter said, as Ronald and Nancy burst into laughter.

I visited Reagan's museum on April 26, 2013. Driving up to the top of the hill, I immediately noticed the attention to detail that would await me inside the facility. There were light posts that bore the banner of each of the 44 presidents. As I rode and witnessed the display, it was like a history lesson in chronological order, one post after the next ending with Reagan at the entrance of the facility. As tourists exit, the banners pick up with George HW Bush down the hill, ending with Barack Obama.

One of the first things you see when you walk in Reagan's library is a 6-foot portrait of him above a bronze presidential seal on a marble floor. I took a photo by this as it was such a nice display. Reagan's tour of exhibits and displays begin with his childhood in Dixon, Illinois to video displays of his funeral ceremonies and burial at the museum. There is a 1965 Ford Mustang from his early campaign days, collectibles from his years as a Hollywood actor, replica ranch scenes, his situation room at the White House, a remake of a Camp David facility, dresses from Nancy Reagan's days as first lady, the suit that he wore during his attempted assassination, all of the vehicles of his presidential transportation service including the helicopter, the limousine motorcade and the massive centerpiece of the entire facility, Air Force One.

The SAM27000 Boeing 202 jet that draws much of the attention to the facility, and of which has been used as the backdrop for many televised political debates, was used by Nixon, Ford, Carter, George HW Bush, Clinton, and George W Bush. It was flown to San Bernadino under "Operation Homeward Bound," disassembled, transported in pieces, and finally placed in its present resting spot of which the pavilion was built around it.

I was able to walk through the jet. It was so surreal that I was on Air Force One. I wasn't allowed to take photos aboard the aircraft but was given a guided tour. There was an opportunity to take photos at the front cabin door. A library photographer was on site to provide the services. I waved as if I were president embarking. The photo was sent to the processing lab and was ready as I exited the library. I also took photos by the President's Cadillac, in the oval office, next to a section of the Berlin Wall, and at Reagan's gravesite on the grounds. First Lady Nancy was still living at the time of my visit. I was told that she lived nearby in residence.

First Lady Nancy died on March 6, 2016 and a ceremony was held on March 11 at the Presidential Library. It was attended by President George W Bush and First Lady Laura, First Lady Michelle Obama, First Lady Hillary Clinton, Arnold Schwarzenegger and Maria Shriver, Wayne Newton, Tom Selleck, Gary Sinise, Mr. T, ABC's Diane Sawyer, and NBC's Tom Brokaw. She was buried next to her husband at the library complex.

The President George W. Bush Library Visit

After leaving the Reagan library, I was inspired and made it a goal to visit all of the libraries. Coincidentally, the day before I visited the Regan library, there was a new library being dedicated in Dallas, Texas. On April 25, 2013, a dedication ceremony was held for the opening of the George W. Bush Presidential Library on the campus of Southern Methodist University. The grand opening for the public was scheduled for May 1, 2013. I made my exit from California and was traveling back to Monroe, Louisiana to teach shortly after the Reagan library visit. Dallas was on the return route, so I made plans to tour my second library. I was one of the first Americans to visit on the grand opening day on May 1st.

Bush's library is the second largest of the National Archives system. At 207,000 square feet, it boasts construction costs of $250 Million. Designed by architect Robert A.M. Stern, the ground was broken on November 16, 2010.

At the dedication ceremony, once again, like that of Reagan's library, five living presidents were gathered at once. Presidents Clinton, George HW Bush, Carter, and Obama were in attendance at the event.

"No matter how much you think you're ready to assume the office of the presidency, it's impossible to truly understand the nature of the job until it's yours, until you're sitting at that desk. That's why every president gains a greater appreciation for all of those who served before them," said President Obama in his remarks.

"There was a time in my life when I wouldn't be likely to be found at a library, much less found one. Beautiful building has my name on it, but it belongs to you," remarked Bush. He later thanked President Obama for making the trip. "I am very grateful to President Obama and Michelle for making this trip. Unlike the other presidents here, he actually has a job," he chuckled.

I immediately felt the spirit of Bush's legacy as I walked in the doors to the facility. The visitors approached a checkpoint almost resembling that of TSA at an airport. While waiting in line, there was a stone wall with names of private donors etched in it to remain forever. There were hundreds of names of those who contributed to the $250 million fundraising effort. As I continued my tour, once pass the "TSA Checkpoint," there were a number of features and exhibits in the library. On display in the library were: Hurricane Katrina, the financial market collapse, Bush's HIV/AIDS initiatives, No Child Left Behind, a piece of the girder from the Twin Towers, the bullhorn used atop the rubble at Ground Zero, and there was a replica of his Oval Office. Unlike Reagan's Oval Office, the Bush library allows visitors to sit at the resolute desk and take photos. Visitors could either let the professional photographer take the photo, or they could use their phones to take their own. It was cool sitting at the president's desk.

The President William Jefferson Clinton Library Visit

I visited the Clinton library on September 29, 2013. I took a day off from work, rented a car, and made the short drive up to Little Rock, Arkansas. As I arrived, I observed this weird looking rectangular structure on the banks of the Arkansas River. The libraries that I'd visited up to that point had a standard traditional look to them. However, this one had a look of its own. I didn't know what to expect when I walked inside.

Construction on this 90,000 square foot facility began on December 5, 2001. It was designed by James Polshek and the construction employed about 1,500 workers. It houses the Clinton Library, the offices of the Clinton Foundation, and the University of Arkansas School of Public Service. The exhibits were designed by Ralph Appelbaum Associates and the entire project cost $165 million, from private funding. The City of Little Rock gave the facility $11.5 million in land.

On the day of dedication, November 18, 2004, it rained. Attendees wore colorful raincoats and held umbrellas. President Clinton even had to have someone hold an umbrella over him as he made his dedication ceremony speech. It was attended by Wille Mays, Robin Williams, Barbara Streisand, and Bono. Presidents Carter, George HW Bush and George W Bush were the only presidents in attendance. In his speech, Clinton thanked President George W Bush for attending the ceremony. "Mr. President, I can't thank you enough for your generous words and for coming to the opening at all. I mean, after all, you just delayed your own library opening by four years," Clinton said. Bush and his wife laughed at the statement, as he had just won re-election a few weeks before the dedication ceremony.

One of the first things I saw when I walked inside the building was Clinton's presidential limousine. The Cadillac One was on display in the lobby. I had to take a photo next to it. I love artifacts, cars, and awesome displays in these museums. The only other real display in the museum was a full-scale replica of Clinton's oval office which was above the theater. A majority of the library exhibits were static displays of photos, artifacts, letters, and documents all centered around the years of Clinton's two terms as president. There was much attention to making the library look more like a library than a museum like the others. It holds more documents and archived material than any of the other libraries in the National Archives system. After leaving the library, I bought a few souvenirs at the Library store a few blocks down the street, as it was not placed inside the library facility.

The Lyndon B. Johnson Presidential Library Visit

Some time passed before I would make my next visit. I wanted to do something "me" for my 36th birthday. Visiting a presidential library was my idea of fun. So on the morning of February 19, 2014, I made the journey to Austin, Texas to the Lyndon B. Johnson library.

The library was dedicated on May 22, 1971. Designed by Gordon Bunshaft, it is housed on the campus of the University of Texas at Austin. At the dedication ceremony, President Richard Nixon was the only other president to join him on the platform. However, there were scores of elected officials and celebrated individuals in the audience including: Henry Fowler, Orville Freeman, Sen. Hubert Humphrey, Gregory Peck, Gen. William Westmoreland, Roy Wilkins, Douglas Dillon, Rep. Hale Boggs, Sen. Barry Goldwater, Ebony Magazine Publisher John H. Johnson, Rep. Jim Wright, Henry Kissinger, and David and Julie Eisenhower.

At the dedication ceremony, President Nixon made comments. "One of the first rules of statecraft is that we can successfully chart the future only if we can understand the past. Libraries such as this can be among our keys to that understanding," he said.

I was awed at the massive structure. Although smaller in total square footage, it was one of the tallest libraries that I had visited. In front of the structure, there are two flags, the American flag and the Texas state flag. Inside, I immediately saw a Lincoln Town Car boasting its suicide doors. I had to take a photo by it. It is almost placed as the Cadillac One is in the Clinton Library in Little Rock. As I continued to tour the facility, I was exposed to almost 40 years of American History beginning with the depression and ending with the Vietnam War. There is a Vietnam War exhibit, exhibits from World War II, the Great Depression, a replica of Johnson's Oval Office with the signature three television screens; there is also a display on Dr. Martin Luther King, whom Johnson spent much time with during the Civil Rights Movement. In the exhibit, there is a telephone cord and handle, and a visitor can hear a phone call made between Johnson and King. There is also a letter on display of which Johnson wrote to Coretta Scott King in the wake of the assassination of King. First Lady "Lady Bird" Johnson also has an exhibit in the facility. Her office and her campaigns are on exhibit. They capture the spirit of the 1960s with its colorful décor. As I ended my tour, I had to take a photo next to the large 12 foot wide photo of Johnson signing the Voting Rights Act into law, with MLK standing behind him. In the photo, I place myself as if I'm in the room looking down at the signing. What a birthday trip it was.

The Jimmy Carter Presidential Library Visit

During my school's 2014 Spring Break, I decided to make a trip to Atlanta, Georgia to visit the Jimmy Carter Presidential Library. I made the trip on April 22, 2014. The 69,750 square foot complex, which sits on 35 acres houses the Library and Carter Center. The former president is known for being on the grounds a few days out of the week as the center is where his office is located.

Construction began on the Carter library on October 2, 1984 and the dedication ceremony was held on October 1, 1986. It probably was not a coincidence that the dedication ceremony was also held on Carter's 62nd birthday, which was also on October 1st. At the ceremony, President Ronald Reagan made remarks. He joked about knowing Andrew Carnegie personally, with Carnegie's passion for libraries and books. He also stated that after seeing Carter's library, he and Nancy had their work cut out for them in preparing his.

"I can think of no other country on Earth where two political leaders could disagree so widely yet come together in mutual respect," said Reagan.

I learned a bit about Carter in my senior year of college when I took a Middle East Politics class. Carter was a central figure in the talks between the Egyptian President Anwar El Sadat and the Israeli Prime Minister Menachem during the Camp David Accords towards the end of the 1970s. The twelve days of negotiations resulted in the signing of agreements on September 17, 1978. However, I did not know that Carter was a naval officer and former governor of Georgia. These things I would learn as I toured the museum. Even a historian can learn something new, well that's the point of the museums.

The museum underwent a $10 million renovation in 2009, so what I saw did not look like the original library and museum. In the museum, I saw a number of exciting exhibits which followed the life of Carter from his early beginnings in his family's Georgia business until his works after he exited the White House. There was a makeshift naval vessel to chronicle his time as a naval officer, gifts he received from world leaders, a display of his Nobel Peace Prize and a display of his Grammy Award, which he won for Best Spoken Word Album. I also took photos in his full-sized Oval Office replica, which included a resolute desk.

It would seem as though President Carter is more active in private life after the White House than he was as president. There are few exhibits which display his work around the world in aid and relief operations through the Carter Center. So essentially, the Library and Museum focus on his past and the Center focuses on the future of his works…all in one complex.

The Richard Nixon Presidential Library Visit

On July 3, 2014, I made a trip out to California for the 4th of July Weekend. One of my stops was the Richard Nixon Presidential Library, the sixth presidential library visit. His library is located in Yorba Linda, California.

Dedicated on July 19, 1990, the 52,000 square foot complex is the site for not only Nixon's library and museum, but it also includes his birthplace. The home in which he was born is on the site and is listed as a National Historic Landmark. It is also the final resting spot for Nixon and his wife, Pat. The complex has a 38,000 square foot wing, which was constructed in 2004, of which has a replica of the East Room of the White House.

At the Nixon Library's dedication, about 50,000 people were present, including Presidents George HW Bush, Gerald Ford, and Ronald Reagan.

Although Nixon's library is not as grand as some of the others, it does boast some pretty cool elements. As I walked into the lobby, there was a miniature Air Force One model with a huge photo of Nixon and his wife waving from the cabin door. On display were photos of Nixon on the plane during his presidency. Although there was no replica of the Oval Office, there was a Resolute Desk on display in the lobby. There are displays throughout the center which begin at Nixon's childhood, his marriage to Pat and a handwritten essay from 1925 in which he wrote that "I would like to study law and enter Politics for an occupation so that I might be of some good to the people."

As I moved throughout the facility, I saw trinkets of his election years when he first campaigned for Senator and when he campaigned for Congressman. There is a classic Mercury car with a sign and horn on the top bearing the words "Nixon for US Senator." The exhibit trail moves on to his Vice Presidency under President Eisenhower. I took a photo of a letter on display from Dr. Martin Luther King, Jr. to President Nixon in 1957 (then Vice-President) of which King explains to Nixon that "we will seek to get at least two million Negroes registered in the south for the 1960 elections." In his letter, he was pleading for the enactment of the Civil Rights Bill long before Johnson was able to sign the Voting Rights Act in the next decade.

Like Reagan's library, Nixon's also had a section of the Berlin Wall on display. Nixon's presidential limousine is on display, by which I took a photo. One of the largest areas of the exhibition in the center was Nixon's moments of scandal. There is a display which outlines the White House's taping system, with a special focus on the 18 ½ minute gap which was mysteriously missing from the Nixon tapes. After the taping system display, I observed another set of displays on the Watergate Break-In from June 1972, the event which eventually led to Nixon resigning from office. There's a moon rock from an Apollo 15 mission on display as is a complete astronaut's uniform.

My visit to the Nixon Library could not be concluded without standing next to the VH-3A "Sea King" helicopter which sat towards the rear of the complex. This is the helicopter that was flown between 1961 to 1976 and was used by Presidents Kennedy, Johnson, Nixon, and Ford before being retired. Nixon's pilot was instrumental in locating the bird and arranging for its transit to the Yorba Linda site. As I stood near the door, I posed with double peace signs, hands stretched, imitating that moment when Nixon entered the bird for the last time on the White House Lawn.

The Abraham Lincoln Presidential Library and Museum

None of the other libraries would prepare me for what I was to see at the Abraham Lincoln museum in Springfield, Illinois. I traveled to Springfield on July 17, 2014 for the museum visit. It would not be a waste of travel, for I was certainly pleased with that to which I was exposed. Of all of the libraries I have visited, Lincoln's has the most attention to detail of which I would give an Academy Award for best costume and best original sets if there were such awards for museums.

Lincoln's library and museum are not one of those operated by the National Archives system. It is operated by the Illinois Historic Preservation Agency, which is an agency of the State of Illinois. The library, which holds Lincoln's papers and documents, opened on October 14, 2004, and the museum opened on April 14, 2005. This 50,000 square foot masterpiece took three gubernatorial administrations to get to a ribbon cutting ceremony. Dozens of scholars, historians, and teachers were instrumental in preparing the museum to make it as authentic and as historically accurate as possible. The museum is a combination of library, museum, Broadway theater, and Hollywood theme park all in one.

On the day of the grand opening, the City of Springfield hosted a number of celebrations honoring President Lincoln. There were parades and gatherings, the residents and visitors dressed in 1860s period clothing and there were dozens of Abraham Lincoln impersonators on site. Aside from the parade, there was a rail splitting contest to celebrate Lincoln as a frontiersman. Politicians from around the state of Illinois gathered to recreate a Lincoln White House dinner and there were actors dressed in Union Soldier uniform standing guard.

So not knowing what to expect in the museum, I began my self-guided tour. Immediately I was taken in by the massive White House recreation. I'd seen many Oval Office replicas, but I'd never seen the outside structure in replication. There is a recreation of the South Portico and standing in front were wax figures of the Lincoln Family of which visitors could take photos. Of course, I took a photo with the Lincoln family. It was fun. Off to the right of the South Portico was a very detailed re-creation of a Lincoln log cabin. Inside I saw a young Abe Lincoln reading by an imitation fireplace. The designers put their work into the display. I was thoroughly impressed.

Another great feature of the museum was not just the outside look of the White House, but a walking tour of Lincoln's White House. Room by room, visitors could peer into the life of the White House during the 1860s. The museum spared no detail in costumes and set design. I saw Lincoln at a meeting with his cabinet in one room and in another room, I saw Lincoln's son Willie on his deathbed. Each of these rooms was re-created to the detail from photographs preserved over time. I took pictures for a short time until I was instructed to cease photography by the museum officials. The only place that visitors were allowed to take photos was in the open area in front of the South Portico. I did get a good number of photos in before I had to stop.

The Ford's Theater was a very interesting re-creation as it was the place where Lincoln was assassinated by John Wilkes Booth. In the re-creation, Lincoln and Mary are seated as they would be watching the drama and there is a wax figure of Booth behind them with a pistol in his hand. My first thoughts were, "These people are very morbid." But it happened. It's history.

As I moved on, the scene became a bit dark and gloomy, almost like I was in a funeral home. Well, that's exactly the mood the creators wanted me to have as they attempted to re-create Lincoln's body lying in state. Using photos from the event in Springfield, museum designers, again, re-created the scene to the detail. It was regal with a full casket, columns, drapery, and the magnificence of the moment.

There is an interactive feature of the museum that utilized state-of-the-art graphics and technology. Museum designers made simulations of the Campaign of 1860. The set is designed like a television station control room. There are nine monitors that display different candidates campaigning for office in a makeshift 1860s election. There are even campaign commercials created which use scripts from the period, but with modern commercial graphics and video editing. It was very interesting to watch on television a period in which humans wouldn't see for another 100 years.

There were plenty Civil War exhibits and displays throughout the museum, as the war was Lincoln's presidency from start to finish. There is a photo gathering of Lincoln's portraits to demonstrate the toll the White House years took on him from the entrance to exit. His face dramatically changed from a fresh representative from Illinois to a tired war worn President. Reality set in to just how much the Oval Office can do to a man's mental and physical state.

Before leaving the museum, I had to visit the Hollywood component on display featuring actual sets from the movie "Lincoln" which starred Academy Award winner Daniel Day Lewis. The outfits Lewis and Sally Field wore during the movie were on display and clips from the feature film were playing as visitors moved throughout the exhibit. What a wonderful way to end my tour of the Lincoln museum, a long trip that was worth my time. Bravo Springfield. Bravo!

The George H.W. Bush Presidential Library

Even though I have visited many libraries at this point, the George HW Bush Presidential Library will be one of my most rewarding adventures. On this trip, I didn't go solo, but I afforded an opportunity for four of my students to travel with me. So, I was able to share this experience with four youth who probably would not have gone otherwise. I contacted their parents and told them the plan and what their students would get out of the experience. I paid for the travel, admission to the museum, and their meals during the trip. Their parents approved and on the morning of November 24, 2014 (during their Thanksgiving school break), I picked up Ricki and Rashad Newton, Nekesia Hamilton, and Kobe Sutton, and headed to College Station, Texas where we would tour Bush's museum.

The 69,049 square foot facility was dedicated on November 6, 1997. It sits on 90 acres on the west campus of Texas A&M University. About 18,000 people assembled for the dedication ceremony. Four US Presidents were present including Presidents George HW Bush, Clinton, Carter, and Ford. A fifth US President was also on the scene (George W). However, he was only the Governor of Texas at the time. In a rare scene, six first ladies were present. First Ladies Hillary Clinton, Barbara Bush, Nancy Reagan, Rosaline Carter, Betty Ford, and Lady Bird Johnson were in attendance. Colin Powell, Kevin Costner, and Arnold Schwarzenegger were also in attendance. World leaders were a big spectacle as Prime Ministers from Canada, Great Britain, Japan, the Netherlands, Poland, and Bermuda were present.

The Rev. Billy Graham gave the invocation, benediction, and blessing over the facility. During the event, President Ford made comments. "George Bush and I have much in common. To begin with, each of us married above himself, thereby demonstrating that behind every great woman, is a man wondering what on Earth she ever saw in him," Ford said. President Bill Clinton also made remarks. He said, "When President Carter spoke, I thought, thank goodness he just reminded the world that presidents have to raise all the money for their library."

My four students and I began our library journey by taking a group photo outside of the building. It had the likes of Thomas Jefferson's Memorial in Washington, DC. On the inside, like Johnson's and Clinton's libraries, there was the presidential limousine in the lobby. I took a photo by Bush's Lincoln Town Car. Walking through the exhibits, I saw a warplane hoisted above me, as Bush was a pilot when he served in the Armed Forces. I took a photo of Barbara's wedding gown, which is on display next to a 7-foot wedding photo of she and George. There are submarine and aircraft carrier models in the World War II exhibit. I thought those were cool.

Unlike the other museums, HW Bush's library had a replica of both Capitol Hill and the outside of the White House. The Capitol Hill replica exhibit focused on Bush the Congressman. There was even a bronzed figure of Bush seated in a chair with a large United Nations room photo behind him. There was an empty chair next to the statue, so visitors could sit and simulate having a conversation with Bush, a cool photo idea.

The Oval Office replica was okay, but it was not a full-scale replica like the others, not even like George W. Bush's library in Dallas. The desk in HW's office is not even a resolute desk. It has the wooded feel, and visitors can sit at the desk and take photos, but a scholar, historian, and frequent visitor of presidential museum notices quickly that the desk is not a Resolute. It was fun watching my students sit at the desk and pose for photos. They enjoyed the experience.

As we made our way through the self-guided tour, the students took photos by a piece of the Berlin Wall, of which this was the third I'd seen in presidential libraries. I began to wonder if any pieces of this wall existed in Germany. I thought it would be beneficial for them to take the photos to use for history projects in high school. Not too many of their peers would be able to say they have stood by and touched a piece of the Berlin Wall. The students also took photos sitting at the table in Bush's situation room. There were exhibits from Bush's term as CIA Director and a few on his term as president and farewell ceremonies.

We bought a few souvenirs in the gift shop, went for lunch, and headed back home. It was a very rewarding experience for the students and I was honored to be with them as they were exposed to history in a way that they could never have within the four walls of a classroom.

The Woodrow Wilson Presidential Museum

Thomas Woodrow Wilson was the 28th President of the United States. I'd made visiting his museum an objective for quite a while. I'm a fan of the 1920s era and Wilson was the president during this decade of American History. When I found that it was in the vicinity of Mr. Vernon and Monticello, the visit became a reality, a rental car trip to be made. His museum is located in Staunton, Virginia.

I didn't previously know that Woodrow was not his first name. It's his mother's maiden name. His name is Thomas. That was mysterious to me but a bit clever. Men don't usually take their mother's names, as if I were to be called Adams Wright. However, that's why these visits are important to me. Much is learned about the presidents and there I was, walking in history.

I visited the Manse (the name of Wilson's birthplace) on February 27, 2017. After a hotel stay the previous night, my visit was early, for I had a long day of travel. After Wilson's visit, I would be moving on to Madison's and Jefferson's place…a day for presidential home visits.

I'd seen photos of the place on the museum's website and became excited about seeing Wilson's presidential limousine. I'd seen the limousines used by Ronald Reagan, George HW Bush, Bill Clinton, and LBJ, but nothing was as unique and fabulous as walking over to the garage and seeing that shiny black 1919 Pierce-Arrow. It was a sight to see and I marveled at it on display. It was Wilson's favorite car and it was waiting for him at the docks in New York when he returned from Paris in 1919 after negotiating the Treaty of Versailles.

In the museum, there are a number of artifacts from Wilson's life not only as President of the United States but also from his term as the President of Princeton University and as Governor of the State of New Jersey. On display was the telephone he used in the White House, a copy of the official program from his inauguration in 1913, newspapers, posters, campaign ribbons, and Rose Medallion china given to Wilson as a gift from the Chinese Ambassador.

In the basement of the home, visitors can prepare themselves to step into a model of World War I. It is made into a bunker. It's a bit dark and dismal, but I think that is the objective of giving guests a sample of what life was like for a doughboy during the great war.

FORTY-FOUR

VISITING GEORGE WASHINGTON'S MT. VERNON

*"I walk on untrodden ground. There is scarcely any part of my
conduct which may not hereafter be drawn into precedent."*
President George Washington

On March 1, 2017, I visited the home of America's first
President, General George Washington. Luckily, on the day I made
my tour, I was the only visitor with the tour guide. So I had a 1:1
teacher-student ratio during each stage of the visit, which was okay
by me. There was not one guide that walked around with visitors.
The guides were divided into sections, and with each portion of the
home, there was someone else there to greet you and tell the story
about that particular part. They essentially were experts of their part
of Washington's history.

The 500-acre estate is located on the banks of the Potomac
River in Fairfax County, Virginia. The mansion is made out of wood
and it has lasted over three centuries. The estate was not named by
Washington, but by his half-brother Lawrence, of whom George
inherited it. Interestingly, the home of the American General who
fought for American Independence is named for an officer, Vice
Admiral Edward Vernon, in the British Royal Navy.

As I learned during my tour, the mansion that I visited was a
culmination of decades of revisions. When Washington began living
on the Potomac facing property, it was a four-room residence. Over
a few decades would see additions to make the Mt. Vernon that sits
today. He inherited the property from his half-brother in the 1730s,
raising the roof to make it two stories. The first tour guide gave me

an overview of the layout and showed me artwork of the stages of construction from the base structure, to the winged additions, and ultimately the top floor.

I moved through the house to the New Room, which was a fashionable 18th-century salon and was used for dining and dancing. The size, the color and the decorations in this room displayed Washington's wealth. The room was big enough to include a full house at the time. When you walk into the room, you think "this is a farmer's house." It was the topic of discussion for Washington and his guests. The room displayed Washington's appreciation for farming and the importance of agriculture. There were many symbolic showpieces in the room that made this point, including the landscaping paintings on display. These were Washington's view for the future of the country...developing a system to get goods to the market. As his home sat on the Potomac River, he was in a good position to be the pioneer in such system. Similar to the foyer of Thomas Jefferson's home, he and Washington took measures in the details to host a museum of sorts, a few centuries before their homes themselves became museums. There are also mirrors in Washington's home that are almost identical to the mirrors that are in Jefferson's home.

After the grand room, I moved to the oldest section of the house, the Central Passage. This section included the front door, where Washington's slave Frank Lee would greet guests. The guide was very knowledgeable about the room and the procedures that took place when guests came to visit Washington. There I was, over 200 years later, standing in Washington's foyer as a guest looking around at what many African-Americans at the time would never see...as a free man. The guide showed me into the West Cove, considered the finest room at the time until the new room was built. This was the room where more distinguished guests would be entertained. There would be chess, card playing, and conversation. It was possibly in this room that discussions took place that shaped the history of our country. There I stood, walking around in the textbook.

In Washington's home on display is the key to the Bastille. The key was given to Washington by Marquis de Lafayette. This was a gift to the American general after the Revolution. Lafayette's job was to demolish the prison. The infamous Parisian prison was demolished on July 14, 1789. The key in the home of America's first president was a symbol of Liberty and Freedom. This was one of Washington's most honored possessions and where it sits today in his home is where it has always sat.

I moved up to the second floor and toured the bedrooms. An original painting of Lafayette, painted by Charles Willson Peale, is on display. There was no record kept of the bedrooms to which dignitaries slept. So no one knows which room Patrick Henry or Thomas Jefferson slept in during their visit. Because Lafayette's portrait is situated near one of the rooms, it is the assumption that that is the room he took up a temporary stay.

Although the record of visitor's names was not kept, Washington recorded several hundred visits to his home after he moved out of the White House. He referred to his home as a tavern because people were always there to socialize and stay over. It was possible that Washington didn't know many of the people who were in his home. However, at that time, it was taboo to ask someone not to stay or to ask when they were leaving. Playing host to all of these guests, providing free room and meals, it must have been a lovely time for the guests. However, not so for the slaves who had to provide the meals, turn down the beds, light the fires, empty out the bath/shower basins, and empty the chamber pots. It must have been a very horrible and unbearable time as a slave working in the President's home. As I observed, I became thankful that such time has come and gone. Looking at the living quarters and seeing it with my own eyes gave me a new perspective on history. There was no deodorant at the time and many went without bathing during the visits. There were even animal smells to add to the mix. The stench of so many people in close quarters had to be very rank and disgusting.

I moved on to the private side of the second floor and saw Mrs. Washington's office. This was far from the Lady Bird Johnson's office setup that I saw in Austin, Texas at the Lyndon Baines Johnson Presidential Library. I saw Mrs. Martha's desk where she wrote letters, plan meals and wrote recipes. Her office, as it turns out, was also she and George's bedroom. In the bedroom is a specially made bed. General Washington stood at 6 foot 2 inches. So, he could not rest in a normal sized bed. Martha had her carpenter build it just for him, sized at 6'6. Solemnly, the bed that I saw was also the one on which the President died. Thirty-six hours after he fell sick, Washington was dead, but not before an agonizing struggle with pain that could not be cured. Looking at his bed, I saw the battlefield that took out the Great General George Washington. There was not a piece of land in the Americas that the British could accomplish such feat, but here before my eyes, was such a place; a 6'6 bed.

It was the first time I would see a bed warmer in context. The Washingtons would heat their beds and pull the curtains to contain the heat, weathering bitterly cold nights. As a child, I'd always seen canopy beds but would wonder about the purpose of the curtains. A relic design, they had a purpose, and now I saw it in practice at Mt. Vernon. Before I left Washington's bedroom, I could not exit without seeing his chamber pot. Across my mind, again, went horrible visions of slaves coming in and out changing pots and human excrements several times a day.

I finally made it to the last room of the tour….Washington's library. His office and study was the most private room of the house. You were only allowed in the room if Washington invited you or summoned you. I had a visual of Washington coming down the stairs at 4 o'clock in the morning and begin his work before breakfast at 7 o'clock. I was reminded that these men did what successful men have always done…rise early and get much accomplished. In Washington's office, I saw the desk where he sat and ran the affairs of the plantation. There is a saying that "the sun never rose with George Washington in bed."

Washington never had a formal education. Because of the lack, he took to reading. Being very aware of his literary deficiency, he was very studious on his own time. There are 900 volumes in his collection. It was interesting to see the private desk of the former President. Although it wasn't the Queen's Resolute Desk, as in the Oval Office, it was the desk of a President. Washington owned around 100 slaves. It was on this desk of which he wrote in his will that they would be freed.

There was much to learn and see during this visit. Although this is not a library, operated by the National Archives, it is the home and personal office of the nation's first President, a tour anyone interested in history should make.

FORTY-FIVE

VISITING THOMAS JEFFERSON'S MONTICELLO

"Whenever you do a thing,
act as if all the world were watching."
President Thomas Jefferson

On February 28, 2017, I visited the home of America's third president Thomas Jefferson. Jefferson was not only the third president, but he also drafted the Declaration of Independence, served as governor of Virginia, Secretary of State, Vice President, minister to France, was a very talented architect and interior decorator and was an owner of slaves. Some would suggest that because he owned slaves, I shouldn't hold him up in such high regard. General Washington owned slaves as well, as did many of the notable men of the time. Knowing this, I was still interested in walking in history at his home of which I would find to be one of the most impressive, even by today's standards, of home décor.

Over a 40-year period, Jefferson personally designed Monticello, the name of his home site. In Italian, Monticello means "little mountain." As tourists travel to the site, they find out where the name originates. Today it is a World Heritage site and one of the best-preserved plantations on the continent.

Jefferson's home is not just the mansion, but a 5,000-acre plantation. The mansion sits at the top of the hill overlooking the Virginia landscape. He began building the house in 1769. After a number of trips to France as Minister, he would often come back and make alterations to the home. He'd tear down and rebuild. The house I visited was as it was when Jefferson retired as President. There was some restoration work taking place during my visit, but it was not taking away from the original layout.

I was on tour with about a dozen other people. The first room we entered was the entrance hall. It was an atypical room in a home. There were no portraits of family members or stairwells to the second floor, as one would find in modern day homes. The entrance hall of Jefferson's home was designed as a museum. There were many maps, charts and collectibles that he wanted to display for his guests. A unique feature of The Hall was the plantation clock. Jefferson designed the clock when he was Secretary of State in Philadelphia. It's powered by cannonball weights. As the balls fell, they would indicate the day of the week and time of the date. There is a painting of Jefferson composed by artist Thomas Sully in 1856, and there are also collectibles from Lewis and Clark's expedition. As scholars know, Meriwether Lewis and William Clark were sent out to explore the newly purchased territory by Jefferson after the nation purchased it from Napoleon in 1803.

From the Hall, we moved from a public area to the private family area. We went to the smallest room in the house, the South Square Room. This is the room that Jefferson's daughter Martha used as a sitting room and office. She became the overseer of the plantation when Jefferson retired. The tour guide focused on the Hemmings family. He talked about Sally Hemmings and the assumed relationship between Jefferson and his slave. The guide made the ironic connection between Jefferson penning the Declaration of Independence saying 'all men are created equal' and him owning over 600 slaves.

We then moved to the library, the cabinet and Jefferson's bedroom. In the library, the guide referred to Jefferson's love of books and his ability to read seven languages. In 1814, the Library of Congress was destroyed by the British. He offered to sell to Congress over 6,000 books of which he was paid over $20,000. He eventually wanted them back, saying "I can't live without my books." He was interested in education and wanted to play an active role in it. Jefferson is the founder of the University of Virginia. Luckily, Monticello was elevated enough that Jefferson could look out with a telescope and observe the construction.

After we left the library, we went into Jefferson's Bedchamber. There were skylights in his bedroom, an uncommon feature of farmhouses in Jefferson's time. However, they were a common feature in the homes in France, of which Jefferson observed during his trips. So, naturally, he brought home the ideas and remodeled his home to resemble what he saw in France.

Jefferson also modeled his alcove bed like the French. It sits between the bedchamber and the cabinet, to save space in the room. Jefferson, like General Washington, stood over six feet tall, so his bed also had to be specially made to accommodate his height. Above his bed was a closet. There was a ladder that was used to climb up to his closet to get his clothing items.

So much of Jefferson's life is preserved because he documented his life and kept detailed records. He wrote over 19,000 letters in his life. There was a polygraph machine in his bedchamber of which allowed him to make the many copies of his work. Seeing all of these features of the president's home made me very intrigued by him. I too was a chronic documenter of my life and kept detailed records. This revelation was a sign that I was on the right track and also gave me insight on how to continue the work that had already been done about my adventures.

Jefferson died on July 4, 1826 in the room of which we were standing. Like Washington, this was becoming a trend of walking in history, for I saw the place where the General died and there I was again, looking at the place where #3 died…in his bed.

After leaving the bedchamber, we entered the Parlor. This was the room where Jefferson's family and his guests met, read together and played games and instruments. Although this was a family room similar to what we'd call a living room in modern home architecture, Jefferson didn't display many portraits of his family, but many of notable people in the history of the world including Lafayette and Washington. There is also a large mirror in his home that is similar to the one in George Washington's home.

We then traveled to Jefferson's dining room. The color on the wall was yellow. This was an expensive paint at the time. However, Jefferson was not known to avoid his luxury tastes. Many of these extravagant tastes left the president in debt at the time of his death. Economists have considered inflation over the years and have put Jefferson's debt close to $2 million in today's money. One can look at his home with today's eyes and question why an old house in the 1700s was considered so luxurious. However, considering what was available at the time, this was the cover of Architectural Digest.

Jefferson's family was forced to sell Monticello because of his debts. The only reason why creditors didn't bother him was likely because he was the president. In today's financial market, I don't think being president would be a safeguard. However, in the 1700s, this was the case. Acquiring the Louisiana Purchase may have been one of the most important factors of his presidency, but regarding human life, many people were affected by his personal affairs. Although slaves were already put in a position of inferior humanity, their lives too were disrupted when Jefferson died. The family, in selling Monticello, also had to separate families, selling off the slaves, because they too were as valuable as the items in the house.

I took a photo in the West Lawn with the mansion behind me. It's the same image one will find on a nickel, as it's been since the US Mint decided to commemorate Jefferson in 1938. I'd learned a lot from my visit to Monticello. What I didn't learn in grade school or college, I learned from my tour. It's one thing to read about history in a textbook, and yet another to walk in history.

FORTY-SIX

VISITING JAMES MADISON'S MONTPELIER

"A well-instructed people alone can be permanently a free people."
President James Madison

James Madison was the fourth President of the United States. He served two terms in office from 1809 to 1817. He is also known as the father of the Constitution and the architect of the Bill of Rights. His wife Dolley is known as America's first First Lady. He, like a few of the other founding fathers, was Virginia-born, and his homesite was near Monticello and President Woodrow Wilson's museum. So when I visited Thomas Jefferson's home, I made the trek to Madison's place as well. It would be equally rewarding.

It is unclear why Madison named his home Montpelier. It has been speculated that it originates from a city in France (Montpellier). The founding fathers were world travelers and normally brought the world to the colonies. The Montpelier property sits in Orange, Virginia, a 50-mile drive from Jefferson's place.

On February 28, 2017, I made the trip to the president's home and was joined on tour with over a dozen other people. We began our tour at the front of the house as the guide explained the many additions to the structure that were not apart of the original house. It was a much smaller mansion than it is today. When Madison and his wife moved there, it was only a townhouse. They enlarged it and when he became President, another renovation took place.

We began in the original house on the right side of the site. We first toured his mother's favorite room. It was called the "Old Lady's Apartment." She had her own set of slaves and her conveniences away from Madison and Dolley on the other side of the house. His mother was his first teacher and she also gave him his first instructions on operating a farm.

Madison went off to boarding school at the age of 11 until the age of 16. He received a classical education and could read in over five languages including Spanish, Latin, French, Italian and Greek. He was also interested in the enlightenment as during the period of his life was known as the Age of Reason. There would be many collectibles in the house that attest to this period, reasons why they were important to the President.

We went to the Drawing Room, similar to Thomas Jefferson's Parlor Room. The room was covered in red wallpaper. Like Jefferson's home, this color, too, was expensive, but it was a favorite of Dolley Madison. The president has many paintings and sculptural busts of his contemporary friends in the Drawing Room. There were paintings of George Washington, John Adams, and James Monroe. Along with the other paintings was a familiar one seen at Monticello, the Penitent Magdalen. It was a gift to Jefferson from Madison, so they both had copies in their social rooms. Madison was 25-years-old when the Declaration of Independence was signed. He has a commemorative copy of it on the wall in his home. They played cards and gambled in the drawing room, despite Dolley formerly being a Quaker.

In the room was a chess board set up, for Madison's favorite pastime was Chess. It was situated next to the bust of Thomas Jefferson, one of whom he shared a friendship for over five decades.

We left the drawing room and traveled to the dining room. Madison called his dining room a "Marketplace of Ideas." In the dining room there was a dining table setup and interestingly, there were cutouts of the people who would be sitting at the table. Some were there at the same time, while others were separated by decades. I was separated by many more decades. There I was, walking in history, standing in the room where President Madison entertained his guests. His cutout was at the center of the table, unlike most situations where the man-of-the-house sat at the head of the table. This was not Madison's way. He wanted to be seen and heard, and of course, people traveled long distances to hear his opinion on constitutional issues. It took Thomas Jefferson eight hours on horseback to travel to Madison's home. I was appreciative of how far we've come, for it only took me an hour to drive in my rental car.

231

Dolley, on the other hand, sat at the head of the table, because she liked to direct the flow of the events. From her position, she could direct the slaves and the conversation all at the same time. She was very politically savvy and purposefully sat her guests in such a way that would spark conversation. The table cutouts included: Thomas Jefferson, James Monroe, Andrew Jackson, Margaret Bayard Smith (Washington gossip columnist), and Marquis de Lafayette. The tour guide said that Lafayette was made to appear grumpy in his cutout because of the types of conversations he may have had with Jefferson and Madison for owning slaves despite all the work done in the name of liberty and freedom. Another significant cutout was of Paul Jennings, the slave who eventually wrote a book about his time with the Madisons.

During his retirement, Madison and Dolley encountered large debts. There was no presidential pension and the plantation was not yielding suitable profits. So, he began selling his notes from the Constitutional Convention. He took notes daily and recorded them in shorthand, of which only he understood. He and Dolley took years to transcribe his notes and prepare them for sale. This took care of her after Madison died.

The last room we visited in the house was my favorite, Madison's library. At one point he had up to 4,000 books in his library. His library was his bedroom as a young child. Out his window, he could look out and be inspired. It was in this room where Madison would come up with a plan he introduced in the Constitutional Convention as the Virginia Plan. This was the idea to have a bicameral legislative government. There I was, not in Philadelphia where the Declaration of Independence was signed, but in the study and library where Madison drafted the plan that gave us the government we now have as Americans. This was also the room where Madison, John Jay, and Alexander Hamilton assembled the Federalist Papers, the documents that were used to support of the Constitution.

There I was....in James Madison's home. I walked around on tour taking in history, walking in history, and wearing a T-Shirt I purchased at a gift shop at Thomas Jefferson's home and museum. On the shirt was a quote by Jefferson that said: "I can't live without books." As I stood in Madison's library, I reflected on George Washington's and Thomas Jefferson's homes. Education is a powerful thing. It's one thing to read and study history. One truly doesn't get the full story until he or she walks around in it. Visiting these homes was a great experience and one that has had a tremendous impact on my perspective of time.

FORTY-SEVEN

MEETING THE
REV. JESSE JACKSON, SR.

"If my mind can conceive it, and my heart can believe it, I know I can achieve it."

Rev. Jesse Jackson, Sr.

We often find ourselves in the right place, at the right time. This couldn't be truer than the time I met the Rev. Jesse Jackson, Sr. I was the photographer at the wedding of Terisa Griffin and John Kendall in Chicago on November 24, 2012. There was a grand reception at the Hyatt Regency and it was filled with lavish decorations, exquisite cuisine, wine, and live music.

Jackson is the founder of the Rainbow/PUSH organization and was the Democratic National Convention's nomination for United States President in 1984 and 1988. He attended the celebration along with other dignitaries who surrounded Terisa, who is a sensation in her own right. You may remember reading about her earlier in the book in the chapter about photographys school. She is a well-known entertainer in Chicago, and the preferred songstress at social gatherings. She appeared on a few episodes of NBC's "The Voice" and has performed for many notable events in Chicago including gatherings hosted by Chicago Mayor Rahm Emanuel and the funeral service of Comedian Bernie Mac. Her husband only added to the special cause for the large gathering. He is a well-known lawyer in Chicago. A brother of the Alpha Phi Alpha Fraternity, he was also at the time, the president of the 100 Black Men of Chicago organization. So it spoke volumes about their relevance and prestige that Jackson was among the attendees at their wedding.

Other notable attendees included: Kim McCullough, Sam Balark, Craig Gilmore, Ralph Hughes, Hermene Hartman, Midge Kimberly, Wynona Redmond, George & Regina Daniels, Stella Foster, Larry Rogers, Sr. and Larry Rogers, Jr., LaRue Martin, Adrienne Jones, Michael House, Darryl Newell, Dr. Terry Mason, Sharron Troupe, Dedry Jones, Art Sims, Spencer Leak, Jr., Dr.

Wayne Watson, Melody Spann and Pierre Cooper, Juanita Passmore, Tracy Williams (Wedding Director) and Tyronne Stoudemire. The recording artist and "VOICE" of Chicago was walked down the aisle by Jerry "The Iceman" Butler at the Beloved Community Church. The wedding was officiated by United States Congressman Rev. Bobby Rush, from Illinois's 1st Congressional District.

As a historian, it was sentimental to shake hands and be in the presence of Jackson, who walked with Dr. Martin Luther King, Jr. and was there in Memphis, Tennessee on the balcony of the Lorraine Motel, where King was assassinated on April 4, 1968.

FORTY-EIGHT

MEETING UN AMBASSADOR ANDREW YOUNG

"You have to start living for something that's worth dying for."
Andrew Young

Tuesday, February 27, 2018, I had a rare opportunity to meet with another historical figure who walked with Dr. Martin Luther King, Mr. Andrew Young, former United States Ambassador to the United Nations. Young was in town to speak to students at the University of Louisiana at Monroe as part of its Black History Month celebration.

Born in New Orleans, LA in 1932, Young holds degrees from Dillard University, Howard University, and Hartford Seminary. While a pastor at an Alabama church, he became active in the Civil Rights Movement of which he would later join forces with Dr. Martin Luther King, Jr. The two were brothers in the Alpha Phi Alpha Fraternity.

In 1960, Young joined the SCLC (Southern Christian Leadership Conference) and later moved to Atlanta. Three years later, he was named the Executive Director of the SCLC. Young was with Dr. Martin Luther King, Jr. in Memphis, Tennessee when King was assassinated at the Loraine Motel.

He served as a U.S. Congressman in Georgia's 5th Congressional District from 1973-1977 and was named by President Jimmy Carter as the US Ambassador to the United Nations. From 1982 until 1990, Young would serve as the mayor of Atlanta, Georgia. He was preceded and succeeded by Maynard Jackson, who was also his brother in the Alpha Phi Alpha Fraternity.

When I heard that Young was coming to town, I became overly excited. I'm naturally interested in the US Presidency and national politics. I've never met a president, but this gentleman worked closely with presidents and sat in the chambers of the United

Nations Headquarters in New York City. Certainly, this was a hand I wanted to shake, a conversation of which I would love to entertain. Before the day was over, I would achieve both.

During the day of his visit, Young spoke to students and faculty at the university. He told the gathering, in response to a question, that America lacks a single vision. He said that the founding fathers had a vision and they wrote it in the first paragraph of the Constitution. He went on to recite the preamble and said that neither Democrat or Republican party has a vision that they could put in a paragraph. As a result, he said, President Trump gave the country an alternative to create one of their own, however misguided it was. He also told the gathering, in response to a question, that to be truly free "you must overcome the love of wealth and the fear of dying." He said that if they truly wanted to get involved in civil rights, they must not go into it seeking to get rich.

Through the efforts of local Alpha Phi Alpha Fraternity men Lavelle Hendricks and former Louisiana State Senator Charles Jones, a dinner was prepared for Young such that he could meet with brothers from the local fraternity chapter. It was an honor to be asked to join in the celebration with men from the Eta Delta Lambda Chapter of Alpha Phi Alpha Fraternity, Inc. to meet the Ambassador. We dined at Genusa's Italian Restaurant and enjoyed discourse with Young. He talked about international politics, some fun times he shared with Dr. Martin Luther King, his travels to various African nations, and he even gave some insight to the way forward as a nation. I asked him about strategies to help young kids gain a global perspective. He told me that youth need to be exposed to the world. He said that I should take them to museums and have them reading books, for that's what shaped his worldview when he was younger.

To sit in the room with the man was a rewarding experience. This man walked with Dr. King, met with presidents, served in Congress, was the mayor of a major American city, and served with over a hundred representatives from around the world in the UN. This was a man with a massive worldview. As he spoke, I listened. There were times when his delivery was slow, as he is in his 80s and his words of reflection are calculated and filled with decades of wisdom. He was not rushed and we waited for the next words that came from his mouth. It was truly an honor to walk in history for just a moment, with a man who helped create it. Not only was it good to be in Young's presence, but it was equally enjoyable to sit among other local men on whose shoulders I stand. A mix of lawyers, a judge, preachers, business owners, teachers and a medical doctor, men active in their community who were sharing in Young's spirit of achievement. It was great being among great men.

FORTY-NINE

EPILOGUE

"Surely God would not have created such a being as man, with an ability to grasp the infinite, to exist only for a day! No, no, man was made for immortality."

President Abraham Lincoln

I spent a considerable amount of time in church throughout my life. In those years, I attended a number of funeral services for people who lived for many years. The obituary was a common thread to these services. I attended the services of people who lived 80 and 90 years and their obituaries were only two or three short paragraphs. How do you submit a summary of 90 years of life in three short paragraphs? The typical funeral program went like this:

"Brother John Doe was born. He is the son of John Sr. and Mrs. Doe. He confessed Christ, joined the church, sang in the choir, and died. He is survived by…."

How depressing is it to live for nine decades and this be the lasting epithet. I've often told people that know me well that when I die and find out that all I'm given is a paragraph or two on the funeral program, I will not be as friendly as Casper. I will be going a haunting. They laugh, but I command my spirit to see it through.

Each of us, whether we live 20 years or 90 years, has a story to tell. We've done something, lived someway, and experienced something. Those years are worth mentioning. Certainly, we can say more about people when they die than "He was just a happy person" or "She knew how to cook." Most of us went to school, worked at some institution or site of business, were someone's child or sibling, voted, traveled, or participated in some form of human life other than to simply exist. Even if we find ourselves in prison or homeless on the street, that experience is a story in itself. However, if our lives aren't important enough to be documented by ourselves, I guess it's not that disheartening that others don't know the details of our existence.

I am a fan of the voice of Billie Holliday and Michael Jackson among others. Their voices are immortal, not only because they worked at their craft and perfected their sounds, but that they took the time and effort to document this gift using the best technology that was available to them in their window of time. The immortality of their talent captivates audiences for infinity. The immortality of what I've done in my short window of life is likewise made possible because I'm recording it and submitting it for collective human memory. The same can be said for the immortality of your life's story. It has to be written. It has to be recorded. Otherwise, as decades and centuries pass, unless a notable Griot includes you in his or her story, what you were able to do with God's gift of life will wither as dust in the wind, never to be recognized.

In many of our lives, there is a constant struggle for identity, for acceptance, and for immortality. We want to do something so remarkable that we are remembered, that we are noticed. Many take to performing feats of offensive and controversial nature because its sensational and it attracts the most attention of the masses. With the invent of social media platforms like Facebook, Instagram, Twitter, and Snapchat, we are given an opportunity to be instant celebrities with thousands or millions of people following our every move. However, that following is only perpetuated if there is something there keeping the follower's attention. It's a pubescent-like state of "out of sight, out of mind." So daily or weekly, we have to concoct a new scheme, a new fad, challenge the social norms, and push the envelope just a little farther to stay relevant. People will write and draw on their bodies because it attracts attention. But what happens when one's body is completely covered and there is no more space for ink? When does it end?

Bruce Lee once stated, "The key to immortality is first living a life worth remembering." God gives us all abilities, whether we locate them within ourselves or not. When we locate them, our zeal in the exercise of these abilities is cause for a memorable life. So you can draw. What did you draw? Did your canvas have a message that can surpass a 48-hour hashtag hype? So you can sing. What was the nature of your song? Was it about sex? Was it about life in the ghetto? Was it about something magical that captivated the hearts and minds of millions?

In the play "Julius Caesar," Act 3, Scene 2, Shakespeare penned "The evil men do lives after them; the good is oft interred with their bones." If this could be said about Rome's champion of war, so too could this be said about any of us. We all have had some dark moments in our lives and we've often attempted to do more good to balance out that disharmony. I don't think a few mistakes should be the lasting description of a man, especially when so many more good deeds were done that are often overlooked. This, however, requires focus. Why do we focus more on the evil that men do than the good that they do? Why is evil more attractive than good?

That may be the test of our humanity, to rise from our basal expectations and passions to that of noble life and appreciation for that which is good, which is pure, decent and wholesome. Bill Cosby is one the greatest artists of my time and he wasn't a painter or graphic designer. The Cosby Show was his art and despite Cosby's flaws, those eight seasons of magic will live in infamy as good work, work that is praised for its wholesomeness and its dignity of purpose, but only if there is an appreciation for this type of expression. If we choose to focus on Cosby's life away from his artist's canvas, then we will lose focus on the good work that he created. I think it is up to all of us to do the best we can with what we can and recognize that none of us are perfect even in our striving to be the best in our fields. I have many personal flaws. I know that no good deed or any collection of good deeds will ever erase the bad ones, I simply choose to keep doing good deeds in spite of the bad ones. I think this is where we go from Shakespeare.

Live your life and write your story. In doing so, make sure the creator gets due credit for your life's existence. Think good things and do good things and in time, your life will be rewarding. Evil is applauded moment by moment. Goodness takes time. The Holy Scripture states "Finally, brethren, whatsoever things are true, whatsoever things are honest, whatsoever things are just, whatsoever things are pure, whatsoever things are lovely, whatsoever things are of good report; if there be any virtue, and if there be any praise, think on these things." Philippians 4:8

I shared with my students at Minnie Ruffin Elementary School that history is like a flashlight in a dark place. The objects in the light's beam may be illuminated, but the other objects in the room are no less in existence. How do you look at the story of human life? It captivates me. I'm just nostalgic like that. I've made many decisions in my life to walk to the left or the right, not knowing where that road will lead. In doing so, I've often been in the right place at the right time. It was my destiny to meet with and dance with time at that moment. It was a choice to create new episodes of life. It was a choice to walk in history.

Choices. We all must make them. I've made many of them. It has been an incredible journey so far, and I'm looking forward to the next forty years or more, God willing. Nevertheless, "I shall be telling this with a sigh, sometime ages and ages hence, two roads diverged in a wood, and I, I took the one less traveled by, and that has made all the difference."

THE BOOK'S COMPANION

Visit my website: www.iamrobertwright.com to see the multimedia companion to this first autobiographical volume. There, you will find photographs and video footage indexed to follow the chapters in this publication. Thank you for purchasing and reading this book. Enjoy!

Made in the USA
Coppell, TX
26 September 2021

63027111R00136